Werner Friesenbichler

Transient Faults in Quasi Delay-Insensitive Logic

Werner Friesenbichler

Transient Faults in Quasi Delay-Insensitive Logic

Effects and Mitigation

Südwestdeutscher Verlag für Hochschulschriften

Impressum/Imprint (nur für Deutschland/only for Germany)
Bibliografische Information der Deutschen Nationalbibliothek: Die Deutsche Nationalbibliothek verzeichnet diese Publikation in der Deutschen Nationalbibliografie; detaillierte bibliografische Daten sind im Internet über http://dnb.d-nb.de abrufbar.
Alle in diesem Buch genannten Marken und Produktnamen unterliegen warenzeichen-, marken- oder patentrechtlichem Schutz bzw. sind Warenzeichen oder eingetragene Warenzeichen der jeweiligen Inhaber. Die Wiedergabe von Marken, Produktnamen, Gebrauchsnamen, Handelsnamen, Warenbezeichnungen u.s.w. in diesem Werk berechtigt auch ohne besondere Kennzeichnung nicht zu der Annahme, dass solche Namen im Sinne der Warenzeichen- und Markenschutzgesetzgebung als frei zu betrachten wären und daher von jedermann benutzt werden dürften.

Coverbild: www.ingimage.com

Verlag: Südwestdeutscher Verlag für Hochschulschriften GmbH & Co. KG
Heinrich-Böcking-Str. 6-8, 66121 Saarbrücken, Deutschland
Telefon +49 681 37 20 271-1, Telefax +49 681 37 20 271-0
Email: info@svh-verlag.de

Approved by: Wien, TU, Diss., 2012

Herstellung in Deutschland (siehe letzte Seite)
ISBN: 978-3-8381-3324-9

Imprint (only for USA, GB)
Bibliographic information published by the Deutsche Nationalbibliothek: The Deutsche Nationalbibliothek lists this publication in the Deutsche Nationalbibliografie; detailed bibliographic data are available in the Internet at http://dnb.d-nb.de.
Any brand names and product names mentioned in this book are subject to trademark, brand or patent protection and are trademarks or registered trademarks of their respective holders. The use of brand names, product names, common names, trade names, product descriptions etc. even without a particular marking in this works is in no way to be construed to mean that such names may be regarded as unrestricted in respect of trademark and brand protection legislation and could thus be used by anyone.

Cover image: www.ingimage.com

Publisher: Südwestdeutscher Verlag für Hochschulschriften GmbH & Co. KG
Heinrich-Böcking-Str. 6-8, 66121 Saarbrücken, Germany
Phone +49 681 37 20 271-1, Fax +49 681 37 20 271-0
Email: info@svh-verlag.de

Printed in the U.S.A.
Printed in the U.K. by (see last page)
ISBN: 978-3-8381-3324-9

Copyright © 2012 by the author and Südwestdeutscher Verlag für Hochschulschriften GmbH & Co. KG and licensors
All rights reserved. Saarbrücken 2012

Preface

Asynchronous *Quasi Delay-Insensitive* (QDI) logic offers an improved fault tolerance compared to common synchronous logic. Its delay-insensitive encoding makes QDI circuits not only robust to varying delays but also highly insensitive to transient faults, as such faults likely generate illegal data that is simply ignored.

To describe these fault effects in a quantitative manner, a model that includes all assumptions and boundary conditions has to be employed on. With existing models one has to make a trade-off between the level of detail they provide and their complexity. In this work, a new *trace based fault model* is developed. It covers both unprotected as well as hardened QDI circuits in the necessary level of detail, while still only moderate computational efforts are required to analyze real-world circuits. A *trace* is the sequence of all signal transitions a circuit receives and generates. As that sequence can be used to synthesize QDI circuits, it only seems to be natural to utilize traces for the description of QDI circuits in a faulty environment as well. Thereby the developed model is used to identify problematic fault scenarios and to derive their relative probability.

In the field of QDI circuits, different hardening strategies exist. Based on the insights gained from the trace based fault model, a new method called *duplication and rail cross-coupling* is derived. The idea is to re-arrange the particular rails of QDI signals in such a way that a transient fault will lead to an illegal code that prevents the fault from being processed. Such a hardened QDI circuit simply waits until the transient fault decays or it deadlocks for indefinite time, but without propagating any data errors. The initial approach was refined and led to the modified *DRXS / DRXX / DRS* methods, which are investigated in more detail.

For a systematic assessment of the proposed hardening methods two complementary approaches using simulation and hardware based fault injection are applied. While related tools are described in literature, these do not appropriately consider the peculiarities of QDI logic. Consequently, two customized fault injection tools are developed, one for *fault simulation* and one for *fault emulation*. These tools allow an adequate investigation of transient fault effects, thereby backing up the theoretic results from both the trace based fault model as well as the proposed hardening methods. Several basic test circuits as well as one moderately complex signal processing application are selected to verify the predicted fault tolerance of the different hardening strategies. It is shown that a clever re-arrangement of a duplicated QDI circuit helps to improve the tolerance against transient faults significantly, while keeping the hardware overhead low.

I would like to thank Andreas Steininger for his advice, experience and patience in the often lengthy discussions. Of course I also would like to thank Heinrich Vierhaus from the Brandenburg University of Technology Cottbus for reviewing the thesis and giving fruitful feedback. Thank you RUAG Space Gmbh for granting sponsoring to attend conferences.

Thanks to my colleague Thomas Panhofer, for all the helpful suggestions, reviews, collaborations on papers, coffee break discussions and especially for the motivation during stressful periods.

Finally, my thanks go to my family, my friends and especially to Stephanie, for supporting my work and giving me the strength and endurance to get the job done.

Werner Friesenbichler

Contents

1 Introduction   1
    1.1 Motivation 1
    1.2 Scope 4
    1.3 Contribution 5
    1.4 Outline and Methodology 6

2 Background   7
    2.1 Asynchronous Logic 7
       2.1.1 General 7
       2.1.2 Classification 9
       2.1.3 Operating Modes 10
       2.1.4 Handshake Protocols 10
       2.1.5 Quasi Delay-Insensitive Logic 12
    2.2 Faults and Errors in QDI Circuits 18
       2.2.1 Definitions and terms 18
       2.2.2 Fault Classification 19
       2.2.3 Logic Fault Models 20
       2.2.4 Masking Effects 21
       2.2.5 Fault Model 23
       2.2.6 Error Classification 26

3 Fault Description   29
    3.1 Related Work 29
       3.1.1 Transition Based Fault Description 29
       3.1.2 Token Based Fault Description 30
    3.2 Circuit Definition 32
       3.2.1 Signal Transition Graph 32
       3.2.2 State Graph 34
       3.2.3 Trace Theory 35
       3.2.4 Delay-Insensitivity 36
    3.3 Nominal Behavior of QDI Circuits 37
       3.3.1 Combinational Circuits 37
       3.3.2 Sequential Circuits 38
       3.3.3 Nominal Trace Description 38

3.4	Trace Based Fault Description	43
	3.4.1	Introduction 43
	3.4.2	Boundary Conditions 44
	3.4.3	Token Classes 45
3.5	Fault Effects	52
	3.5.1	Effects at Block Interconnections 52
	3.5.2	Effects in Combinational Logic 54
	3.5.3	Effects in Sequential Logic 58
3.6	Summary	60

4 Fault Mitigation — 65

4.1	Introduction	65
	4.1.1 Soft Error Rate	66
	4.1.2 Fault Trace Propagation	68
	4.1.3 Assessment of Soft Error Probability	70
	4.1.4 Principle of Redundancy	71
4.2	Related Work	72
	4.2.1 Hardware redundancy methods	72
	4.2.2 Duplication	72
	4.2.3 Rail synchronization	73
	4.2.4 Re-calculation	75
	4.2.5 Forcing deadlocks	76
	4.2.6 Concurrent error detection	77
4.3	Trace Based Fault Assessment	78
	4.3.1 Evaluation of Fault Propagation	79
	4.3.2 Trace Re-ordering	83
	4.3.3 Dependency on the encoding	86
	4.3.4 Impact of the handshake protocol	88
	4.3.5 Multiple rail transitions	89
4.4	Duplication and Rail Cross-coupling	94
	4.4.1 Principle	94
	4.4.2 Evaluation of Fault Masking	95
	4.4.3 Synchronized rail cross-coupling	101
	4.4.4 Tolerance against multiple errors	107
	4.4.5 Fault propagation and storage in cross-coupled circuits	112
	4.4.6 Rail comparison	116
	4.4.7 Summary	120
4.5	Fault Injection Overview	123

5 Simulation — 125

- 5.1 Related Work 125
- 5.2 Fault Simulation in QDI Logic 130
- 5.3 The FOSTER Tool 133
    - 5.3.1 Description of the Tool 134
    - 5.3.2 Error detection 137
    - 5.3.3 Random Tests 138
    - 5.3.4 Evaluation of Token Classes 140
    - 5.3.5 Interpretation of Soft Error Probability 141
- 5.4 Simulation of DRXS Hardened Circuits 149
    - 5.4.1 Test Setup 149
    - 5.4.2 Test Circuit Selection 151
    - 5.4.3 Results 154
- 5.5 Summary 163

6 Emulation — 167

- 6.1 Related Work 167
- 6.2 Fault Emulation in QDI Logic 171
    - 6.2.1 Error Coverage 171
    - 6.2.2 Reproducibility 173
- 6.3 The STEFAN Tool 174
    - 6.3.1 Description of the Tool 174
    - 6.3.2 A Versatile Saboteur 177
    - 6.3.3 Usage 182
- 6.4 Application: The GAIA Video Pre-Processing Algorithm 185
    - 6.4.1 The GAIA Mission 185
    - 6.4.2 The GAIA Pre-Processing Algorithm 185
    - 6.4.3 FSL Implementation 187
    - 6.4.4 Emulation of the GAIA Algorithm 188
- 6.5 Summary 198

7 Conclusion — 201

- 7.1 Summary 201
- 7.2 Outlook 203

Bibliography — 205

1

Introduction

This chapter gives an overview of the motivation behind this thesis. It briefly describes the main objectives and the contribution that is made.

1.1 Motivation

Today's modern integrated circuits are still facing a continuing down-scaling process. The smaller feature size has led to several improvement trends as shown in Table 1.1. The most remarkable trends are higher integration, faster operation and decreasing cost per function, which has led to significant improvements microelectronic products [1]. At the same time, the supply voltage is reduced as well leading to a higher power efficiency.

Table 1.1: Improvement Trends for ICs Enabled by Feature Scaling from [1]

TREND	EXAMPLE
Integration Level	Components/chip, Moore's Law
Cost	Cost per function
Speed	Microprocessor throughput
Power	Laptop or cell phone battery life
Compactness	Small and light-weight products
Functionality	Nonvolatile memory, imager

That higher integration and improved performance is paid by an increased fault sensitivity as the amount of electric charge that defines a logical value in a digital circuit (critical charge) is becoming smaller. Fig. 1.1(a) depicts the critical charge versus the circuit technology. As the circuit's environment is not affected by that trend, it becomes more easy to disturb the logic state of a circuit node [2,3] and soft errors mainly caused by high-energy cosmic neutrons are becoming a major source of errors in modern integrated circuits [4].

1. Introduction

The effect of the reduced critical charge is an increased soft error rate as depicted in Fig. 1.1(b). Thereby the soft error rate for SRAM cells did not change significantly. The reason for this is the compensation of the smaller critical charge by a disproportionate reduction in the cell area and an improvement in technology. However, for logic elements and latches, the soft error rate grows as predicted by the critical charge reduction.

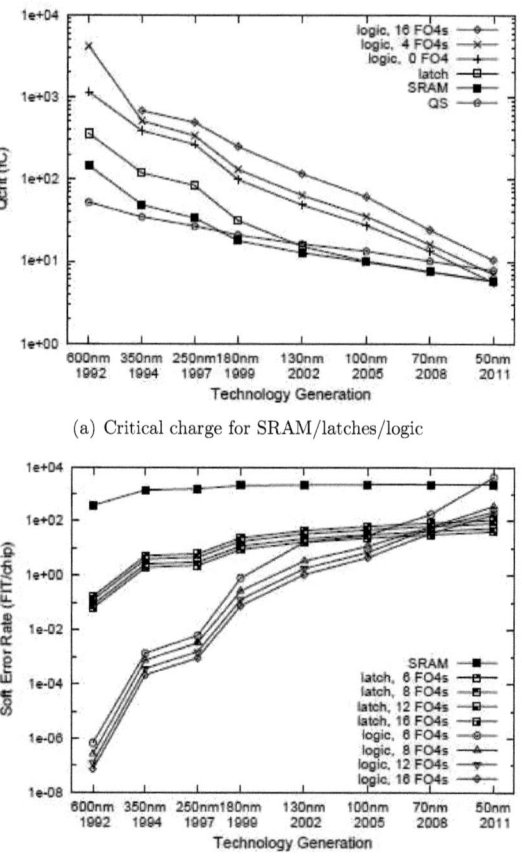

(a) Critical charge for SRAM/latches/logic

(b) Soft error rate / chip for SRAM/latches/logic

Figure 1.1: Critical charge and soft error trends versus technology [5]

Although the analysis in [5] has already been performed in 2002, the results are confirmed by recent research [6]: The soft errors in logic cells start to overtake the soft errors in SRAM cells and will become the dominating source of errors in future technologies. Table 1.2 compares the SEU (single event upset, soft error) rates in microprocessors that are designed in different technologies. The failures in time (FIT) per bit are declining, while the higher integration density leads to an overall increase in the SEU rate for the complete device. Even worse, it was shown that shrinking feature sizes lead to an increase of multi-cell upsets, i.e. a single particle incident will disturb several logic cells. These multiple upsets primarily affect memory cells, thus more complex error correcting codes are required to minimize the system level effects [6].

Table 1.2: Raw SEU Rate per Microprocessor from [6]

Tech. (nm)	Relative SEU rate in FITs/kbit	Approx. Mbits per microprocessor	Relative uncorrected SEU rate per microprocessor (kFIT)
250	3.2	1.52	4.95
180	3.0	1.52	4.29
130	2.4	3.28	10.24
90	1.0	33.6	33.60
65	0.7	44.3	30.46

Especially for high reliability (hi-rel) applications, an improvement in circuit performance that is accompanied with a reduction in dependability is not acceptable. Moreover, radiation effects that have been known for a long time in fields such as space engineering or radioactive applications for science, medicine or military have now found their way into commercial products. Soft errors, induced by e.g. irradiation with high energetic particles are becoming a concern for terrestrial applications [7–10].

Aside these reliability issues, modern highly integrated microcircuits make it harder to distribute a low skew central clock signal across a chip and to maintain the necessary timing margins for synchronous technology. Providing a reliable communication between particular on-chip modules is getting more challenging as well [1].

Within this field, asynchronous circuits are becoming more popular [11]. They show some properties that make them superior to their synchronous counterparts. The clock distribution problem is eliminated, the obtained performance is more an average case than a worst case as every single module runs at its own maximum speed and no timing margins have to be considered. Further the asynchronous modules are easy to compose as they are based on a local handshake that autonomously adapts to the slowest device. Transitions take place only when they are needed, which reduces electromagnetic emission and susceptibility as well as dynamic power consumption. Asynchronous designs also offer an improved fault tolerance, not only to internal process variations but also to external faults.

On the other hand, asynchronous circuits have a clear disadvantage in terms of area compared to equivalent synchronous circuits. The design market thinks and acts synchronously. Tools for developing asynchronous circuits are in the minority compared

1. Introduction

to synchronous tools and often limited to university usage. Although synchronous tools can be utilized, their outcome and performance is not as satisfactory.

While there is a lot of research done on fault tolerance in synchronous systems, less attention has been paid to asynchronous circuits. Well established error detection techniques applied to synchronous circuits cannot be directly applied to asynchronous designs. Further, the different classifications of asynchronous circuits [12] – bounded delay (Huffman), speed independent, (quasi) delay-insensitive circuits – entail different methods of error detection.

1.2 Scope

The main objective of this work is the investigation of transient fault effects in asynchronous *Quasi Delay-Insensitive* (QDI) circuits [12] and the development of hardening strategies to mitigate these faults. Thereby both the fault effects and their countermeasures are applied at the register level, which regards general combinational logic and registers as primitive items. That level of abstraction provides more simplicity as well as yields general, technology independent results compared to more fine grained levels such as the gate or transistor level. Similarly, as the mitigation of faults is also applied to the register level, higher level hardening methods such as checksums or parity protection are not applicable. Therefore the developed mitigation strategies will be system independent as well.

Although this work provides a general treatment of QDI circuits, a focus is set on a special member of the QDI family, namely *Four-State Logic* (FSL) [13], which describes one possible implementation of the *Level Encoded Dual-Rail* (LEDR) [14] protocol. The robustness of an asynchronous FSL processor was investigated in [15] and showed a high inherent robustness to transient faults, which is based on the delay-insensitive encoding of QDI logic. Basically, the fault mitigating feature of QDI logic relies on its inherent tendency to block manipulated data: A fault rather stops a QDI circuit instead of producing any functional errors. If the circuit is stopped forever, it is said to be deadlocked. It depends on higher level requirements, whether such a deadlock is preferable not.

While a deadlock can be assumed for nearly all kinds of permanent faults, that is not necessarily true for transient faults and it has been shown that transient faults have become the major source of errors [16]. Traditional methods applied to synchronous circuits cannot be directly mapped to asynchronous circuits [17, 18]. There is no global clock that produces a new set of valid data each clock edge that can be used for e.g. comparison with a redundant data set. The absence of a clock also prevents synchronous fault injection test methods to be applied to asynchronous designs [19]. This thesis aims to improve both, simulation and hardware based transient fault injection in QDI logic. Thereby the characteristics of QDI circuits are taken into account, especially when using commercial design tools that have been developed for synchronous circuits.

1.3 Contribution

Within this thesis a comprehensive investigation of transient fault effects in QDI logic is performed:

Trace Based Fault Model – A new fault model is developed to describe the effect of transient faults in QDI logic and to derive proper hardening techniques. Contrary to existing models that are based on transition [20] or token level [21], this model is based on trace theory [22]. The trace based approach is well suited for the description of events in asynchronous circuits and it combines the benefits of transition (high level of details) and token based methods (simplicity).

Duplication and Rail Cross-coupling – Various methods are examined to mitigate transient faults in asynchronous QDI logic. A new method called *duplication and rail cross-coupling* was derived. It is based on duplication but comes along with a minimum amount of supplemental hardware by modifying the signal trace during a transient fault. Thereby the hardware overhead is minimized, which is one of the main drawbacks of asynchronous circuits. The properties, benefits and drawbacks of this new method are discussed and compared to established hardening techniques such as duplication and double checking [18].

Consideration of latching effects in QDI simulation – A widely used technique to evaluate different fault effects, hardening methods or the robustness of a system is fault simulation. One key difference between synchronous and asynchronous circuits is the transparent phase of a storage element. In flip-flop based, synchronous logic that phase is very short, limited by the rise time of the clock and the internal delays. In asynchronous circuits a storage element may be transparent for a considerable amount of time, leading to different effects. A special *fault injection tool* for VHDL simulation was developed that considers these peculiarities. It allows to simulate both soft errors and transient errors without modifying the underlying circuit architecture and may be used for all kind of synchronous and asynchronous circuits if transient faults shall be examined. The benefit of this tool over existing methods is its simplicity and a minimum computation effort.

QDI fault injection considering controlled traces – Contrary to simulation, emulation offers improved performance as the circuit's operation takes place in real hardware and does not need to be simulated. A common practice is to add invasive elements, or saboteurs, that provoke faults. The problem with asynchronous circuits opposed to synchronous circuits is to achieve a full fault coverage. In a synchronous design the clock is the only event that generates a new state. In an asynchronous design each signal event triggers a new state, which requires not only to control the logic value of a fault and the moment of its occurrence but also to control the sequence when events take place – the trace. A new *hardware fault injector* has been designed that allows to control that trace. Thereby, a deterministic and reproducible fault investigation of QDI circuits in hardware is obtained, which takes care of the state coverage problem that is commonly disregarded in other tools.

1. Introduction

1.4 Outline and Methodology

The thesis is structured in different chapters, which are – as far as possible – self-standing parts providing the interested reader a more efficient way to study the subjects he is interested in without working through the whole document.

Chapter 2 gives a brief introduction in asynchronous logic especially in QDI logic. It comprises the idea behind the asynchronous design style and introduces the peculiarities it is accompanied by. A general overview of the different faults and fault models in QDI logic is provided. Fault tolerance and its application in QDI logic is described.

Chapter 3 presents an overview of the different fault models that are suited for QDI logic. It describes the *trace based model* that has been developed during this thesis and applies that model to different circuit parts, especially interconnections as well as combinational and sequential circuits. The chapter derives the necessary rules and boundary conditions of the trace based model, which are then applied in the following chapters to determine the mitigation of transient faults.

Chapter 4 handles the general aspects of soft errors and what mitigation strategies may be applied. It introduces the concept of *duplication and rail cross-coupling* and investigates the properties of this method applying the trace based fault model that has been developed in Chapter 3. The duplicated and rail cross-coupled method aims to improve the logical masking capability of a system. Several implementations of this concept are compared with respect to fault tolerance but also in terms of hardware overhead.

Chapter 5 describes the simulation of QDI circuits that are subjected to transient faults. Thereby the characteristics of QDI logic is highlighted, which lead to the design of the **FO**ur **ST**ate **ER**ror injection tool (FOSTER). Originally, that tool was developed to simulate transient faults in Four State Logic (FSL), which is a special design style of QDI logic. In principle it can be also mapped to other common styles such as 4-phase dual-rail. This chapter investigates the theoretically derived results from the previous chapters by means of simulation based experiments using typical building blocks of digital systems.

Chapter 6 deals with the fault emulation of QDI circuits, focusing on an optimum error coverage and reproducibility of the fault injection. Thereby the trace based model is applied to real hardware by means of the **S**ynthesizable **T**est **E**nvironment **F**or **A**synchronous **N**etworks (STEFAN). That tool allows to test QDI circuits in a deterministic manner by presenting a new type of saboteur that takes over the control over a circuit's trace. The new fault injection method is applied to a real signal processing application. Thereby the fault tolerance of the different duplication and rail cross-coupling architectures is investigated.

Chapter 7 draws a conclusion and gives an outlook to remaining fields of investigation on this subject.

2

Background

This chapter provides the necessary background for this thesis. First an introduction to asynchronous logic, especially into *Quasi Delay-Insensitive* (QDI) circuits is given. The different types of faults in asynchronous logic are presented and an overview of the state of the art in fault tolerant QDI circuits is reviewed.

2.1 Asynchronous Logic

2.1.1 General

Digital logic deals with binary signals. An analog signal, typically a voltage, is assigned to discrete boolean values TRUE/FALSE or 1/0. Fluctuations in the analog nature of information are not relevant as long as the boolean value remains unchanged. Another simplification in the design of digital circuits is the assumption of a common, discrete time – defined by the clock signal [23]. A discrete time resolves many problems, since the actual behavior of a signal between two consecutive clock edges is of no importance. Properties such as different propagation delays (skew), glitches or hazards do not alter the logic function as long as all transients have settled to a stable state before the next clock edge occurs. That fundamental constraint manifests in the setup and hold time known from synchronous flip-flops. If these timings are violated a correct operation is not guaranteed and metastability may occur. As long as the circuit operates solely in a synchronous domain, which means that no asynchronous signals have to be processed, the setup and hold problem can be solved by simply reducing the clock frequency. Thereby the transients have a longer time to settle. An asynchronous signal does not follow a discrete time, i.e. events on such a signal may occur at any time and are not related to the clock signal.

Asynchronous circuits neither assume a discrete time nor do they have a common clock signal. The communication between the sender and the receiver of data is based on a local handshake between these two instead of a global clocking scheme. Thereby the actual speed of the circuit depends on the actual propagation delays of the particular circuit elements and not on an externally imposed clock frequency. Any communication actually takes place when it is needed and not at pre-defined time intervals such as clock edges. This fundamental principle generally results in considerable benefits compared to synchronous circuits [11, 12, 23, 24]:

- *Less dynamic power* – Asynchronous circuits only perform an action when such an event is requested by the local handshake and not at every clock edge. Fewer switching reduces the dynamic power consumption.

- *Average case performance* – In synchronous circuits, the clock frequency must be selected according to the worst case delay for a correct operation. Asynchronous circuits, especially those which are insensitive to delays show an average case performance as they regulate their operational speed inherently.

- *Adaptivity* – Asynchronous circuits are not affected by environmental variations that change the operating speed of the circuit. They simply adapt their local handshake protocol to the new conditions.

- *Modularity* – The local handshaking as well as the reduced impact of actual delays makes asynchronous circuit highly modular. Components may be simply replaced without considering synchronization issues or making worst case timing analyzes.

- *No clock skew problem* – The distribution of a low skew, high-speed clock signal is not needed any more.

- *Reduced electromagnetic emission* – Since there is no dominant regular switching operation at every clock edge but rather a distributed, smooth activity across the circuit the electromagnetic emissions are reduced.

- *Security* – Less emissions of asynchronous circuits make them more rugged to security attacks. It is harder to both scan as well as disturb a system that operates at rather arbitrary time instants.

- *Robustness* – The reduced susceptibility to delays, environmental impacts and the lack of a common clock signal that affects all parts of a design makes asynchronous circuits inherently very robust.

- *Reliability* – The clock signal constitutes a single point failure in a synchronous circuit. Asynchronous circuits eliminate that source of errors, since no clock is needed. As the circuit operation is more evenly distributed across a chip, the wear-out of specific circuit parts is reduced, which improves the life time of a component.

Of course, all the above items are more general statements that have to be treated on case-by-case basis. Detailed information about asynchronous logic can be found in various books and articles such as [12, 23–30] to name a few.

However, asynchronous circuits also face considerable drawbacks. In general, they are not as efficient as an equivalent synchronous circuit especially in terms of area overhead. Although they consume less dynamic power and offer average case performance, their increased area and complex design may annul these benefits when overall power and performance is compared. The design methodology is more complex and asynchronous circuits are neither easy to test nor easy to develop due to the lack of commercial CAD tools. For prototyping tasks, these drawbacks become much more evident as typical platforms such as FPGAs are optimized for synchronous designs. Although a synchronous FPGA can be used for asynchronous designs the resulting design may even have a worse efficiency than predicted, which makes a fair comparison asynchronous versus synchronous even harder.

This thesis focuses on the investigation of transient fault effects and their mitigation in asynchronous circuits. The deficiencies such as area overhead are of secondary concern, although they are briefly tackled.

2.1.2 Classification

Asynchronous logic is not a new principle and lasts back to the 1950s. Pioneers in that field, such as *D. A. Huffman* [31, 32] and *D. E. Muller* [33], derived different methods of digital asynchronous circuit design. There exist several possibilities to classify asynchronous circuits. One of the most obvious methods is the delay model the system adheres to. In principle, there are two disjunctive models:

1. The *Bounded Delay* model places certain constraints on the propagation delays of gates and wires in a circuit.

2. The *Unbounded Delay* model allows arbitrary delays for at least some parts of a circuit.

Within the unbounded delay model, two main families can be distinguished: *Speed Independent* (SI) and *Delay-Insensitive* (DI) circuits. SI circuits assume positive, unknown delays in gates but zero delays on wires. DI circuits do not apply any delay restrictions, neither in gates nor on wires. Unfortunately, the class of DI circuits is limited to circuits that only consist of inverters and so called *Muller C-gates* [34]. A less restrictive sub-class of DI circuits are *Quasi Delay-Insensitive* (QDI) circuits, which allow unbounded delays in all elements except in *isochronic forks*. Such forks assume the difference in the delay of each branch is negligible, i.e. a transition that starts at the root of the fork will arrive at the end of each branch at the same time. With that limitation the class of QDI circuits becomes bigger and thus more practicable than pure DI logic. If all forks in a QDI circuit are required to be isochronic, the circuit essentially becomes a SI circuit. In this case, the wire delays are transferred into their associated gates, as the SI paradigm allows arbitrary gate delays. In practical QDI circuits, such isochronic forks are applied to the gate level implementation of basic building blocks (gates, registers), where the matched delays are more easy to control, while at a higher level the connection between these blocks is truly DI [12].

Synchronous circuits also adhere to the bounded delay model. The synchronous paradigm assumes that all transient states have settled to a steady state by the next clock edge. Asynchronous circuits that follow the bounded delay model require certain timing assumptions and operation modes. They are also referred to as *Self-Timed* [23].

2.1.3 Operating Modes

The classification of asynchronous circuits according to their delay model does not define the interaction with their environment. There are two basic operating modes [24]:

1. Fundamental Mode

2. Input-Output Mode

The *fundamental mode* was developed by D. A. Huffman [31,32]. This mode requires that the next input must not be applied until the circuit has settled to a stable state. Thus an upper limit must be placed on the delays of the circuit as the internal states of the circuit are not visible to the environment. Fundamental mode circuits always adhere to the bounded delay model. The classic fundamental mode only allows one single input to be changed at a time. The *burst mode* [35] extends that single-input limitation and allows several inputs to be changed at once. The environment still has to wait until the circuit has stabilized before the next input burst may be applied. The completion of an operation in a fundamental mode circuit cannot be concluded by solely looking at the outputs as these may change due to transient, intermediate states as well.

In the *input-output mode* developed by D. E. Muller [33], the environment may apply the next input as soon as an output change has been observed. So there exists a causal relation between input and output transitions. The internal signals as well as internal states of the circuit are not regarded, so each output transition must be a valid one. No transient or intermediate output transitions are allowed. Therefore a circuit that operates in the input-output mode must be at least speed-independent.

2.1.4 Handshake Protocols

In a synchronous circuit, the clock signal determines when data is valid. So new data will be sampled at the clock edge only. Asynchronous circuits have no clock that

2.1. Asynchronous Logic

defines the validity of data and triggers the capture process. Thus some kind of handshake protocol between the circuit and its environment is needed to decide when data is valid and may be captured. In general, two handshake events are required as shown by Fig. 2.1:

1. A *request* event, which signals the receiver that new data is available.

2. An *acknowledge* event, which signals the source that data has been captured.

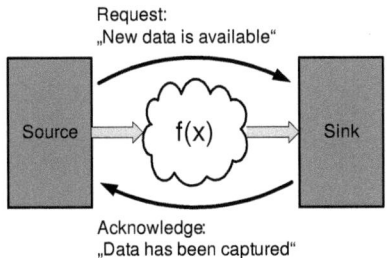

Figure 2.1: Principle of handshake

In the nominal case, i.e. without any faults, these two events will alternate. A request is followed by an acknowledge, which will be followed again by a request and so on. In synchronous circuits, the clock serves as global request event that triggers the storage of new data. An acknowledge signal is not needed as the synchronous principle requires that data is processed by the next clock event. In asynchronous circuits, there exist several handshake implementations.

In bounded delay circuits, such as Huffman state machines operating in the fundamental mode, the handshake is implicitly provided by the delay of the environment before consecutive data is applied. Therefore, fundamental mode circuits operate similar to synchronous circuits. Other types of bounded delay circuits and especially circuits that operate in the input-output mode, require dedicated handshake signals.

In *bundled data* circuits, the handshake information is explicitly transmitted together with the data. The handshake signals comprise one request signal and one acknowledge signal for N data signals. Thereby the request signal has to be delayed to guarantee that data is valid when the request event is received. Therefore, bundled data circuits follow a bounded delay model and require a positive timing margin between the propagation delay on the request line and the worst case propagation delay on the data lines. For the acknowledge signal, no such timing constraint is required. Other asynchronous design techniques, such as SI and (Q)DI circuits do not require a dedicated request line. In these circuits, the validity of data is implicitly determined by the data encoding.

2. Background

The request and handshake events may be level or edge encoded. The type of encoding defines whether the event is defined by the logic state (*level signalling*) of the handshake lines or by the change of that state (*transition signalling*) [36]. In general, level signalling results in simpler circuits as transition signalling requires the circuit to react on signal events rather than on signal states.

Within the handshaking, either the sender or the receiver may initiate the communication. In general, the sender performs this task by means of providing new data. This standard configuration is known as *push channel*. On the other hand, the receiver may also control the handshaking by asking for new data, which is referred to as *pull channel*.

The handshake protocol can be classified by the number of operation phases it consumes. The *four phase protocol* (4-phase) uses a simple return-to-zero encoding for the handshake. Although this protocol does not convey any information in the return to zero phases, the 4-phase protocol allows to design quite simple circuits and is therefore the most popular one. Second, the computation time in an asynchronous circuit may be much longer than the transmission time, so the return to zero phases do not have a large weight in the overall budget and justify the more simple circuit design. The *two phase protocol* (2-phase) is a good choice when this is not the case. It uses a non return-to-zero encoding. That protocol does not waste the time of the reset phases, however, a 2-phase circuit design is generally more complex than a 4-phase circuit. Some asynchronous designs utilize the benefit of both protocols by applying the 4-phase protocol to the computational part of the circuit and the 2-phase protocol to the interconnection parts [37, 38]. Another improvement of data throughput for asynchronous handshake protocols is *Level Encoded Transition Signalling* (LETS), which combines a return-to-zero encoding with 1-of-N codes [39]. An example for a practical 4-phase realization that has been placed commercially on the market in the 90's is *Null Convention Logic* (NCL) [40].

The classification of an asynchronous circuit does not define its physical implementation. For instance, a DI circuit may use a 4-phase or a 2-phase protocol. Additionally, the properties of bounded and unbounded delay can be combined as in the *Micropipeline* [41], which uses a DI control circuit for the handshaking but bounded-delay data path.

2.1.5 Quasi Delay-Insensitive Logic

As already highlighted, real DI circuits do not comprise a lot of practical applications. Thus QDI logic is applied instead, provided the limitation of isochronic forks is acceptable – which is often the case considering practical designs. Due to the unbounded delay the sender does not know when the receiver has captured the requested data. Therefore the receiver must explicitly inform the sender about such an event by means of an acknowledge signal. The sender is not allowed to transmit the next data until it has received an acknowledge.

2.1. Asynchronous Logic

On the other hand, the receiver must only process valid data. Bundled data circuits solve that problem by attaching a dedicated request signal to the data signals. That request signal must always be late compared to the data, which requires a bounded delay model. In case of arbitrary, unbounded delays a temporal order between any signals is not guaranteed anymore. Therefore, data must be transmitted using a *delay-insensitive* or *unordered code*. Thus the receiver is able to detect new, valid data by simply evaluating its code. There is a variety of delay-insensitive codes [42]. The combination of a delay-insensitive code and a handshake protocol allows different styles.

The most widely applied handshake scheme is the 4-phase protocol, which is shown in Fig. 2.2(a). Actually only two phases carry valid data and acknowledge events while the other two phases are used to reset the data and the acknowledge signal to their initial value. The drawback of this protocol is invalid data (I) between the valid code words (V). The advantage is a rather simple circuit implementation. More efficient is *Level Encoded Dual-Rail Signalling* (LEDR) [14] that uses a 2-phase protocol. Data is transmitted in two alternating *phases*, $\varphi 0$ and $\varphi 1$, as depicted by Fig. 2.2(b). No invalid codes are needed, however, the circuit implementation is in general more complex.

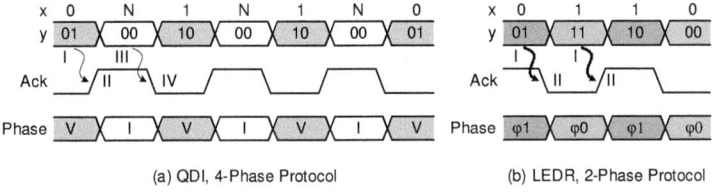

(a) QDI, 4-Phase Protocol (b) LEDR, 2-Phase Protocol

Figure 2.2: Data sequence using a 4-phase and a 2-phase protocol

Table 2.1 shows two possible implementations of QDI logic. Both map a boolean variable $x \in \{0,1\}$ to a dual-rail variable y comprising the two rails a and b: $x \mapsto y_a y_b$ with $y_a, y_b \in \{0,1\}$. The most widely applied style is a *1-of-2 one hot* or simple *dual-rail* code together with a 4-phase protocol. In *4-phase dual-rail*, data alternates between the valid code set $V = \{01, 10\}$ and the invalid code $I = \{00\}$. The remaining code $\{11\}$ is not used, which means only three of the four possible code states are used.

Table 2.1: Truth table of 2- and 4-phase dual-rail logic

$y_a y_b$	2-ph. dual-rail (four-state coding)		4-ph. dual-rail (three-state coding)	
	x	code set	x	code set
0 0	0	$\varphi 0$	-	I
0 1	0	$\varphi 1$	0	V
1 0	1	$\varphi 1$	1	V
1 1	1	$\varphi 0$	-	Not used

2. Background

The invalid code in a 4-phase dual-rail protocol does not convey any information and is purely used to separate consecutive code words or *tokens*:

Definition 2.1.1. A token describes any legal data in an asynchronous system that can be interpreted.

To be legal, data must be *consistent* as well. During the transition between the code phases, the encoding reaches intermediate states that are *inconsistent*. Both terms are detailed later on. In addition to illegal codes, such as '11' in 4-phase dual-rail, there is a second reason for illegal data. Once a token has been consumed, the data held by the predecessor becomes obsolete. In this case the token in the predecessor is transformed into a *bubble*.

Definition 2.1.2. A token is transformed into a bubble after it has been consumed, i.e. acknowledged, by the successor.

Any QDI circuit may only receive a token if it holds a bubble. During the operation, tokens travel from the source to the receiver, while at the same time bubbles travel from the receiver to the source. This token – bubble game describes the data flow in an asynchronous circuit. For more details refer to [12].

Within this thesis, the term *illegal* means any code that does not comply with the circuit's protocol, while the term *inconsistent* means that the code word cannot be evaluated. In general, a QDI circuit shall be designed such that it will never process inconsistent data. Regarding illegal codes, it depends on the circuit implementation whether it will process such data or not. For example, the illegal code '11' in 4-phase dual-rail may be used for error detection [17, 43], but it can as well be simply ignored to save area.

In LEDR a more efficient dual-rail encoding together with a 2-phase protocol is used. As this style uses all four possible states of a dual-rail code it is also called *four-state coding* compared to the previously described *three-state coding* [13]. One way to implement the LEDR protocol is *Four State Logic* (FSL) or *2-phase dual-rail*. In FSL, data alternates between the two codes sets $\varphi 0 = \{00, 11\}$ and $\varphi 1 = \{01, 10\}$ as shown in Table 2.1 and Fig. 2.3. Each phase uniquely defines the boolean states FALSE and TRUE. Phase $\varphi 0$ is also called the even phase and $\varphi 1$ is called the odd phase, which stems from the modulo-2 sum of the two rails in the code. Contrary to the 4-phase protocol, both FSL code sets carry valid information. The benefit of the 2-phase protocol is higher speed [44], thereby LEDR allows to build circuits with more acceptable complexity compared to classical transition signalling [36]. Within this thesis the terminology FSL refers to the design style of a LEDR encoded QDI circuit.

The most promising application of LEDR lies in the realization of asynchronous interconnections. For example, a single buffer implemented in LEDR has 187% higher throughput but consumes only 62% of the energy compared to an equivalent 4-phase

2.1. Asynchronous Logic

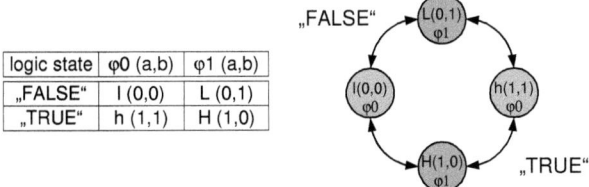

logic state	φ0 (a,b)	φ1 (a,b)
„FALSE"	l (0,0)	L (0,1)
„TRUE"	h (1,1)	H (1,0)

Figure 2.3: FSL encoding and state transitions

dual-rail buffer [38]. In [45] a very fast asynchronous shift register designed for high speed bit serial on-chip interconnection channels is presented. The interconnection channel was implemented using LEDR signalling. Simulations showed a speed of 67 Gbps in 65 nm CMOS and at the same time an immunity to in-die process variations in the order of 10σ, with σ being the standard process variation.

In Fig. 2.2, the boolean sequence $x = \{..., 0, 1, 1, 0, ...\}$ has been transferred to both common 3-state QDI logic using a 4-phase protocol and to FSL using a 2-phase protocol. From that example, two fundamental properties can be derived, which have to be satisfied by all types of QDI circuits:

(I) Data is always processed in alternating code phases, which is called the *alternation property*.

(II) Any QDI function $z = f(Y)$ with $Y = \langle y_1, ..., y_n \rangle$ will produce a *consistent* output z if and only if its input Y is also *consistent*. Otherwise the current output is preserved, which is called the (strong) *completeness property*.

Property (I) allows to distinguish consecutive data, while property (II) prevents the mixture of code phases. The concept of consistency is an important property that distinguishes QDI from common synchronous logic. To formally describe consistency, the *code set* Φ is introduced:

Definition 2.1.3. The code set Φ holds all legal codes that can be processed by a QDI function.

Similarly, the code set can be split into subsets that only hold legal codes of their own code phase. For dual-rail and 1-of-N codes there are two subsets Φ_0 and Φ_1:

Definition 2.1.4. The code subset $\Phi_p \subset \Phi$ holds all legal codes of the code phase p. For dual-rail and 1-of-N codes one can state $\Phi_0, \Phi_1 \subset \Phi$ and for complete codes such as FSL $\Phi_0 \cup \Phi_1 = \Phi$, i.e. the complete code set is covered by two subsets. Further the code sets are disjoint, i.e. $\Phi_0 \cap \Phi_1 = \emptyset$.

2. Background

The code phase of a signal vector $Y = \langle y_1, y_2, ..., y_n \rangle$ can be calculated by the *consistency function* $\varphi(Y)$:

$$\begin{aligned} \varphi(Y) = 0 &\Leftrightarrow \forall y_i \in Y : y_i \in \Phi_0 \\ \varphi(Y) = 1 &\Leftrightarrow \forall y_i \in Y : y_i \in \Phi_1 \\ \varphi(Y) = \mathtt{X} &\Leftrightarrow \exists y_k, y_l \in Y | y_k \in \Phi_0 \wedge y_l \in \Phi_1 \end{aligned} \quad (2.1)$$

For a one-bit dual-rail signal y the code phase can be calculated with a simple XOR function of the two rails: $\varphi(y) = y_a \oplus y_b$. For an $(n > 1)$-bit signal vector the code phase is logical 1/0 if and only if the code phase of each bit in the vector is logical 1/0. Otherwise the code phase is not defined, which is expressed by X. For a completion detection circuit that is used in all types of QDI logic to determine the current code phase, no unknown state is defined. Thus if a completion detector cannot evaluate its output because at least two bits are not in the same code phase, the last known output is maintained.

In LEDR, all possible members of the code set are used, while 4-phase dual-rail does not have this property. Here, the code '11' is not used. Depending on the actual implementation, '11' may be a legal code or not. In the first case, $\{11\} \in \Phi$ and the code is processable. In the latter case, $\{11\} \notin \Phi$ and the circuit will not be able to evaluate the next code phase. So for a QDI function to process a code, it is mandatory that the code is legal and consistent. This requirement applies to all bits of the code word.

Definition 2.1.5. A code word $Y = \langle y_1...y_n \rangle$ is called *consistent* if all bits y_i are member of the code set and have the same code phase:
$\{\forall y_k, y_l \in Y : k, l = 1...n : y_k, y_l \in \Phi \wedge \nexists y_k, y_l | \varphi(y_k) \neq \varphi(y_l)\}$.

The definition of consistency does not define whether the data is valid or invalid. In QDI circuits, only valid data conveys information. It is mandatory that valid data must be both legal and consistent. However, the same applies for invalid data, which is used as a spacer in e.g. 4-phase dual-rail or 1-of-N circuits. For these codes we can derive another property that is helpful in the analysis of QDI logic.

Definition 2.1.6. The transition between consecutive dual-rail code words is performed by one single rail transition for each bit of the code, which is called the *single-event property*.

The above properties can be used to describe the behavior of combinational and sequential QDI circuits. The completeness property implies that even combinational QDI circuits require state holding elements. Any inconsistent code must not be interpreted and lead to the completion of an output. The word completion is important in this context because the completeness property only applies to atomic QDI gates. An atomic gate performs any boolean function, no matter how many terms it is composed of, in one distinct computation step without requiring any intermediate results. If circuits composed of atomic gates adhere to the completeness property they are called *strongly*

2.1. Asynchronous Logic

indicating [12]. In this case, the outputs will be only computed if all inputs have the same code phase. On the other hand, QDI combinational functions can also be designed *weakly indicating*, i.e. they will begin to produce valid outputs even if not all inputs are in the same code phase. Nevertheless, the complete output will not be created before the complete input is in the same phase. A simple example for a weakly indicating circuit is a ripple carry adder. The adder may start to produce an output on its lower bits provided the associated input bits are consistent. The complete result will only be generated if the complete input is consistent.

For sequential QDI circuits, that prerequisite for processing an input must be extended by the handshake protocol.

Definition 2.1.7. Any sequential FSL function will process its input if and only if (i) it is consistent, (ii) its code phase is inverse to the code phase of the currently stored token and (iii) the successor has already acknowledged the current token, which is called the *acknowledge property*.

Sequential gates or registers control the data flow in a QDI circuit, while combinational functions are transparent to the handshaking. The acknowledge property is one of the fundamental properties of any QDI design.

A typical implementation of a QDI circuit is the pipeline in Fig. 2.4. Data is passed from stage (i) to stage $(i+1)$ via the (optional) combinational function $f(x)$. The handshake is controlled by the registers, while the combinational functions are transparent to the handshake. More details, especially on the implementation of FSL in synchronous FPGAs are given in [46, 47].

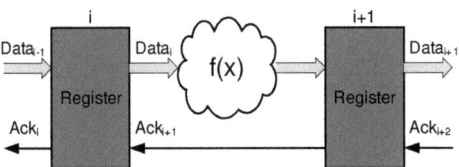

Figure 2.4: Generic QDI pipeline

The physical implementation of QDI circuits is often combined with certain delay assumptions especially when regarding the basic building blocks such as plain registers or simple combinational gates. For the internal design of a practical QDI circuit nearly all forks are required to have matched delays. Additionally, the control signals of latches need to have a minimum pulse width for a correct operation [37, 39, 47]. If these timing constraints are fulfilled, the QDI function can be treated as atomic gate and any circuit that is composed of such functions will be delay-insensitive.

2. Background

2.2 Faults and Errors in QDI Circuits

2.2.1 Definitions and terms

Some frequently used terms related to fault tolerance and error detection shall be clarified. The terms *failure*, *error* and *fault* are understood as established in the Working Group 10.4 (WG10.4) on Dependable Computing and Fault Tolerance of the International Federation For Information Processing (IFIP), summarized in [48]:

- A *failure* occurs when the delivered service deviates from the correct system function, the latter being what the system is aimed at.

- An *error* is that part of the system state which is liable to lead to a subsequent failure. An error is an observable discrepancy between the computed and the correct value due to the activation of a fault.

- A *fault* is the adjudged or hypothesized cause of an error.

The chain in Fig. 2.5 describes the causal relationship between faults, errors and failures: A fault will generate an error provided the fault is activated and not dormant. The produced error will lead to a failure provided the error changes the intended behavior of the system. Basically, an error must propagate to the system boundaries to trigger a failure. This causal chain is continued on the next higher level. A failure in a subsystem may be regarded as fault on the higher system level.

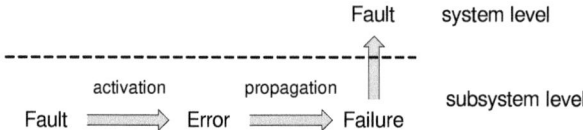

Figure 2.5: Fault-Error-Failure Chain (adapted from [49])

When applying *error detection* the result of a function is checked to validate its correctness. The detection of errors can be conducted during the operation of a system, which is called *Concurrent Error Detection* (CED). On the other hand, when *preemptive error detection* is applied, the operation has to be stopped while the error detection takes place. In this thesis, whenever the term error detection is used, it is regarded as CED.

Example 2.2.1: Let's consider a simple serial protocol where a message of 8 bits is followed by one parity bit. Due to electromagnetic interference, a transient fault occurs and corrupts one data bit during the transmission. We assume the receiver will detect a parity error and ignore the message. Although the error has been identified, the

2.2. Faults and Errors in QDI Circuits

system has failed if we consider the delivery of the message as an integral requirement of the system.

In contrast, *fault tolerance* means the system is able to provide the correct service despite the presence of faults. Fault tolerant systems require error detection to identify the error plus some kind of recovery mechanism to correct the error and to re-establish the correct function or service.

Example 2.2.2: Memories of reliable computing systems are often equipped with an *Error Detection And Correction* (EDAC) code that stores the information together with check bits. Typically, an EDAC code not only allows to detect errors but also to correct them. The number of detectable and correctable errors must not necessarily be the same and varies with the EDAC code structure. In this example, the system is fault tolerant as the error will not propagate and become a failure.

The main purpose of error detection schemes is to improve a system's *dependability*, which defines the ability to deliver a service that can be justifiably trusted [49]. Dependability is seen as an integrative concept that includes attributes such as reliability, availability, safety and security.

2.2.2 Fault Classification

Faults can be classified according to their persistence in *transient* and *permanent* faults. Sometimes the term *intermittent* fault is added to this collection, which is used to describe faults that occur repetitive but not continuously [50].

Transient faults may be introduced by three main radiation effects [9]: High-energy cosmic neutrons that interact with the silicon nuclei of semiconductor devices [51], low-energy cosmic or thermal neutrons that interact with insulation layers [52] and alpha particle radiation due to package imperfections [53]. As today's integrated circuits generally use advanced processes with purified materials, high energetic cosmic neutrons are the dominating radiation effect [9]. Beside radiation, transient faults could also be provoked by *electromagnetic interference* (EMI) due to external sources or signal integrity problems such as ground bounce. Transient faults, especially those generated by particle strikes can be modeled by an electric charge injected to or removed from a circuit node that is represented by the boolean signal x. Thereby the charge is typically described by a double exponential current pulse [54]. Together with the total node capacitance, the injected current pulse modifies the electric voltage of the node. If the injected charge is high enough, the logic threshold of the circuit's technology may be exceeded in either direction and a positive $x\uparrow$ or negative $x\downarrow$ logic transition is generated. At the same time, the injected charge is restored by the node's driver, thus the disturbed signal will return to its initial state after the fault duration t_f depending on the amount of charge, the circuit

2. Background

technology and the node's driver strength. Eventually, the transient fault manifests itself either as a positive or negative digital pulse on the subjected signal x. Our main interest lies in this secondary effect – the corruption of the boolean value of x. The shape or the amplitude of the induced current are not important in the digital domain.

Cosmic rays or other charged particles will induce transients with a pulse width t_f of 100 to 200 ps. In modern microcircuits with feature sizes below 0.35 μm, these transients are no longer attenuated within the gates and will propagate like normal digital signals [55]. At high energies, transient faults longer than 1 ns are predicted for 100 nm bulk CMOS at both proton-rich space environments but also for terrestrial neutron environments [56]. At 90 nm the nodal capacitance and the supply voltage are further reduced, decreasing the critical charge that defines the logical value of a node to a few femto-coulomb. That increases the probability that a charged particle induces a logical disturbance of a few hundred picoseconds [57]. Faults that originate from e.g. glitches on the supply voltage or due to EMI can be described similarly although their underlying primary source is different.

If a transient fault is injected into a circuit without feedback elements, it will only generate a logic pulse at the output of the circuit. Especially in space engineering, such pulses are called *Single Event Transients* (SET) [58]. In circuits with feedback elements, e.g. in a latch, a transient fault may be memorized and generate a permanent upset or error, which is also referred to as *Single Event Upset* (SEU) or simply as *soft error* [59].

Permanent faults are typically used to model physical defects, such as fabrication imperfections, malfunctions due to excessive voltage, current, power or wear out effects such as electro migration [60] or gate oxide break down [61]. Contrary to transient faults, a permanent fault cannot be restored or removed. This fact has to be observed, especially when permanent faults are compared with soft errors. For example, both a transient and a permanent fault may corrupt a memory cell. The transient fault may result in a soft error that can be restored by updating the affected memory with the correct value. If a permanent fault corrupts the memory cell, it cannot be restored, therefore the effect of a permanent fault is also called a *hard error*.

Intermittent faults are assumed to be a sub-class of transient faults, since they occur regularly but will disappear after some time. Thus they can be described the same way as transient faults.

Within this thesis, only the effects and mitigation of transient faults are treated.

2.2.3 Logic Fault Models

At the logic level, faults can be modeled in different ways. One popular method is the *Single Stuck-At Fault* (SSAF) model [62], which disconnects a circuit node from its surrounding elements and forces the isolated node either to the power supply or to ground. The result is either a stuck-at-1 (s@1) or stuck-at-0 (s@0) fault. The SSAF model was originally defined for permanent faults, but can be applied to transient faults as well. The difference lies in the fault duration t_f. Although the SSAF model is simple, it can cover at least 70% of all fabrication defects [17]. Therefore this model is widely applied.

A drawback of using the stuck-at model for transient faults is its inherent activation problem. If a s@0 or s@1 fault is applied, there is a certain probability that the fault will force the subjected signal to its anticipated value. That probability has to be taken into account in the analysis as well as in the practical conduction of fault experiments, otherwise the results could be falsified. As an alternative, *bit-flip* faults are popular because they invert the logic value of the victim signal and therefore avoid the activation problem of stuck-at faults [63]. However, a simple inversion of the fault-free signal is not a good representation of a physical transient fault. Consider a logic signal that is forced to its opposite value. Now, during the fault duration t_f the original signal changes its logic state. The bit flip model will again invert that value. Thus any transition of the fault-free signal will be inverted by the bit flip model. Such a behavior deviates from the original physical effects of transient faults that will rather hold the subjected signal at either logical value until the disturbed charge has been removed by the signal's driver.

A more realistic representation is a pulse that forces the fault-free signal to the inverse value at the fault occurrence and maintains that state during the complete fault duration [64]. This *pulse model* requires the knowledge of the fault-free signal before the fault is applied. Although such a behavior is easy to simulate it is more difficult to emulate in real hardware. Here, a pure combinational saboteur function is not sufficient anymore. The pulse model requires a state holding element that maintains the faulty state during the fault duration.

In the past, gate delay was the major delay source in an integrated circuit. However, with smaller feature sizes, the delays in wires and interconnects are becoming the dominating source of delay and determine a circuit's performance. Thus *delay faults* are gaining more importance, especially for devices with very high quality and reliability requirements [1]. This is also due to the parameter variations in gates.

Other types of faults that are getting more important are *open faults*. This fault just disconnects and isolates a circuit node from its environment. Since the node has no associated driver anymore its logic state is controlled by the surrounding noise and may fluctuate and probably lead to oscillations. A *bridging fault* occurs, when the logic state of a node called victim is controlled by another signal called aggressor. For example, a s@0 fault could also be described as a bridging fault to the lower supply voltage rail, typically ground.

2.2.4 Masking Effects

Masking prevents a fault from becoming active and generating an error. In general, there are three main reasons for fault masking [5]:

2. Background

1. *Electrical masking*: Although a fault is injected on the electrical level, it does not have an impact on the logical level. For example, the current pulse induced by a charged particle, see 2.2.2, is not large enough to corrupt the boolean value. Or there is a glitch on the subjected node but this glitch is attenuated by subsequent gates or wire and eventually has no effect.

2. *Logical masking*: The fault corrupts a boolean signal, however, the logic function that is connected to that faulty signal does not take it into account. An example is implicit logical masking: e.g. a faulty logic 1 pulse at one input of an AND-gate will only propagate if the other input is also at logic 1. Hence, implicit logical masking also depends on the input data of the affected circuit as well. Another example is explicit logical masking: adding a majority voter to replicated functions will block an erroneous replica as long as the fault-free replicas are in the majority.

3. *Temporal (latching-window) masking*: The fault disturbs a signal but the fault is not captured. That type of masking only applies in circuits with state holding elements. For example, a transient fault between two clock edges in a synchronous circuit has no effect as long as its effect is removed by the next clock event. In a QDI circuit, a faulty input will not be captured if the successor circuit has not yet sent its acknowledge.

Fig. 2.6 illustrates these basic masking effects. One might regard fault masking as a separate mechanism that allows to mitigate a fault without explicit error recovery measures [49].

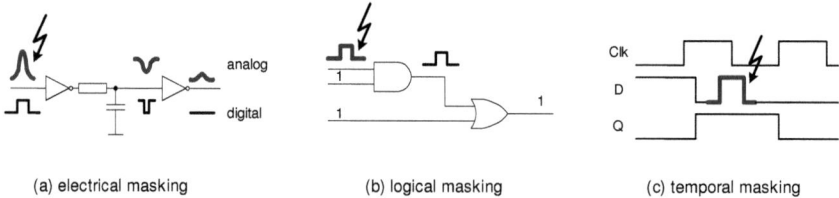

Figure 2.6: Classical fault masking

For this thesis, another masking effect is introduced that deals with QDI logic, namely *code masking*. Fig. 2.7 shows a QDI OR-gate that receives a transient fault at one of its inputs. The fault generates a logic 1 value that would propagate to the output due to the logic OR function. However, as the second input is not in the same code phase, the faulty input is masked and the output remains in its current state. Code masking considers the fundamental property of processing only consistent tokens, while inconsistent tokens – independent whether their content is correct or wrong – are rejected:

22

2.2. Faults and Errors in QDI Circuits

4. *Code masking*: A fault is rejected by a QDI circuit, if it leads to an inconsistent token. Such a token is prevented from propagating any further as long as it persists.

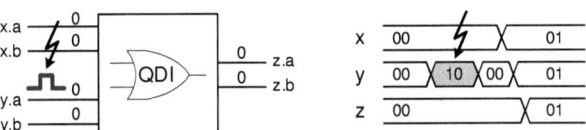

Figure 2.7: Principle of code masking

Code masking may also be interpreted as logical masking, since the logic function of the receiver does not evaluate the token. Contrary to the logical masking as described above, it is not the data content that leads to the masking effect but the code phase of that data. Therefore, the term code masking has been introduced to highlight that fundamental difference. A similar approach has been presented in [65], where the terminology C-element masking is used. However, that masking effect is described solely for C-elements that receive different inputs, while the definition of code masking is more generally applicable to any type of QDI logic. The authors also mention the masking of delay faults, which is not explicitly highlighted in this work as QDI logic is immune to this type of faults by definition.

Fig. 2.8 shows a boolean tree of how masking effects help to mitigate faults. Small graphics highlight the masking effect. The electrical masking branch attenuates a faulty glitch. The logical masking branch blocks the positive going pulse via the implicit AND-gate masking. The temporal masking branch rejects the fault as the receiving circuitry is not yet ready for any data at all. The code masking shows a QDI circuit that holds data in code phase $\varphi 0$ and therefore waits for the opposite code phase $\varphi 1$. A fault corrupts one bit to the old phase $\varphi 0$, which produces inconsistent data that is not processed. The figure can be read as an inverse fault tree, i.e. it is sufficient to have at least one valid branch through the tree to mask the fault.

Electrical masking is not further dealt at all within this thesis as it is concerned with the transistor level and with the design of semiconductor processes. Other types of masking effects as well as their application to prevent any fault propagation will be handled in 4.1.2.

2.2.5 Fault Model

The fault model collects all previously defined boundary conditions under which faults are assumed to occur, such as the fault classification (2.2.2), the logic model (2.2.3) and the applicable masking effects (2.2.4). Additionally, the number of faults that occur per time as well as the rate of their occurrence has to be defined for a comprehensive fault

2. Background

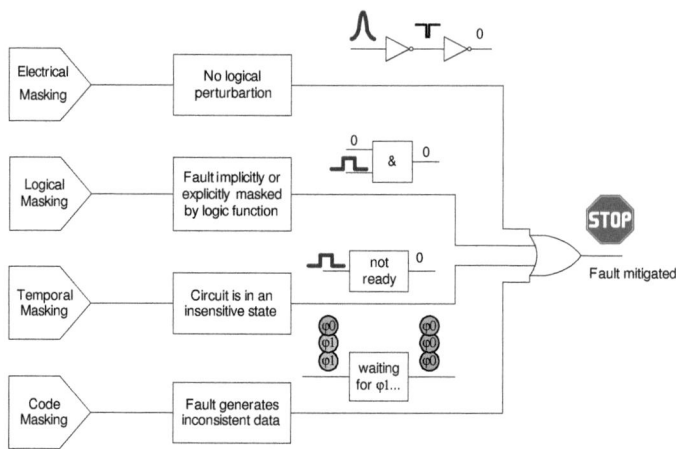

Figure 2.8: Fault masking tree

model. A common approach is to limit faults to one single physical net per time, which is referred to as the *single fault model*. In single-rail logic, such as the common synchronous logic, this restriction means that only one single boolean variable is affected by the fault. In asynchronous QDI logic, a boolean variable is composed of multiple physical rails. To utilize the single fault model, only one single rail must be affected by a fault per time. When comparing dual-rail with single-rail designs that bias has to be considered by e.g. assuming twice the fault rate in the dual-rail circuit to obtain a fair comparison.

The single fault model also assumes that consecutive faults are *separated in time* and are not interleaved. In synchronous logic that separation means that two distinct faults are separated at least by one clock period. That temporal restriction can be transformed to QDI logic, by assuming that only one transient fault occurs per handshake cycle. Alternatively, when hardening methods are deployed, the single fault assumption often means that the next single fault is not applied before a potential recovery has been completed.

Finally, it should be mentioned that the single fault model only limits the fault itself as being a singular event. It does not tell anything about its effects, e.g. it might be possible that a single fault leads to multiple errors.

Within this thesis only *input faults* are considered, while output faults are not treated. This restriction stems from two main reasons:

1. Primarily, we want to examine how a circuit reacts to a faulty input.

2. A faulty output is hard to prevent especially at register level as it requires hardening of the internal structure. Eventually, all output faults will occur at the input of the next component and are therefore covered by item (1).

Like in synchronous circuits, only the sequential circuits define the progression of states. If a state is not altered the fault has no effect. Therefore the end-effect of a fault is always projected to the primary input of a *sequential circuit* independent of where the fault occurs. Although combinational QDI functions are state-holding, the evolution of these states is defined by the sequential circuits that control the handshake in the asynchronous pipeline. For example, a faulty result of the combinational function in the QDI pipeline given in Fig. 2.4 will not lead to an error as long as it is not captured by the receiving register. The effect is the same as the latching-window masking in a synchronous pipeline.

Finally, the *abstraction level* of the faults has to be defined. This abstraction may range from transistor level, to gate level, register level or even system level. The abstraction level defines the least significant granularity of a circuit from a fault's perspective. At each level, faults may be considered differently. For instance, on transistor level it is common to investigate the effect of transient faults by taking into account its analog properties, such as the injected charge as well as the effective node capacitance and impedance at the fault location. At system level, modeling a fault as an analog signal is impractical. Here, higher level fault abstractions such as a corrupted operand may be used. In this thesis faults are solely considered at *register level*, which regards general combinational logic and registers as primitive items of a circuit. Thereby the design of a logic function or a register – their actual composition by means of logic gates or even transistors – is not of interest. That abstraction has some benefits:

- Faults can be applied as logic disturbances, which allows to use fast digital simulation tools and modeling languages such as VHDL.

- Rather complex systems can be treated with still acceptable insight.

- The internal design of basic building blocks or gates need not to be tackled, which allows to examine fault tolerant systems if the internal structure of these blocks is not accessible. For instance, the gate library in an ASIC or FPGA cannot be changed by the user without detailed modifications on transistor level.

- Some physical properties of faults, such as a logic glitch on a particular net, can still be taken into account, which is not possible at higher level where faults are modeled with less physical background.

Investigating fault at the register level does not consider the physical design of a gate or a register. Therefore it lacks a detailed insight as it would be available at finer abstraction levels such as the gate level or even at the analog transistor level. Applying hardening methods at register level also excludes modifications of the internal gate structure as these details are regarded invisible. Investigation at gate or transistor level not only provides a more detailed investigation of fault effects but also allows to place mitigation strategies more directly in the gate design. The fine resolution of gate and transistor level has to be paid by a much higher computation effort, which soon hits practically infeasible boundaries when more complex systems have to be investigated, such as a complete processor for example. Finally, the gate and transistor level depend on the circuit technology, which may not be available at all or which will not allow to draw generic conclusions.

2.2.6 Error Classification

When the different transient faults described in section 2.2 are applied to a QDI circuit, they may – according to literature [17] – result in a deadlock, synchronization failure, token generation or token consumption. Within this thesis, the errors in QDI circuits are classified slightly different as *token error*, *synchronization error* and *deadlock*.

Definition 2.2.1. A *token error* describes the appearance of syntactically legal (see 2.1.5) but semantically erroneous data.

Definition 2.2.2. A *synchronization error* describes a disturbance in the order of consecutive tokens in a way that violates the protocol.

Eventually, both a token error and a synchronization error lead to wrong data. However, their immediate effect is different. Regarding a sequence of N tokens, a token error takes any of these N tokens and replaces it by wrong data. A synchronization error does not touch the token contents. It takes $k > 1$ tokens from that sequence and either deletes them or inserts copies. A simple example shall illustrate these properties.

Example 2.2.3: Let's assume a 2-bit wide pipeline implemented in 4-phase dual-rail that transmits the sequence $\{0, 1, 2, 3, 0, 1, 2, ...\}$ as given by the top waveform in Fig. 2.9. The token error in the middle waveform corrupts the code $\langle 1001 \rangle \rightarrow \langle 10\overline{10} \rangle$ or $2 \rightarrow \overline{3}$ using a binary representation. So the received sequence is changed to $\{0, 1, \overline{3}, 3, 0, 1, 2, ...\}$. The bottom waveform shows a synchronization error. We assume the token $\langle 0110 \rangle$ is applied to the receiver, which is not yet ready to capture that token. A transient fault on the handshake forces the sender to issue the next token pair $\langle 0000, 1001 \rangle$. Now the receiver becomes ready. It detects a valid token in the correct code phase and continues its operation. The handshake fault has led to an unintended consumption of the token $\langle 0110 \rangle$ and its associated null token, which are both removed from the sequence. The received sequence is $\{0, 1, (), 3, 0, 1, 2, ...\}$.

2.2. Faults and Errors in QDI Circuits

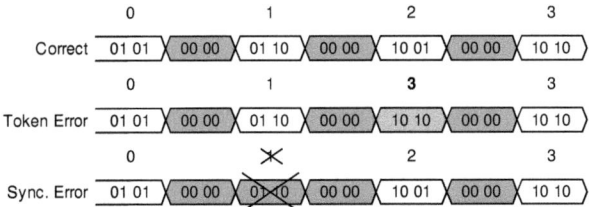

Figure 2.9: Token and Synchronization Errors

Contrary to token and synchronization errors, a deadlock stops the circuit. A deadlock may also be regarded as infinite delay error that originates either from (i) a permanent fault or from (ii) a soft error that freezes the handshake:

Definition 2.2.3. A *deadlock* defines a state of a circuit that has no successor state that belongs to the set of reachable states of the circuit.

This definition of a deadlock originates in trace theory (see 3.2.3), which investigates the state evolution of asynchronous circuits. If the state cannot evolve any further, i.e. no successor state applies to the current state, the circuit has stopped. More practically, a QDI circuit will deadlock if it stops producing output transitions although the circuit's environment does produce or is ready to produce input transitions. This definition stems from the fact that all input transitions are controlled by the circuit's environment – which is not related to the circuit's state.

3

Fault Description

This chapter takes a closer look at the description of faults and their effects in QDI circuits. A new method to describe single faults is derived. It is based on trace theory, a tool set which is already used quite a long time in the development of QDI circuits. The trace based method is used to describe the various effects of faults and to assess the inherent fault tolerance of QDI logic.

3.1 Related Work

The treatment of faults in QDI logic can be classified in either transition based methods or token based methods. The main difference is the used abstraction level.

3.1.1 Transition Based Fault Description

In the *transition based* model, transient faults are directly applied to the external and internal signals of a QDI circuit, depending whether the analysis takes place on register, gate or transistor level, respectively. For instance, the hardened properties of a duplicated double checking architecture on register level is extensively analyzed in [18]. Another example, which investigates the effects of transient faults in QDI network-on-chip links on gate level is described in [20]. Fig. 3.1(a) shows a 1-of-3 QDI pipeline where a transient fault is applied to one input of the middle latch. The effect of this glitch is analyzed by means of a STG in Fig. 3.1(b) and tabulated in Table 3.1.

The transition based method investigates the impact of a transient fault or hazard on an arbitrary signal rail in an arbitrary state of the circuit and its environment. This method seems to be the most natural one as it directly models the primary effect of a transient fault – the perturbation of a logic signal.

3. Fault Description

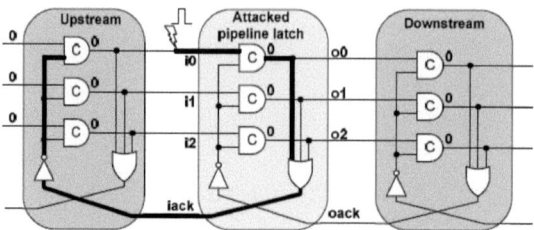

(a) Glitch on a data wire of a 1-of-3 RTZ QDI pipeline

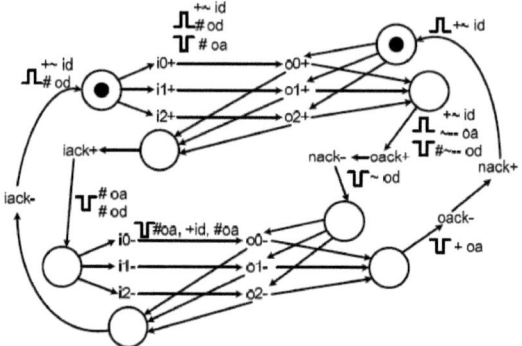

(b) STG of the affected pipeline latch

Figure 3.1: Investigation of a transient fault using a transition based description [20]

The benefit of a transition based fault investigation is a high level of details. It also considers the actual design of the circuit. Especially for hardening methods that are applied on transistor level, such as transistor sizing [66, 67] or on gate level [20], a transition based analysis is mandatory as the effect of this measure are not observable at higher abstraction levels. On the other hand, the state space that has to be covered grows rapidly especially if all possible scenarios shall be covered. Thus the transition based method involves elaborate computations even at moderate complex circuitries.

3.1.2 Token Based Fault Description

In *token based* methods faults are applied at a higher abstraction level that regards the token as an atomic unit. For example, a formal analysis of QDI circuits in the presence of SEUs using a token based fault model is presented in [21]. The authors develop a rule set that describes how the different types of tokens (valid, invalid, bubble) are corrupted by an SEU. The resulting soft error leads to token vanishing, token generation, bubble

Table 3.1: Resulting effects of a glitch in a 1-of-3 QDI pipeline latch [20]

Glitch	Location	Expected next activity	Effect possible
+	ack	New 1-of-n code	Temporary lockout
+	ack	Ack assertion	Symbol loss (race through)
+	code-wire	New 1-of-n code (same wire)	Additional symbol
+	code-wire	New 1-of-n code (different wire)	Additional symbol, Illegal symbol
+	code-wire	Ack assertion	Illegal symbol (2-of-n)
+	code-wire	Ack deassertion	Additional symbol, Illegal symbol
-	ack	code rtz	Temporary lockout
-	ack	Ack rtz	Illegal symbol (race through)
-	code-wire	code rtz (0-of-n)	Additional symbol
-	code-wire	Ack assertion	No effect
-	code-wire	Ack deassertion	Additional symbol

vanishing, bubble generation and valid token corruption. The rule set is described using 4-phase dual-rail QDI logic but it may be also adopted to other design styles such as FSL that is used in this thesis. The benefit of the token based approach is its simplicity compared to the transition based method. In Fig. 3.2(a), a 3-stage state machine is investigated on token level. The 3 stages are described in a column vector. In each stage, one of the previously defined soft error representations is applied and the effect is evaluated. Fig. 3.2(b) shows such a fault injection example.

The token based method efficiently describes the end effect of a transient fault, such as a soft error or SEU. Contrary to a transition based analysis, it already assumes that an SEU is generated by some kind of hidden transient fault. Although this approach eases a formal investigation of the effect of soft errors it does not allow a detailed investigation in the presence of transient faults as it disregards this primary cause of an error.

3. Fault Description

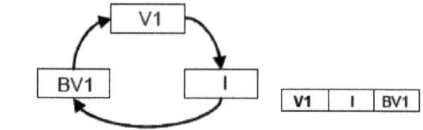

(a) 3 stage state machine and state representation

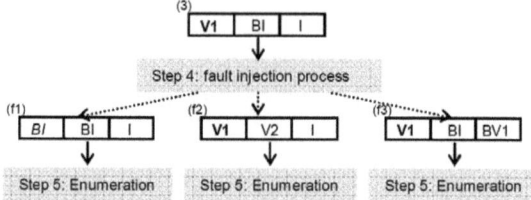

(b) Fault injection in one of the possible circuit states

Figure 3.2: Investigation of a transient fault using a token based description [21]

3.2 Circuit Definition

To understand a trace oriented description as it is developed in this thesis, the temporal definition of QDI circuits is briefly presented. Fundamental and burst mode circuits can be described similar to synchronous sequential circuits by means of a *state graph* (SG) because the occurrence of signal transitions is well defined. SI and (Q)DI circuits work in input-output mode and signals may change in an arbitrary order. These circuits need to be described considering all allowed sequences of signal transitions or *traces*. A common method for specifying such circuits are *signal transition graphs* (STG) [24]. Contrary to a SG, the STG also specifies the behavior of the circuit's environment, which is necessary for all circuits operating in input-output mode.

3.2.1 Signal Transition Graph

A STG is a variant of a *Petri Net* that models the causal relations between the signal transitions of a system [24]. A petri net is a directed graph for modeling concurrent systems. The graph has two types of nodes that are connected via arcs: *places* and *transitions*. The transition nodes are interpreted as a signal transition, either as a rising $(x+)$, a falling $(x-)$ or an arbitrary transition $(x*$ or simply $x)$. The places describe the condition or prerequisite for a transition to take place. Regarding the modeling of a (Q)DI circuit, a transition will happen only if all places that are connected to that transition hold legal data – or simply a token.

For completeness, a STG must satisfy special conditions to describe a meaningful circuit. It must be 1-bounded (only one token can be held in a place), deadlock-free (the circuit will never halt inherently) and contain only simple forms of input choices (inputs must be mutually exclusive) [12]. In addition, to describes a SI circuit, a STG must be both consistent and output-persistent [68]. Consistency means that transitions must alternate, i.e. a rising edge must always be followed by a falling edge. Persistency means that once a transition has been enabled the condition must be maintained until the transition has taken place. The circuit design has to ensure persistency for all internal signals and for all outputs, while the environment is responsible for persistent inputs. To describe a (Q)DI circuit, no input transition must directly precede another input transition [69], i.e. before the next input transition may be applied by the environment the circuit must have generated an output transition. This constraint applies to the external interfaces of a module and assumes the internal design being practically delay-insensitive. Throughout this thesis the same assumption is made – the practical QDI approach assumes the delays within a circuit can be tightly controlled, while the external interfaces have to be DI. The visual representation of the transition sequences in a STG eases the understanding of the trace theory. Further details on delay-insensitivity is provided in 3.2.3.

Example 3.2.1: Fig. 3.3 shows the STG of an arbitrary two-input combinational FSL gate (a) compared to the STG of a 4-phase dual-rail gate (b). Typically only the transitions between the particular places of the graph are shown, while the places (especially implicit places having only one input and output transition) are omitted.

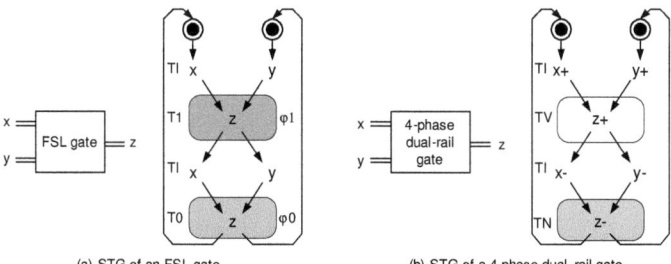

Figure 3.3: STG of 2-input QDI gates

Both gates have dual-rail inputs and outputs. The STG only shows the composite inputs but not their particular rails. The STGs are nearly identical. In the FSL gate, we consider either falling or rising transitions on any rail of the inputs and outputs. The STG in Fig. 3.3(a) also marks the code phase of the tokens that alternates between $\varphi 1$ (T1) and $\varphi 0$ (T0). The output token sequence can be expressed as trace $t_o = \{T1; T0; T1; ...\}$. The situation on the inputs can be generalized when all inputs are collected in the input vector $I = \langle x, y \rangle$. Since there is more than one input, the intermediate *inconsistent token* TI is introduced, which is produced when only

3. Fault Description

one of the two inputs has a transition. The input token sequence would be then $t_i = \{T0; TI; T1; TI; T0; ...\}$, where the duration of the inconsistent phase can be arbitrarily short or long depending on the circuit's environment. Both the input and output traces have been started with the initial marking in Fig. 3.3(a). Note that the common notation is used, where a semicolon marks the temporal order of events.

In the STG of the 4-phase dual-rail gate in Fig. 3.3(b), the rising and falling transitions can be explicitly marked. All rising transitions will eventually lead to a valid code phase, while all falling transitions will eventually lead to an invalid code phase. Consequently, if there is a rising transition on one rail in a 4-phase dual-rail circuit there must be a falling transition on the same rail in the next invalid code phase. The temporal behavior of a 4-phase dual-rail gate is similar to the FSL gate. The invalid or *Null Token* TN means that all rails are logical 0. A valid token TV occurs when exactly one rail per bit is logical 1, while the inconsistent token TI marks any intermediate configurations between TN and TV in case of multiple bit. Considering the initial marking in Fig. 3.3(b) the output trace is $t_o = \{TV; TN; TV; ...\}$ and the input trace is $t_i = \{TN; TI; TV; TI; TN; ...\}$.

The previous example has shown how the behavior of a QDI circuit and its environment can be visualized in a STG. To derive a circuit implementation from such a STG specification, the corresponding SG has to be derived. The SG comprises all reachable states and transition sequences described by the STG. This conversion can be done manually for simple circuits or by means of CAD tools such as Petrify [70] for more complex circuits.

3.2.2 State Graph

A SG models the temporal behavior of a circuit implementation, where each node of the graph describes a unique state of the circuit and each edge describes the transition between these states. Each state is defined by a binary encoded vector that at least comprises all input and output signals but may also contain additional internal signals to guarantee a unique state assignment. The latter is important as each state of the SG must only correspond to one unique marking in the STG.

Contrary to a STG, the SG expands all possible state transition sequences, thus in general the SG is more complex than its associated STG. The edges of the SG are labeled with signal transitions using the same conventions as in the STG. In a SG, only one transition is allowed to occur at a time. To model concurrent events all possible transition sequences have to be considered, e.g. if two inputs x and y may change concurrently, the SG must include the two possible orderings $\{x; y\}$ and $\{y; x\}$, respectively. Section 3.3 gives an example for a SG of both a combinational and a sequential QDI circuit. A good overview of state graphs and their application in asynchronous circuits is given by [24, 36].

3.2.3 Trace Theory

Trace theory is a method to describe concurrent computation using formal language theory compared to the graph theory applied to STGs [22]. In the design of asynchronous circuits, trace theory has been used for both circuit specification and synthesis. Thereby, all possible communication between an asynchronous circuit and its environment can be described by means of *directed trace structures* [71].

Definition 3.2.1. A *directed trace structure* describes the behavior of a circuit C by a triple $\mathcal{P} = \langle I, O, T \rangle$, where I is the set of input transitions, O is the set of output transitions and T is the *trace set* of C. The trace set $T \subseteq (I \cup O)^*$ comprises all finite-length sequences of input and output transitions, where the asterisk (*) expresses arbitrary repetitions. Each *trace* in the trace set T defines one possible finite sequence of such input and output transitions.

In the description of traces, the concatenation of signal transitions is either explicitly marked with the caret operator (^) or more commonly the concatenation operator is omitted, e.g. $x\hat{\ }y \equiv xy$. An example shows the application of a directed trace structure.

Example 3.2.2: A two-input Muller-C gate, one of the basic building blocks of SI and (Q)DI circuits can be described by the following directed trace structure $\langle I, O, T \rangle$: $I = \{a, b\}, O = \{c\}, T = \{\varepsilon, a, b, ab, ba, abc, bac, abca, ...\}$, where ε describes the empty trace. The output of a Muller-C gate will be logic 1/0 only if both inputs are logic 1/0, otherwise it will maintain its current state [33].

A trace structure is directed if it clearly separates input and output transitions. Thereby it expresses that delay has a direction, i.e. a signal's sending must precede its reception [72]. Whenever speaking about trace structures in this thesis, a directed trace structure is meant. To describe a delay-insensitive circuit the trace set T must be *prefix-closed*:

Definition 3.2.2. A trace set T is called prefix-closed if $ts \in T \Rightarrow t \in T \land s \in I \cup O$. It means that any prefix t of a trace in T must be a member of the trace set T as well.

The idea behind a prefix-closed trace is that any trace of a circuit can be extended during the circuit's communication with the environment. A trace may be extended by an input transition received from the circuit's environment or the trace may be extended by an output transition generated by the circuit itself. This definition applies to both combinational circuits as well as to sequential circuits having internal feedback structures. Internal signal transitions are not considered. The practical meaning of prefix-closure becomes evident if components are connected to delay-insensitive networks.

3. Fault Description

3.2.4 Delay-Insensitivity

Several components are connected together to describe a system or network. The trace set is a convenient tool to check whether the communication between the particular components is delay-insensitive (DI) or not. Thereby two fundamental properties must be fulfilled [73]:

1. There must be no *computation interference*, which means a new output must only be generated when the receiver is ready. Assuming the receiver is a valid DI component, its specification must not be violated within a DI system. Therefore, only traces that belong to the (prefix-closed) trace set of the receiver are allowed, otherwise an input may be received at the *wrong moment*:
$\forall s \in I \cup O \wedge t \in T : ts \in T$.

2. The system must be free of *transmission interference*, which means that successive events on a wire must not interfere with each other. That restriction ensures that no new event is sent over a wire before the previous event has been received and acknowledged:
$\forall s \in I \cup O \wedge t \in T : tss \notin T$.

The absence of computation interference ensures that the component's specification is not violated, while the absence of transmission interference ensures that information is not corrupted during the journey between the particular components. Both restrictions are quite similar (a wire may be regarded as a simple component) and eventually require some kind of handshake between communicating components.

Example 3.2.3: Let's examine a two-input Muller-C gates within a DI network. The DI trace structure of such a gate was described in Example 3.2.2. Regarding a trace $t_{ci} = \{aba\}$, the next input transition on a is received before the gate has produced its output transition on c. Computation interference has occurred. On the other hand, the trace $t_{ti} = \{abcc\}$ implies that the C-gate produces two consecutive transitions on its output. Transmission interference is generated.

The definition of delay-insensitivity is also closely related to the so called *Foam Rubber Wrapper* postulate [74]. A circuit is surrounded by a foam rubber wrapper where all inputs and output must pass. That wrapper arbitrarily affects the propagation delays of each signal between the environment and the circuit. So the temporal order of events at the environment and at the enclosed circuit may be changed by the wrapper. For a DI circuit a re-ordered event sequence must not have any consequences on a circuit's and system's behavior – which is ensured by using a DI code. On the other hand, if certain timing constraints are applied on that event ordering, a DI encoding is not necessary. The most popular constraint is an isochronic fork.

Another simplification is to apply local delay constraints on the internal construction of gates and registers. In such a case the internal design is not DI anymore although a system that is composed of such gates may still be DI. The restriction of DI to the interfacing level eases the development [47], reduces the hardware overhead [69] as well as simplifies the design of fault tolerant systems as will be shown in chapter 4. The internal delays of a module can be more tightly controlled, since the particular components are placed closely together. However, the connection between these modules, e.g. in a system-on-chip design, is much harder to control and to predict, especially as the wire delays are gaining more importance in the design of integrated circuits [1]. A DI inter-module communication interface guarantees the correct functionality between the modules, while the correct intra-module functionality is ensured by more easy to control local timing constraints.

3.3 Nominal Behavior of QDI Circuits

3.3.1 Combinational Circuits

The STGs of two-input combinational QDI gates have been depicted in Fig. 3.3. Their corresponding SGs are shown in Fig. 3.4. The graphs have been derived with write_sg, which is included in Petrify. For such simple examples a manual conversion from the STG to the SG would be as quick as the automatic method. For the FSL gate, the two code phase regions of the output z are marked, since they are not related to an event direction (rising or falling edge). In the 4-phase dual-rail gate, the valid code phase transition is related to the rising edges and the invalid phase is related to the falling edges. They are not highlighted for visibility.

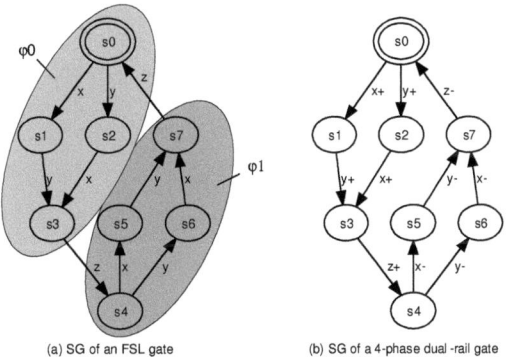

(a) SG of an FSL gate (b) SG of a 4-phase dual-rail gate

Figure 3.4: SG of 2-input QDI gates

3. Fault Description

The trace structure of the FSL gate can be described by $\langle I, O, T \rangle = \langle \{x_a, x_b, y_a, y_b\}, \{z_a, z_b\}, \{\varepsilon, x_a, x_ay_a, x_ay_az_a, x_ay_az_ay_b, x_ay_az_ay_bx_a...\} \rangle$ where the event direction is not specified. The trace structure of the 4-phase dual-rail gate is similar but here the event direction can be unambiguously stated, e.g. $\langle I, O, T \rangle = \langle \{x_a, x_b, y_a, y_b\}, \{z_a, z_b\}, \{\varepsilon, x_{a+}, x_{a+}y_{b+}, x_{a+}y_{b+}z_{a+}, x_{a+}y_{b+}z_{a+}y_{b-}, x_{a+}y_{a+}z_{a+}y_{b-}x_{a-}...\} \rangle$.

3.3.2 Sequential Circuits

In the STG of a sequential QDI circuit, the handshake protocol has to be considered. The reception of a token must be explicitly acknowledged by a dedicated signal. Fig. 3.5 shows the schematic of an FSL register together with its associated STG and SG. The graphs were generated with `draw_astg` and `write_sg` from Petrify. The register uses the *Done* signal to acknowledge when *Dout* has been captured and that a new input *Din* may be applied by the predecessor. To store a token the successor must be ready, otherwise computation interference may occur. So the acknowledge signal *Ack* from the successor determines whether a new input can be processed or not. The trace structure of a 2-bit FSL register looks as follows:

$$\langle I, O, T \rangle = \langle \{Din(2)_a, Din(2)_b, Din(1)_a, Din(1)_b, Ack\},$$
$$\{Dout(2)_a, Dout(2)_b, Dout(1)_a, Dout(1)_b, Done\},$$
$$\{\varepsilon, Din(1)_a, Din(1)_aDin(2)_b, Din(1)_aDin(2)_bDone,$$
$$Din(1)_aDin(2)_bDoneAck, Din(1)_aDin(2)_bDoneAckDout(2)_b, ...\} \rangle.$$

Note that the order of the output transitions *Dout* must not necessarily correspond to the order of the input transitions *Din*.

The STG and SG for a 4-phase dual-rail sequential circuit is nearly identical. The difference is the same as for a combinational circuits, i.e. in FSL the direction of the transitions on the rails of *Din* and *Dout* is arbitrary, while for the 4-phase dual-rail circuit, the rising and falling transitions are clearly defined by the invalid and valid code phase.

3.3.3 Nominal Trace Description

In the sequel, the usage of traces to describe the nominal behavior of QDI circuits is examined in more detail. A simple index notation is introduced that eases the processing and visualization of traces. All n input signals of a circuit are collected in the input vector $I = \langle i(1)_a, i(1)_b, i(2)_a, ..., i(n)_b \rangle$. At the moment only dual-rail signals are treated, where the rails are labeled a and b. The input vector is ordered starting with the a-rail of the most significant bit $i(1)_a$ and ending with the b-rail of the least significant bit $i(n)_b$. A numeric index $1...2n$ is assigned to each rail. All a rails get the odd index $2k-1$ and

3.3. Nominal Behavior of QDI Circuits

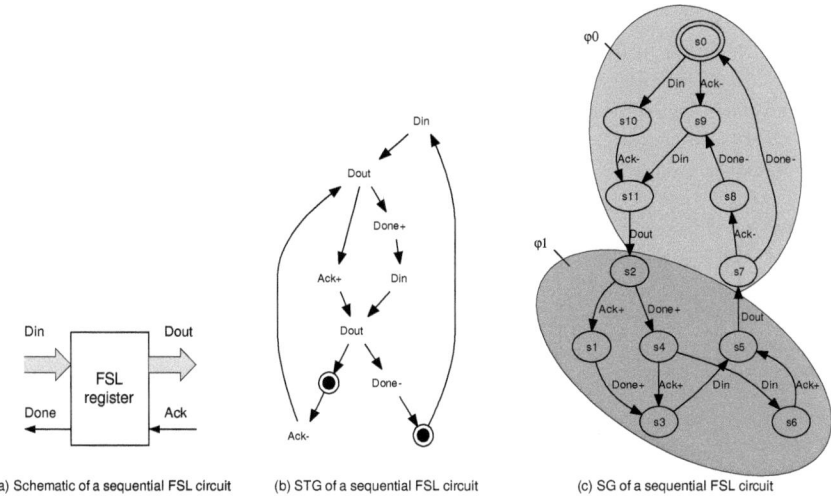

(a) Schematic of a sequential FSL circuit (b) STG of a sequential FSL circuit (c) SG of a sequential FSL circuit

Figure 3.5: FSL sequential circuit with corresponding STG and SG

all b rails get the even index $2k$ with $1 \leq k \leq n$. When building the input trace, all alphanumeric rail labels are replaced by their corresponding indices.

Example 3.3.1: Let's assume a 4-phase dual-rail XOR gate with the logic function $f(x,y) : z = x \oplus y$. The input vector of this gate $I = \langle x_a x_b, y_a y_b \rangle$ is described by the numeric vector $I = \langle 1,2,3,4 \rangle$. The gate may be in the state $\langle x,y,z \rangle = \langle 00,00,00 \rangle$. Constructing the operation $f(x,y) : 01 \oplus 01 = 01$ (or $0 \oplus 0 = 0$ in single-rail notation) eventually leads to the state $\langle x,y,z \rangle = \langle 01,01,01 \rangle$. For the input trace there exist two possibilities. If y precedes x ($y \prec x$): $t_1 = \{y_{b+}x_{b+}\}$ or $t_1 = \{42\}$ using the index notation as shown in Fig. 3.6(a). If x precedes y ($x \prec y$): $t_2 = \{x_{b+}y_{b+}\} = \{24\}$ as given in Fig. 3.6(b).

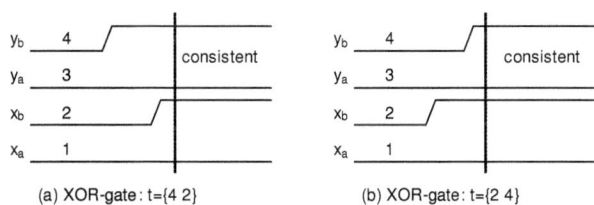

(a) XOR-gate: t={4 2}   (b) XOR-gate: t={2 4}

Figure 3.6: Possible traces of a simple XOR-gate

39

3. Fault Description

As introduced in 2.1.5, data in a (Q)DI circuit is transmitted in alternating code phases, which can be illustrated as infinite long sequence $\{...; \Phi_0; \Phi_1; \Phi_0; \Phi_1; \Phi_0; ...\}$. Any trace t_{01} that leads from the code set Φ_0 to Φ_1 must be a member of the circuit's trace set T. The same applies to any trace t_{10} that leads from the code set Φ_1 to Φ_0. All possible *code phase traces* t_{01} and t_{10} that lead from one code phase to the next one are collected in the *code phase set*.

Definition 3.3.1. The *code phase set* T^φ comprises all legal input traces that lead from a stable consistent state in one code phase to a stable consistent state in another code phase.

The code phase set is a subset of the circuit's trace set: $T^\varphi \subset T$. For the trace based fault model that has been developed in this thesis, it is sufficient to use the much smaller code phase set than the circuit's trace set, which may be theoretically infinitely long. To construct the complete code phase set T^φ, each valid circuit state must be extended by all legal transitions described by the delay-insensitive coding rules in 2.1.5. Thereby the rules for a *simple deterministic* input-output behavior in [75] are adopted:

1. The initial state is stable.
2. The final state is stable.
3. Only one signal transition takes place per time.

A stable initial and a stable final state ensure a deterministic behavior. The limitation to single transitions avoids to deal with concurrent events. This limitation is a fundamental property of STG and trace based models in general. Concurrent events cannot be expressed. Considering two signals x and y, one could construct the trace $\{xy\}$ or $\{yx\}$. Thus one signal will always precede the other one, i.e. $x \prec y$ or $y \prec x$ but $x \preceq y$ or $y \preceq x$ do not hold. The exclusion of concurrent events may be regarded as a limitation to the unbounded delay model. However, a small deviation in any delay is sufficient to change concurrent events to sequential ones, which also simplifies the handling of such events [75].

Considering concurrency requires the analysis of out-of-spec behavior of components, such as metastability, which is another field of research [76–78]. The relative probability of a true concurrent signal transition is estimated to be very low. Thus for this work it is assumed that metastability is not an issue as long as the circuit is properly designed and no faults occur. Finally, in a real, physical circuit one might observe what is called *pseudo-concurrency*, which means that two events take place within such a small time window that the detecting circuit is not able to separate them. Thus even the received trace has a defined sequence of the transitions, that sequence is not detectable. The practical meaning of this pseudo-concurrency is illustrated on a concrete example.

3.3. Nominal Behavior of QDI Circuits

Example 3.3.2: Consider a realistic XOR-gate where a rising edge is applied to both inputs that are tied together. Even if the two inputs are received a few picoseconds apart, the finite propagation delay of the gate will not be able to separate them and the output will not change its value.

Taking into account the previously defined constraints, the construction of the code phase set T^φ for a given QDI circuit with n inputs is demonstrated. A simple but illustrating example is selected to highlight the meaning of this fundamental trace set.

Example 3.3.3: Let's assume a 2-input QDI gate $\langle xy \rangle$, which has 4 possible input states. There are $4 \times 4 = 16$ possible input state transitions between the two code phases and 32 state transitions taking either code phase as the initial one for these state transitions. The input is actually defined as dual-rail vector $\langle x_a x_b, y_a y_b \rangle$. Each state transition can take place on any of these 2 rails, thus in total there are $32 \times 2! = 64$ possible input traces as shown in Table 3.2. The table applies to any 2-input QDI function.

Eventually, the code phase set only includes the unique traces. For a 2-input QDI function it becomes $T^\varphi = \{13, 31, 23, 32, 14, 41, 24, 42\}$.

The size of the code phase set is calculated as follows: Having n inputs, there exist $n!$ possibilities to arrange the input transitions. For each transition either rail a or b can be selected, which results in 2^n variations. Thus the total number of traces in T^φ is

$$|T^\varphi| = 2^n n!. \tag{3.1}$$

That equation applies to all dual-rail codes including 4-phase and FSL. For other codes, (3.1) has to be modified accordingly. For example, in the general 1-of-m code, the code phase set has $m^n n!$ entries. A k-of-m code can be described by $\binom{m}{k}^n n!$ code phase traces.

Next, the *expected trace set* is introduced as a subset of the code phase set. Contrary to the code phase set, the expected trace set depends on the current circuit operation that has to be processed.

Definition 3.3.2. For a specific code phase transition, the *expected trace set* $T^e \subset T^\varphi$ holds all expected traces that lead from one stable code phase to the next one.

Similarly, the *unexpected trace set* describes the remaining members of the code phase set that include unexpected rail transitions for the observed code phase transition:

Definition 3.3.3. For a specific code phase transition, the *unexpected trace set* $T^u \subset T^\varphi$ describes all traces that lead from one stable code phase to the next one and where at least one unexpected rail is excited.

3. Fault Description

Table 3.2: Trace assignment of a 2-input XOR gate

Initial state $\langle x_a x_b, y_a y_b \rangle$ $\langle 12, 34 \rangle$	Final state $\langle x_a x_b, y_a y_b \rangle$ $\langle 12, 34 \rangle$	Traces	Unique traces
00,00	01,01	{2 4, 4 2}	{1 3, 3 1}
	01,10	{2 3, 3 2}	{2 3, 3 2}
	10,01	{1 4, 4 1}	{1 4, 4 1}
	10,10	{1 3, 3 1}	{2 4, 4 2}
00,11	01,01	{2 3, 3 2}	
	01,10	{2 4, 4 2}	
	10,01	{1 3, 3 1}	
	10,10	{1 4, 4 1}	
11,00	01,01	{1 4, 4 1}	
	01,10	{1 3, 3 1}	
	10,01	{2 4, 4 2}	
	10,10	{2 3, 3 2}	
11,11	01,01	{1 3, 3 1}	
	01,10	{1 4, 4 1}	
	10,01	{2 3, 3 2}	
	10,10	{2 4, 4 2}	
01,01	00,00	{2 4, 4 2}	
	00,11	{2 3, 3 2}	
	11,00	{1 4, 4 1}	
	11,11	{1 3, 3 1}	
01,10	00,00	{2 3, 3 2}	
	00,11	{2 4, 4 2}	
	11,00	{1 3, 3 1}	
	11,11	{1 4, 4 1}	
10,01	00,00	{1 4, 4 1}	
	00,11	{1 3, 3 1}	
	11,00	{2 4, 4 2}	
	11,11	{2 3, 3 2}	
10,10	00,00	{1 3, 3 1}	
	00,11	{1 4, 4 1}	
	11,00	{2 3, 3 2}	
	11,11	{2 4, 4 2}	

The above definitions ensure that

$$T^e = T^\varphi \setminus T^u$$
$$T^u = T^\varphi \setminus T^e$$
$$T^\varphi = T^e \cup T^u. \tag{3.2}$$

For an n-bit dual-rail QDI circuit, any legal code phase transition can be described by exactly n rail transitions. Therefore, the size of T^e can be calculated as

$$|T^e| = n!. \tag{3.3}$$

Note that the T^φ, T^e and T^u only consider legal traces. For example, the trace $\{x_{a+}x_{b+}\} = \{12\}$ is illegal as two consecutive transitions on any dual-rail signal are prohibited. Such a trace requires a fault to be produced. In the next section, the single fault model according to 2.2.5 is used to extend the code phase set.

3.4 Trace Based Fault Description

3.4.1 Introduction

Trace theory has been used in the previous section to describe the nominal properties of QDI circuits. In a similar way, the same theory can be used as well to describe the behavior when the circuit is subjected to faults. A concrete example illustrates the application of traces to describe transient faults and how the effect of such a fault can be evaluated.

Example 3.4.1: Fig. 3.7 shows a portion of the state graph of the 4-phase dual-rail XOR gate from the previous example given in Fig. 3.6. Let's assume the circuit is in the stable state $s0$. Now the state graph is scanned to find a legal path to the next code phase. Fig. 3.7(a) highlights one possible code phase trace starting in $s0$: $t_1 = \{y_{b+}x_{b+}\} = \{42\}$. Thereby only the input transitions are considered and the output transition z_{b+} is excluded so far. The figure also depicts a transient fault $y_{a+} \equiv \overline{3}$, which is indicated by the dotted lines. The fault can be inserted at any position in t_1. It will either generate an invalid code and delay the execution if the output z has not yet been calculated or the fault will be ignored. In any case, no token error is generated.

Fig. 3.7(b) shows another trace of the circuit's code phase set, namely $t_2 = \{x_{b+}y_{b+}\} = \{24\}$. Although both t_1 and t_2 lead to the same result, a different trace will have a significant impact on the fault tolerance. Let's assume the fault y_{a+} occurs in state $s16$. It will modify the trace to $t_3 = \{x_{b+}y_{a+}\} = \{2\overline{3}\}$ and lead to the wrong output transition z_{b+} provided y_{b+} is late. The result of the calculation will be wrong and a token error has been generated.

To enhance the readability of traces, faulty transitions are highlighted with an overline, e.g. $\{\overline{1}\}$ or $\{\overline{x_{b+}}\}$. That notation is maintained throughout the complete thesis.

The goal of the trace based model developed in this thesis is to combine the benefits of the transition based approach (high level of details) and the token based approach (simplicity). Thereby the various effects of single transient faults that are superimposed to the nominal circuit trace are analyzed. First the boundary conditions of the trace based fault description are defined.

3. Fault Description

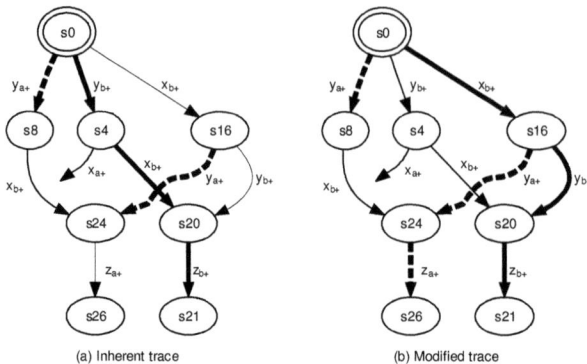

Figure 3.7: Dependency of the fault sensitivity on the circuit's trace

3.4.2 Boundary Conditions

The trace based model considers transient faults on the token level. Thereby the token based model in 3.1.2 is extended beyond the treatment of soft errors. For this extension, there are certain boundary conditions that have to be obeyed. The model comprises all possible tokens

1. that are received at the primary inputs of a sequential QDI circuit
2. in the stable state
3. if the handshake would be opened
4. due to single faults.

Item (1) only considers faulty inputs at register level (see 2.2.5). Items (2) and (3) ensure that all faults eventually arrive at the circuit input and cannot be masked by the handshake protocol. Finally, item (4) restricts the model to single faults only.

The faults are assumed to occur at the locations given in Fig. 3.8. We consider faults that are directly applied to the primary inputs of the sequential circuit under investigation. Thereby a primary input can be either the handshake (1) or the data path (2). This location will efficiently simulate faults in pure interconnection buses between two pipeline stages. Especially in network-on-chip designs, the long interconnection wires between the particular units are susceptible to glitches as they are typically too expensive to be hardened by technological measures [20]. Further, faults are applied to the combinational function that calculates the input for the circuit under investigation (3) and (4). Such an architecture is typically encountered in processing systems. The handshake is not affected by this fault location as the combinational function is transparent to the handshake.

3.4. Trace Based Fault Description

Finally, the faults are applied to the predecessor sequential circuit stage (5) including the handshake (6).

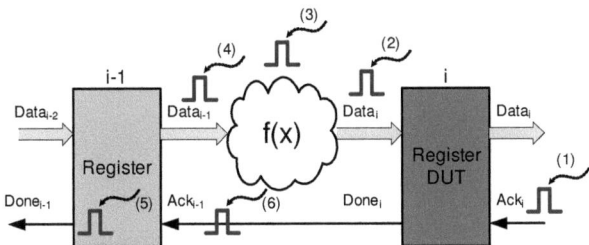

Figure 3.8: Transient fault locations

Now that the boundary conditions of the trace based fault description are defined, the effect of transient faults can be examined on token level. Thereby so called token classes are introduced.

3.4.3 Token Classes

Single transient faults are applied on top of the nominal trace based definition of a QDI circuit. Such a fault manifests as logic glitch, which can be described by two consecutive transitions on the subjected signal. Using a trace definition, a transient fault on a signal x can be described by the *single fault trace* $t_{xx} = \{xx\}$. Two consecutive transitions one the same signal may lead to transmission interference as described in 3.2.4. Thus a transient fault trace alone already violates one of the fundamental constraints of delay-insensitivity.

All possible single fault traces are collected in the *single fault trace set*:

Definition 3.4.1. The *single fault set* $T^{sf} = \{11, 22, 33, 44, ..., 2n2n\}$ contains all possible single fault traces. Its size depends on the encoding. In an n-bit dual-rail circuit it is

$$|T^{sf}| = 2n. \tag{3.4}$$

Merging a single fault trace with a code phase trace leads to the *simple fault set*:

Definition 3.4.2. The *simple fault set* T_y^{xx} describes all traces that are obtained when the single fault trace t_{xx} is merged into a code phase trace t_y: $T_y^{xx} = \{t | t = t_{xx} \cup t_y\}$.

The size of T_y^{xx} is calculated as follows: There are n dual-rail signals that build the trace. The first faulty transition can be placed before any of the n expected transitions as well as after the last one, which leaves $n+1$ possible locations. The second fault transition

3. Fault Description

must be placed after the first one. If the first fault transition is set to the beginning of the trace, there are $n+1$ possible locations for the second one. If the first fault transition is set as second transition, there exist only n possible locations for the second one, etc. In case the first fault is placed after the last expected transition, only one possibility remains to place the second transition. That situation is depicted in Fig. 3.9 for $n = 4$. Eventually, all different configurations are summed, which yields

$$|T_y^{xx}| = (n+1) + n + (n-1) + ...1 = \frac{(n+1)(n+2)}{2}. \tag{3.5}$$

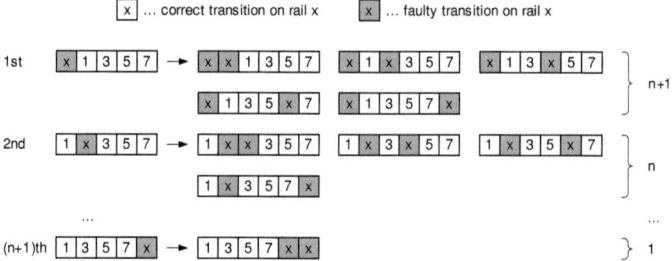

Figure 3.9: Size of the simple fault set

Example 3.4.2: Let's assume an arbitrary 2-input QDI function, with the input vector $I = \langle x_a x_b, y_a y_b \rangle = \langle 1, 2, 3, 4 \rangle$ and the following input trace $t_1 = \{13\}$. Now, a transient fault on rail index 2 (x_b) is added, which will extend t_1 to the fault set $T_1^{22} = \{\overline{22}13, \overline{2}1\overline{2}3, \overline{2}13\overline{2}, 1\overline{22}3, 1\overline{2}3\overline{2}, 13\overline{22}\}$. The set contains 6 traces, which could also be found by applying (3.5): $3 \cdot 4/2 = 6$.

Similarly, T_e^{xx} is obtained when a single fault trace is merged with the expected trace set. Thereby (3.5) has to be multiplied with (3.3):

$$|T_e^{xx}| = |T^e| \cdot |T_y^{xx}| = n! \cdot \frac{(n+1)(n+2)}{2} = \frac{(n+2)!}{2}. \tag{3.6}$$

That result could also be obtained analytically by considering that the faulty trace has $n+2$ transitions, i.e. in general it may comprise $(n+2)!$ permutations. Since the order of the two faulty transitions cannot be reversed only half of these permutations remain. In the next step, the complete single fault set according to (3.4) is merged with the code phase set T^φ. The resulting *phase fault set* $T^f(\varphi)$ describes all possible fault scenarios an n-input QDI circuit receives due to a single fault trace on one signal rail.

Definition 3.4.3. The *phase fault set* $T^f(\varphi)$ merges the single fault set T^{sf} with the code phase set T^φ: $T^f(\varphi) = \{t | t \in T^{sf} \cup T^\varphi\}$. The size of the phase fault set can be

46

3.4. Trace Based Fault Description

calculated considering (3.1):

$$|T^f(\varphi)| = |T^{sf}| \cdot |T^\varphi| \cdot |T^{xx}_y| = 2n \cdot 2^n n! \cdot \frac{(n+1)(n+2)}{2} = 2^n \cdot n(n+2)!. \tag{3.7}$$

Example 3.4.3: Table 3.3 depicts all 192 traces in the phase fault set $T^f(\varphi)$ of an arbitrary 2-input QDI circuit. That overview can be better visualized by listing the excited rail indices for each combination of phase trace versus single fault trace, which is shown in Table 3.4, or by simply counting the number of unexpected excited rails as given in Table 3.5.

Table 3.3: Phase fault set of a 2-bit QDI signal

Phase Trace	Single Fault Trace			
	11	22	33	44
13	$\overline{11}13, \overline{1}1\overline{1}3, \overline{1}13\overline{1}$ $1\overline{11}3, 1\overline{1}3\overline{1}, 13\overline{11}$	$\overline{22}13, \overline{2}1\overline{2}3, \overline{2}13\overline{2}$ $1\overline{22}3, 1\overline{2}3\overline{2}, 13\overline{22}$	$\overline{33}13, \overline{3}1\overline{3}3, \overline{3}13\overline{3}$ $1\overline{33}3, 1\overline{3}3\overline{3}, 13\overline{33}$	$\overline{44}13, \overline{4}1\overline{4}3, \overline{4}13\overline{4}$ $1\overline{44}3, 1\overline{4}3\overline{4}, 13\overline{44}$
31	$\overline{11}31, \overline{1}3\overline{1}1, \overline{1}31\overline{1}$ $3\overline{111}, 3\overline{1}1\overline{1}, 31\overline{11}$	$\overline{22}31, \overline{2}3\overline{2}1, \overline{2}31\overline{2}$ $3\overline{22}1, 3\overline{2}1\overline{2}, 31\overline{22}$	$\overline{33}31, \overline{3}3\overline{3}1, \overline{3}31\overline{3}$ $3\overline{33}1, 3\overline{3}1\overline{3}, 31\overline{33}$	$\overline{44}31, \overline{4}3\overline{4}1, \overline{4}31\overline{4}$ $3\overline{44}1, 3\overline{4}1\overline{4}, 31\overline{44}$
23	$\overline{11}23, \overline{1}2\overline{1}3, \overline{1}23\overline{1}$ $2\overline{11}3, 2\overline{1}3\overline{1}, 23\overline{11}$	$\overline{22}23, \overline{2}2\overline{2}3, \overline{2}23\overline{2}$ $2\overline{22}3, 2\overline{2}3\overline{2}, 23\overline{22}$	$\overline{33}23, \overline{3}2\overline{3}3, \overline{3}23\overline{3}$ $2\overline{33}3, 2\overline{3}3\overline{3}, 23\overline{33}$	$\overline{44}23, \overline{4}2\overline{4}3, \overline{4}23\overline{4}$ $2\overline{44}3, 2\overline{4}3\overline{4}, 23\overline{44}$
32	$\overline{11}32, \overline{1}3\overline{1}2, \overline{1}32\overline{1}$ $3\overline{11}2, 3\overline{1}2\overline{1}, 32\overline{11}$	$\overline{22}32, \overline{2}3\overline{2}2, \overline{2}32\overline{2}$ $3\overline{22}2, 3\overline{2}2\overline{2}, 32\overline{22}$	$\overline{33}32, \overline{3}3\overline{3}2, \overline{3}32\overline{3}$ $3\overline{33}2, 3\overline{3}2\overline{3}, 32\overline{33}$	$\overline{44}32, \overline{4}3\overline{4}2, \overline{4}32\overline{4}$ $3\overline{44}2, 3\overline{4}2\overline{4}, 32\overline{44}$
14	$\overline{11}14, \overline{1}1\overline{1}4, \overline{1}14\overline{1}$ $1\overline{11}4, 1\overline{1}4\overline{1}, 14\overline{11}$	$\overline{22}14, \overline{2}1\overline{2}4, \overline{2}14\overline{2}$ $1\overline{22}4, 1\overline{2}4\overline{2}, 14\overline{22}$	$\overline{33}14, \overline{3}1\overline{3}4, \overline{3}14\overline{3}$ $1\overline{33}4, 1\overline{3}4\overline{3}, 14\overline{33}$	$\overline{44}14, \overline{4}1\overline{4}4, \overline{4}14\overline{4}$ $1\overline{44}4, 1\overline{4}4\overline{4}, 14\overline{44}$
41	$\overline{11}41, \overline{1}4\overline{1}1, \overline{1}41\overline{1}$ $4\overline{111}, 4\overline{1}1\overline{1}, 41\overline{11}$	$\overline{22}41, \overline{2}4\overline{2}1, \overline{2}41\overline{2}$ $4\overline{22}1, 4\overline{2}1\overline{2}, 41\overline{22}$	$\overline{33}41, \overline{3}4\overline{3}1, \overline{3}41\overline{3}$ $4\overline{33}1, 4\overline{3}1\overline{3}, 41\overline{33}$	$\overline{44}41, \overline{4}4\overline{4}1, \overline{4}41\overline{4}$ $4\overline{44}1, 4\overline{4}1\overline{4}, 41\overline{44}$
24	$\overline{11}24, \overline{1}2\overline{1}4, \overline{1}24\overline{1}$ $2\overline{11}4, 2\overline{1}4\overline{1}, 24\overline{11}$	$\overline{22}24, \overline{2}2\overline{2}4, \overline{2}24\overline{2}$ $2\overline{22}4, 2\overline{2}4\overline{2}, 24\overline{22}$	$\overline{33}24, \overline{3}2\overline{3}4, \overline{3}24\overline{3}$ $2\overline{33}4, 2\overline{3}4\overline{3}, 24\overline{33}$	$\overline{44}24, \overline{4}2\overline{4}4, \overline{4}24\overline{4}$ $2\overline{44}4, 2\overline{4}4\overline{4}, 24\overline{44}$
42	$\overline{11}42, \overline{1}4\overline{1}2, \overline{1}42\overline{1}$ $4\overline{11}2, 4\overline{1}2\overline{1}, 42\overline{11}$	$\overline{22}42, \overline{2}4\overline{2}2, \overline{2}42\overline{2}$ $4\overline{22}2, 4\overline{2}2\overline{2}, 42\overline{22}$	$\overline{33}42, \overline{3}4\overline{3}2, \overline{3}42\overline{3}$ $4\overline{33}2, 4\overline{3}2\overline{3}, 42\overline{33}$	$\overline{44}42, \overline{4}4\overline{4}2, \overline{4}42\overline{4}$ $4\overline{44}2, 4\overline{4}2\overline{4}, 42\overline{44}$

Table 3.5 shows that a single fault trace will either excite zero or exactly one additional unexpected rail. That situation remains the same even for multiple faults in a circuit as each dual-rail signal is exposed to one single fault only. In fact the entry +1 means that the fault affects one rail that would have made no transition in the observed code phase change, while +0 means two extra transitions on a rail that would have been excited anyhow. Although this property seems quite obvious at the moment, it will be helpful later on when checking the delay-insensitivity of a system under faults. The observation of the number of excited rails has led to the introduction of *token classes*:

3. Fault Description

Table 3.4: Excited rails of a 2-bit QDI signal with a single fault

	Single Fault Trace			
Phase Trace	11	22	33	44
13	1,3	1,2,3	1,3	1,3,4
31	1,3	1,2,3	1,3	1,3,4
23	1,2,3	2,3	2,3	2,3,4
32	1,2,3	2,3	2,3	2,3,4
14	1,4	1,2,4	1,3,4	1,4
41	1,4	1,2,4	1,3,4	1,4
24	1,2,4	2,4	2,3,4	2,4
42	1,2,4	2,4	2,3,4	2,4

Table 3.5: Unexpected number of excited rails of a 2-bit QDI signal with a single fault

	Single Fault Trace			
Phase Trace	11	22	33	44
13	+0	**+1**	+0	**+1**
31	+0	**+1**	+0	**+1**
23	**+1**	+0	+0	**+1**
32	**+1**	+0	+0	**+1**
14	+0	**+1**	**+1**	+0
41	+0	**+1**	**+1**	+0
24	**+1**	+0	**+1**	+0
42	**+1**	+0	**+1**	+0

Definition 3.4.4. The *token class* is a set that is defined for each single bit according to the number of additionally excited rails during the transitions from one code phase to the next one compared to a legal code phase transition. The notation is *T(# of additionally excited rails)*.

The token classes are defined for each bit of an n-bit signal separately. The reason will become clear later on in 3.5 where the effect of a single transient fault in block interconnections as well as in combinational and sequential logic is investigated. The fault scenarios in Table 3.4 and Table 3.5 were created for all single fault traces T^{sf}, where a logical glitch was assumed to occur on one single rail. The general definition of the token classes also allows to include faults that will inhibit an expected rail transition or that generate a single edge on a signal rail. Such cases are not covered when a fault is modeled as glitch that has two transitions. However, it depends on the circuit implementation what effect that single transient pulse has on the primary outputs of the circuit.

This theoretic part shall not be restricted to any implementation constraints. Thus for generality, inhibited transitions and single edges are considered, which finally creates three different token classes:

3.4. Trace Based Fault Description

- **T(-1)**: one expected transition is inhibited. That class will be inherently masked by all QDI circuits as it prevents the code phase completion. However, it requires redundant gates in the function to inhibit an output transition.
- **T(+0)**: the expected number of rails is excited. Although the class describes legal tokens, it also contains token errors if unexpected rails are excited.
- **T(+1)**: one additional rail is excited. That class is not delay-insensitive anymore. Although unexpected rail transitions are involved, not all members of this class lead to a token error.

Example 3.4.4: Fig. 3.10 defines the three different token classes using simple examples. The expected waveform is illustrated in (a). Wave (b) shows a $T(-1)$ token. As the code phase cannot be completed by an inhibited transition, no token error is produced. Wave (c) illustrates a $T(+0)$ token, where the expected rail is hit by the fault. The effect is a premature completion of the code phase and the expected token is received. Wave (d) gives another possibility of the $T(+0)$ class. Here the transition takes place on the unexpected rail, while no transition occurs on the expected rail. Such a constellation will lead to a token error. In wave (e) a fault generates a glitch on the unexpected rail, which is described by the class $T(+1)$. A token error is generated if the glitch completes the code phase before the expected transition is received. A similar scenario is depicted in wave (f), where the fault leads to a single edge on the unexpected rail. Right to the waveforms both the number of observed transitions and the number of additional excited rails compared to a correct dual-rail code are shown.

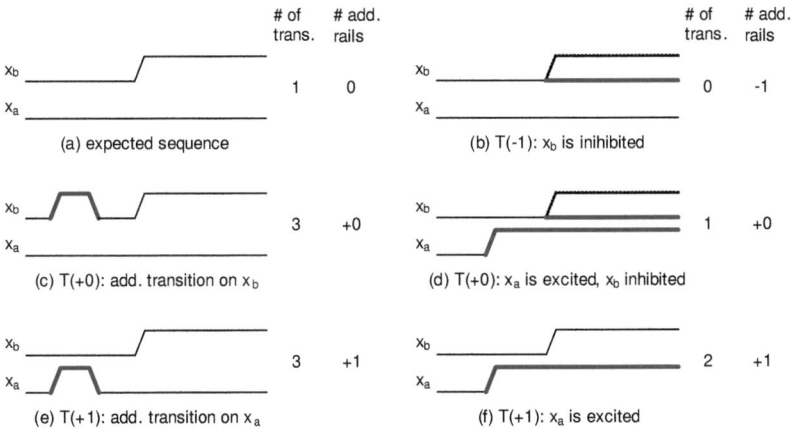

Figure 3.10: Definition of token classes

3. Fault Description

The token classes describe all types of single-faults in a single-bit QDI signal. The model is independent of the applied code, since it only counts the number of excited rails and not the overall number of transitions. As long as a fault only affects one rail in a bit, the token class description is exhaustive.

Especially the class $T(+1)$ has different effects, which is examined in more detail in Fig. 3.11: In Fig. 3.11(a) the fault occurs just after the capture event and is not activated, while in Fig. 3.11(b) the correct and the erroneous transition occur nearly at the same time. Therefore, it depends on the actual delay of the circuit whether it senses the correct token $\langle 01, 01 \rangle$ or the token error $\langle \overline{10}, 01 \rangle$. The scenario in Fig. 3.11(c) leads to a token error as the fault is active during the capture event. Finally, a $T(+1)$ has no impact at all if the fault has already gone before the capture event takes place as shown in Fig. 3.11(d). These list of $T(+1)$ effects is complete and also applies if the fault does not appear as glitch but as edge as shown in Fig. 3.10(f). In this case Fig. 3.11(d) does not apply.

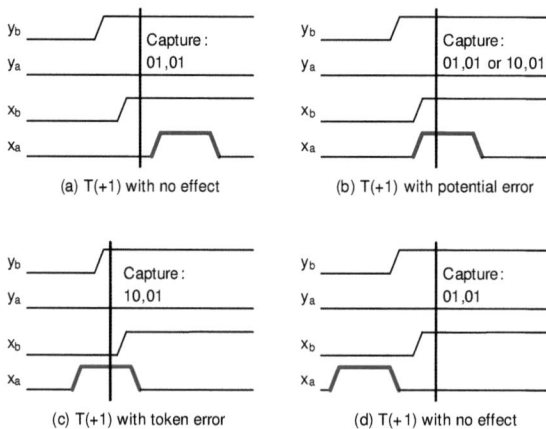

Figure 3.11: Example of a $T(+1)$ token

To examine the effect of a transient fault more formally the properties of the token classes are investigated more closely. First, the *prefix* relation is introduced.

Definition 3.4.5. For any two traces $t_1, t_2 \in T$, $t_1 = \text{pref}(t_2)$ or $t_1 \sqsubseteq t_2$ if there exists another trace $t_3 \in T$ such that $t_1 t_3 = t_2$ [22].

The above definition is generally applicable and also holds if $t_1 = t_2$ as any trace may always be extended by the empty trace $\varepsilon \in T$. Similarly, the empty trace can be regarded always as prefix of any trace. A practically relevant prefix must be not empty and has to contain signal transitions. For this thesis, the term trace is understood as all rail transitions that lead from one code phase to the next, see 3.3.3, while it generally

3.4. Trace Based Fault Description

may be used to describe an arbitrary number of code phase transitions. Similarly, the above definition is restricted to the scope of one single code phase.

Example 3.4.5: Let's consider a 4-bit QDI circuit that receives the code phase trace $t_1 = \{1368\}$. All valid prefixes shall be collected in the trace set T^p, which results in

$$T^p = \text{pref}(t_1) = \{1; 13; 136; 1368\}. \tag{3.8}$$

Note that e.g. $t_2 = \{36\} \neq \text{pref}(t_1)$ as t_2 cannot be extended to obtain t_1. Although $t_2 \subset t_1$, $t_2 \not\sqsubseteq t_1$ as the traces do not have the same initial rail transition.

The limitation of single code phase transitions applies throughout the complete thesis. Finally, the prefix relation can also be applied on two trace sets.

Definition 3.4.6. For any two trace sets T_p and T, $T_p = \text{pref}(T)$ or $T_p \sqsubseteq T$ if T_p only contains prefixes of T: $T_p = \{t_p | \exists t \in T : t_p = \text{pref}(t)\}$.

Finally, it can be shown that the token classes form disjoint sets:

$$\begin{aligned} T(-1) \cap T(+0) &= \emptyset \\ T(-1) \cap T(+1) &= \emptyset \\ T(+0) \cap T(+1) &= \emptyset. \end{aligned} \tag{3.9}$$

A $T(-1)$ trace cannot be described by a $T(+0)$ or $T(+1)$ trace, as the traces in these two classes have no inhibited transitions. Similarly, a $T(+1)$ trace has one additional rail excited, therefore it cannot be described by a $T(+0)$ trace that has one rail less. There exist *no common traces* in disjoint token classes. Consequently, the behavior of a QDI circuit can be examined separately for each token class.

Finally, the token classes have a different susceptibility to metastability, which has already been briefly discussed in the frame of concurrent events in 3.3.3. Now, faults are imposed on the nominal traces of a circuit. As long as the fault provokes the token classes $T(+0)$ or $T(-1)$, it does not violate the fundamental operation principles of QDI logic and metastability is not an issue, provided the circuit and especially the internal structure of gates and registers is properly designed. The class $T(+1)$ violates the DI encoding of the data. Thus closely spaced events on the same dual-rail signal may lead to unexpected short glitches that cannot be properly resolved by a QDI gate or register. The three possible manifestations of metastable behavior are excessive delay, an undefined signal amplitude in between the values of logic 1 and 0 for an unbounded time or output oscillation [78]. It mainly depends on the internal circuit design on transistor level how a circuit generates or reacts on such events. A detailed investigation of metastability goes beyond the scope of this thesis and it is assumed that any metastable behavior will eventually provoke either a token or delay error.

3. Fault Description

For a comprehensive examination of the trace based model, all applicable token classes need to be considered. Thereby it will be shown that the applicability of the three token classes depends on the fault location (as defined in Fig. 3.8) as well as the circuit implementation.

3.5 Fault Effects

This section investigates the effects of transient faults in different areas of a QDI circuit, such as interconnections, combinational and sequential logic. It shows how the token classes can be used to conveniently describe these fault effects.

3.5.1 Effects at Block Interconnections

First, the effects of transient faults that are directly applied to the primary inputs of a sequential circuit are examined according to locations (1) and (2) of Fig. 3.8. A transient fault injected at such a wire will trigger a transient error or SET. Soft errors or SEUs are not an issue for these fault locations. Fig. 3.12 shows the different effects on the dual-rail signal x when the fault hits the rail x_a, which is expected to receive a transition. The top waveform depicts the original, fault-free signal and the superimposed fault. The bottom waveform shows the corresponding result. Three different cases can be distinguished:

1. The fault is injected before the expected transition as shown in Fig. 3.12(a). The fault terminates the code phase on the subjected signal too early, which is referred to as *premature firing*.

2. The fault coincides with the expected transition, as shown in Fig. 3.12(b). In that case, the faulty event prolongs or delays that expected transition.

3. The fault occurs after the expected transition as given by Fig. 3.12(c), which is called *late firing*.

Scenarios (1) and (2) solely affect the duration of the disturbed code phase and are recognized as *delay error*. No token error is generated as only expected rails receive a transition, thus the value of a token is not changed. For instance, the trace $\{\bar{1}1\bar{1}3\}$ merely describes a premature firing on the lowest a-rail of the subjected signal vector. No fault is described by such cases, although they belong to the token class $T(+0)$. Scenario (3) constitutes an exception. The fault occurs after the code phase was completed on the subjected signal, therefore it either has no effect at all or it is already transferred to the next code phase where its effect has to be evaluated from scratch.

3.5. Fault Effects

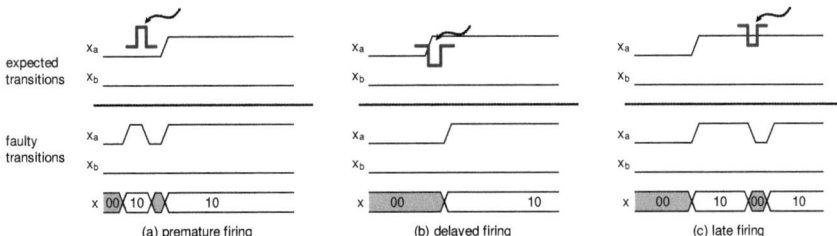

Figure 3.12: Transient fault effects at expected inputs

A different situation emerges when the fault hits a rail that is not expected to be excited, such as x_b in Fig. 3.13. Three additional cases are added to complete that analysis:

4. The fault occurs before the expected rail transition on x_a, so it will generate the token error $\langle x_a x_b \rangle = 01$. The effect of this premature firing is shown in Fig. 3.13(a).

5. The fault occurs after the expected transition as given in Fig. 3.13(b). The effect is the same as in scenario (3) given in Fig. 3.12(c).

6. The fault occurs nearly at the same time as the expected transition as shown in Fig. 3.13(c). Such concurrent events are excluded in trace theory as discussed in 3.3.3. Thus it is assumed that such a scenario will either tend towards a premature or late firing as shown in Fig. 3.13(a) and Fig. 3.13(b), respectively.

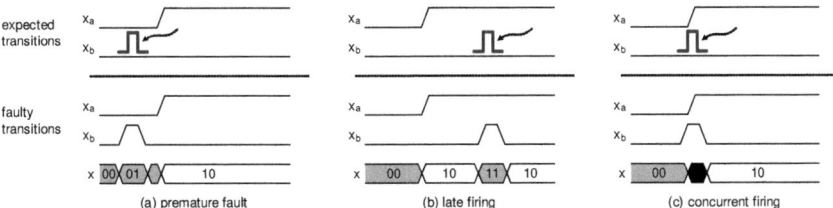

Figure 3.13: Transient fault effects at unexpected inputs

The effect of hitting an unexpected rail can be described by the class $T(+1)$ as there are $n+1$ excited rails, n expected and one unexpected rail.

A different situation emerges when the fault hits the handshake line of the interconnection according to location (1) of Fig. 3.8. The fundamental properties of (Q)DI logic require a handshake transition to acknowledge each new code phase. The fault effect list is continued:

53

3. Fault Description

7. A handshake fault occurs around the completion of the current code phase. In this case, it is will lead to a premature acknowledge. The number of handshake events is not altered, so the fault has no effect.

8. The handshake fault occurs at an unexpected time and is interpreted as additional acknowledge events. If the receiver of the handshake signal processes these additional events, a synchronization error occurs and two consecutive tokens are vanished.

Example 3.5.1: Fig. 3.14 shows a simple QDI pipeline with the consecutive tokens being numbered 1,2,3,... The transient fault on $Ack(i)$ loads the tokens 3 and 4 into the register $x(i)$. The successor stage $x(i+1)$ is not fast enough to process these two tokens and they are eventually removed from the data sequence.

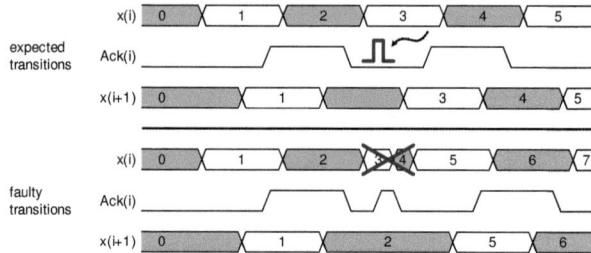

Figure 3.14: Token vanishing due to a synchronization error

A synchronization error does not disturb the content of a single token – it corrupts the content of a token sequence. As the next token that is received after such an error looks like an expected token with respect to its protocol properties, a synchronization error is described by the class $T(+0)$.

3.5.2 Effects in Combinational Logic

Next, the effects of transient faults injected at the combinational logic corresponding to locations (3) and (4) in Fig. 3.8 are examined. As introduction the effect of a transient fault that hits some internal node of a basic gate is examined. Thereby, two different effects can be distinguished:

9. The fault affects a gate that receives a consistent input as shown in Fig. 3.15(a). Provided the fault generates any output response, the correct output will be re-established after the fault duration due to that consistent input. The effect of such a scenario is a logic glitch or SET at the output.

10. The fault occurs while the gate receives an inconsistent input as shown in Fig. 3.15(b). Provided the fault generates any output response, the circuit will not autonomously recover when the fault has expired. An inconsistent input cannot be processed, thus whatever effect the fault has, that state will be maintained until the output is recalculated by a consistent input. As the fault effect persists beyond its duration, the transient fault has led to a static soft error or SEU.

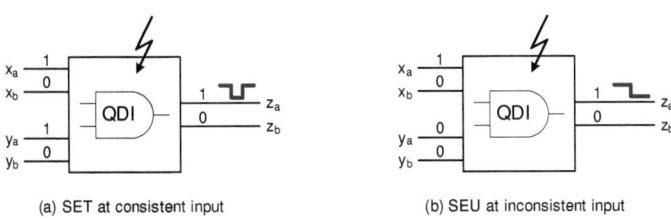

(a) SET at consistent input   (b) SEU at inconsistent input

Figure 3.15: Effect of transient fault depending on input state

These two basic fault effects are independent of the design style of the gate and have already been published in other research [65, 79, 80]. The reason for this architecture-independent behavior lies in the fundamental property of combinational (Q)DI logic that must be adhered by any implementation style: Consistent inputs lead to an update of the output, while inconsistent inputs are ignored and the current output is maintained. That fundamental property means that combinational (Q)DI gates will even recover from multiple internal faults as long as the input is consistent. A different situation emerges, when the fault is applied directly to a primary input:

11. The fault as well as the other inputs produce a consistent code, as shown in Fig. 3.16(a). The circuit will update its output, which is maintained even after the fault has gone. The effect is a static soft error or SEU.

12. The fault occurs while the gate receives a consistent input as shown in Fig. 3.16(b). Provided the fault affects only a single data rail, it will generate an inconsistent input, which is rejected by the circuit. The fault is masked.

Finally, a fault may directly hit a primary output. Thereby it is assumed that the output has no direct feedback to some internal node, otherwise the fault could be regarded as internal fault covered by scenarios (9) and (10) as presented above.

13. The fault directly hits a primary output of a circuit. It will propagate as logic glitch or SET the same way as it is produced.

3. Fault Description

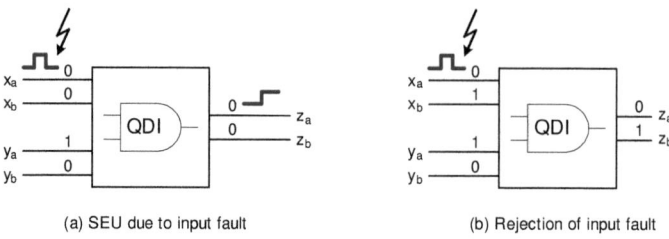

(a) SEU due to input fault (b) Rejection of input fault

Figure 3.16: Effect of transient fault directly hitting an input

It was shown that any consistent, correct input will also produce a correct output as well. However, that property requires a *non-redundant* circuit design [81], which has been assumed so far. In a non-redundant combinational circuit all internal nodes are a direct function of the primary inputs. On the other hand, in a redundant combinational circuit, at least one gate also relies on some internal feedback and cannot be calculated exclusively from the primary input. If a fault affects a redundant gate, a soft error is generated that persists even after the fault is removed and the primary inputs are consistent.

The effect of redundant gates is shown using the optimized full adder in Fig. 3.17 [79] that is designed in *Null Convention Logic* (NCL), a special design style based on a 4-phase dual-rail protocol. In the popular implementation of [40], NCL utilizes so called *threshold gates*, where n of m inputs must be logic 1 in order to produce a logic 1 at the output, while all m inputs must be logic 0 to produce a logic 0. The asymmetric behavior of these threshold gates reduces the circuit complexity.

Example 3.5.2: Let's regard the full adder in Fig. 3.17 [79], which implements the function $\langle x + y + c_i \rangle = \langle c_o + s \rangle$. The threshold levels of the particular gates are indicated by the enclosed numbers, e.g. gate $G1$ has level 2 so it requires at least two inputs being logic 1 to produce a logic 1 at its output. Fig. 3.17(a) shows the calculation $\langle 01 + 01 + 10 \rangle = \langle 01, 10 \rangle$. In this state, only gates $G1$ and $G4$ have reached their threshold level and produce a logic 1. Gates $G2$ and $G3$ do not react on the consistent input and are redundant. In Fig. 3.17(b) a transient fault is injected at c_i^0 and generates the inconsistent input $\langle 01 + 01 + 11 \rangle$. According to effect (12) from the above list that input should be rejected. However, the fault exceeds the threshold of the redundant gate $G3$ and produces a static soft error on s^0. That error remains even if the fault on c_i^0 is removed as $G3$ will only switch back if x^0 and y^0 are logic 0 as well.

Up to now a single transient fault is expected to produce only a single error. However, if the circuit under investigation comprises *forks*, a single fault may even trigger

3.5. Fault Effects

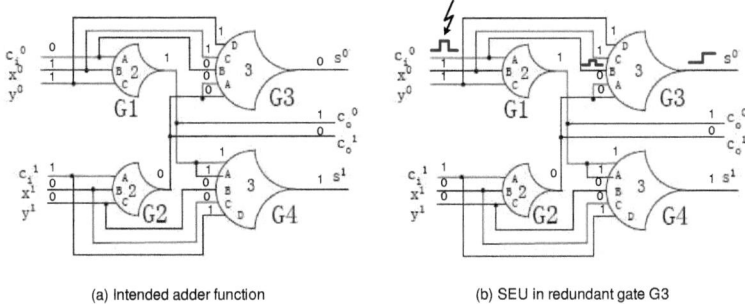

(a) Intended adder function   (b) SEU in redundant gate G3

Figure 3.17: SEU in optimized NCL full adder

multiple errors such as in Fig. 3.18. The single transient fault at the internal node B generates SETs at the two primary outputs X and Y.

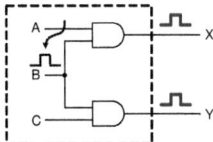

Figure 3.18: Multi errors due to a fork

The previous figure has shown a scenario where the fork is directly visible. Another example is given, where that fork is not that obvious.

Example 3.5.3: A 2-bit adder shall calculate $x + y = z : 2 + 1 = 3$ or in dual-rail $\langle 10, 01 \rangle + \langle 01, 10 \rangle = \langle 01, 10, 10 \rangle$ as given by Fig. 3.19. During the intermediate, inconsistent input state $\langle x(1)x(0), y(1)y(0) \rangle = \langle 10, 00, 01, 10 \rangle$ a transient fault hits $x(0)$ and produces the wrong input $\langle 10, \overline{10}, 01, 10 \rangle$. The adder calculates the corresponding result $\langle \overline{10}, \overline{01}, \overline{01} \rangle = 4$. Compared to the expected result, all three outputs are wrong.

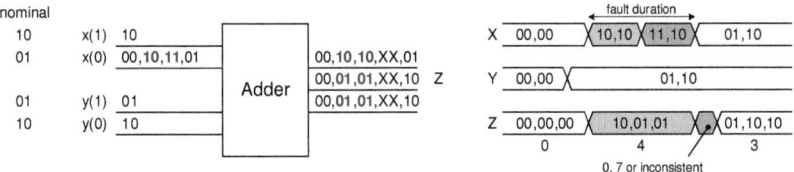

Figure 3.19: Multi errors due to a single fault that completes the code phase transition

57

3. Fault Description

That error persists until the input fault vanishes and the correct input is applied. Now the adder calculates the expected result. However, the transition from the wrong to the correct output is not delay-insensitive anymore. In the given example, the output transition is $\langle 10, 01, 01 \rangle \to \langle 01, 10, 10 \rangle$, which has two rail transitions per bit and thus violates the single event property of the dual-rail code, see 2.1.5. Those multiple transitions may lead to different intermediate states depending on the delays of the circuit. As long as these intermediate states only generate inconsistent outputs they have no impact. If intermediate states generate consistent data additional valid tokens are formed that can lead to token or synchronization errors. As shown in Fig. 3.19, the adder may generate the intermediate tokens $\langle 00, 00, 00 \rangle$ or $\langle 11, 11, 11 \rangle$ when the output is recalculated after the fault has vanished.

To summarize, a transient fault in a combinational circuit may result in single or multiple SETs or SEUs, depending on the circuit's state. Applying the token class model, that means that all fault effects can be described by the sets $T(+0)$ and $T(+1)$. These classes also cover multiple fault effects, since the token class itself is defined for each dual-rail signal separately.

It was also shown that any non-redundant QDI circuit will eventually calculate the correct output as long as the correct, consistent input is applied. This property does not hold in redundant QDI circuits, as there are internal nodes that rely also on feedback signals and are not exclusively defined by primary inputs. Mapped to the token class model, a redundant QDI circuit may also inhibit transitions and generate a $T(-1)$ fault. In this thesis, all combinational functions are designed using non-redundant gates only, which excludes the fault effect (11) from the above list. Consequently, inhibited transitions are excluded and non-redundant combinational QDI circuits are deadlock-free with respect to transient faults. Additionally, a transient fault may also not produce a static soft error on one rail, which appears as single edge as shown in Fig. 3.10(f). That kind of fault effect is excluded from the class $T(+1)$ and not covered in this work.

3.5.3 Effects in Sequential Logic

Location (5) of Fig. 3.8 considers transient faults in the preceding sequential circuit. As for combinational logic, the effect of a fault is strongly influenced by the physical implementation. Below, two possible implementations of a general n-bit register are shown, one for FSL and one for 4-phase dual-rail logic.

Fig. 3.20 depicts the FSL register design primarily used in this thesis [47]. Its function is as follows: Let's assume the register and its successor hold a token in code phase $\varphi 0$, $Ack_i = Ack_{i+1} = 0$. Now the predecessor applies a token in $\varphi 1$. Due to skew (1), the transitions arrive at different times. As the last transition is completed, $Data_{i-1} = \langle 10, 01 \rangle$, the input phase detector (φ_{in}) enables the internal latch by asserting

$en = 1$ (2). The transitions propagate through the latch (3) until $Data_i = \langle 10, 01 \rangle$. The output phase detector (φ_{out}) is triggered and it disables the internal latches, $en = 0$ (4). This event also acknowledges the storage of the token, $Ack_i = 1$ (5). A dedicated acknowledge latch guarantees that the token is stored before the acknowledge signal is toggled.

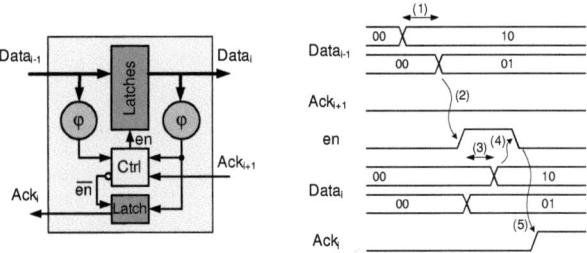

Figure 3.20: Timing of an FSL register

Fig. 3.21 shows a typical implementation and the operation of a 4-phase dual-rail register. We assume the register and its predecessor hold an invalid token, which is indicated by $Ack_i = Ack_{i+1} = 1$. The predecessor applies the next valid token and the skew on the data bus leads to different arrival times of the rail transitions. This design does not have an input phase detector. As soon as a consistent bit in the new code phase is received, the corresponding output bit is generated (2) and (3). Only after the complete output has changed to the new code phase, the output phase or completion detector will acknowledge the reception of the token, $Ack_i = 0$ (4).

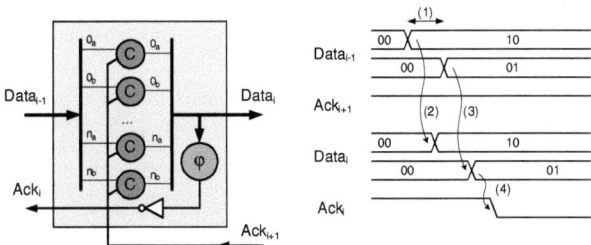

Figure 3.21: Timing of a 4-phase dual-rail register

Contrary to combinational logic, the operation of sequential logic is based on the consistency of the data path *and* the state of the acknowledge input that is driven from the subsequent sequential cell. This basic property is independent of the actual design style or implementation. As a result, one can distinguish the effects of a fault either in the data path (such as the latches in Fig. 3.20 or the Muller-C gates in Fig. 3.21) or in the control part of the cell (such as the acknowledge control logic including the phase detectors in Fig. 3.20 or the completion detector in Fig. 3.21):

14. The fault hits some internal node of the data path. The result is similar to hitting an internal node of a combinational circuit described by items (9) and (10). Since sequential circuits control the handshake, an SEU may additionally generate a deadlock.

15. The fault hits the data path input. The result is similar to hitting an input of a combinational circuit described by items (11) and (12). Again, there exists the possibility to generate a deadlock due to an SEU.

16. The fault hits a primary data path output. The same result as for item (13) applies.

17. The fault hits some internal node of the control path. That part does not have a direct impact on the data path but on the handshake protocol. Therefore a fault in this section may either have no effect if it is acceptable for the handshake protocol or the fault may result in a deadlock if it violates that protocol.

18. The fault hits the input or output of the control path, which are formed by the acknowledge signal, as shown by location (6) in Fig. 3.8. The effect is the same as for items (7) and (8). Either the handshake fault is ignored or a synchronization error is generated.

The possibility of deadlocks is examined in more detail. From a higher level point of view, the control path of a (Q)DI register can be regarded as a redundant function. For instance, even if a consistent input is applied and the subsequent register stage signals ready, it depends on the state of the output completion detector whether this consistent input will be processed. Thus there exist internal nodes that are not a direct function of a consistent input – which has been defined as basic property of redundant circuits in 3.5.2. As a direct consequence, a transient fault may inhibit an output transition and thereby generate a deadlock.

Sequential circuits have no forks that branch to several outputs, therefore no multiple outputs can be disturbed by a single fault. Applying the token classes to the previous findings, all possible class fault sets may occur in a sequential circuit due to a single transient fault, i.e. $T(+0)$, $T(+1)$ and $T(-1)$.

3.6 Summary

In this chapter a new fault description based on trace theory has been introduced. The particular traces that occur due to a fault can be generally characterized by three different token classes $T(-1)$, $T(+0)$ and $T(+1)$, depending on the number of additionally excited rails. Previously, the phase fault set $T^f(\varphi)$ was used as an introduction how to derive the token classes by merging the single fault set T^{sf} into the code phase set T^φ. Thereby, it was assumed that a transient fault eventually manifests as logic glitch being described by two transitions on the same rail. The token classes are more general and also allow the removal of a rail transition, which is entirely described by the class $T(-1)$, replacing an expected transition by a faulty one, which can be described by the class $T(+0)$, as well as faults that lead to one single edge on an unexpected rail, which is covered in $T(+1)$.

As the token class model describes all kinds of fault effects on a trace between two consecutive code phases, it does not distinguish whether the fault hits a rail that is anyhow expected to be excited or a rail that is not expected to produce a transition. To evaluate the what kind of fault may lead to an error, all traces that have an error generation capability are collected in the *class fault sets*:

Definition 3.6.1. The *class fault sets* $T^f(-1)$, $T^f(+0)$ and $T^f(+1)$ contains all traces that may result in a token error, synchronization error or deadlock due to a transient fault on a single rail. These sets can be derived from the expected trace t_e as well as from the expected trace set T^e:

$$T^f(-1) = \{t|t = \text{pref}(T^e) : |t_e| - |t| = 1\}$$
$$T^f(+0) = \{t|t \in T^\varphi : |t_e \cap t| = n - 1\}$$
$$T^f(+1) = \{t|t \in (T^e \cup T^{usf}) : T^{usf} \subset T^{sf} : \forall t \in T^{usf} : t \cap t_e = \emptyset\} \quad (3.10)$$

with the magnitude $|x|$ describing the length of a trace x.

The set $T^f(-1)$ removes one single expected transition. A convenient way to derive that set is to take all expected traces, remove the last transition and collect the unique remaining traces in a set. The set $T^f(+0)$ describes all expected traces, where exactly one rail transition of a signal is replaced by its companion rail. To generate that set, use those traces from the code phase set T^φ that share n-1 rail transitions with the expected trace T^e. In $T^f(+1)$, the expected trace set is merged with all single fault traces that contain unexpected rail transitions T^{usf}. That trace collects all rail transitions that do not occur in t_e.

The size of the class fault sets can be determined by means of combinatorics. In $T^f(-1)$, each of the n rails may be removed, leaving $n - 1$ transitions in the trace. Regarding $T^f(+0)$, there exist n possibilities to replace an expected transition, while the remaining trace still comprises n transitions in total. The size of $T^f(+1)$ is obtained by merging an expected trace with a single fault trace as described in (3.6) and multiplying by all n possible unexpected rails. Thereby, it is assumed that all faults in $T(+1)$ manifest as logic glitch that adds two additional rail transitions, which is justified by only using

3. Fault Description

non-redundant combinational QDI functions:

$$|T^f(-1)| = n \cdot (n-1)!$$
$$|T^f(+0)| = n \cdot n!$$
$$|T^f(+1)| = \frac{n(n+2)!}{2} \qquad (3.11)$$

Example 3.6.1: For a 3-bit QDI circuit with the expected trace $t_e = \{135\}$, the class fault sets describing single faults, are then:

$$T^f(-1) = \{13; 31; 15; 51; 35; 53\} \qquad |T^f(-1)| = 3 \cdot 2! = 6$$
$$T^f(+0) = \{(\overline{2}35)!; (1\overline{4}5)!; (13\overline{6})!\}! \qquad |T^f(+0)| = 3 \cdot 3! = 18$$
$$T^f(+1) = \{(1\overline{22}35)!; (13\overline{44}5)!; (135\overline{66})!\}! \qquad |T^f(+1)| = 3 \cdot \frac{5!}{2} = 180 \qquad (3.12)$$

Thereby the operator $(t)!$ defines all permutations of the trace t.

There exists the following relationship between the token class and its associated class fault set:

$$T^f(-1) \equiv T(-1)$$
$$T^f(+0) \subset T(+0)$$
$$T^f(+1) \equiv T(+1) \qquad (3.13)$$

That relation becomes obvious when the nominal behavior of QDI circuits described in 2.1.5 is reconsidered. The suppression of a rail transition as expressed in $T(-1)$ cannot produce a legal code phase transition, therefore $T(-1)$ is equivalent to $T^f(-1)$. Similarly, adding an unexpected rail transition as in $T(+1)$ violates the single event property, since it does not describe a DI code phase transition. Thus $T(+1)$ must be equivalent to $T^f(+1)$. Finally, the token class $T(+0)$ describes various effects, such as replacing an expected transition but also generating additional transitions on an expected rail. Replacing an expected transition with an unexpected one might lead to an error, while hitting an expected rail will only generated a premature or delayed code transitions, which complies with the DI protocol. Therefore, the traces that describe potential errors $T^f(+0)$ are only a subset of $T(+0)$.

The applicability of the token classes depends on the circuit type and the fault location. As described in 3.5 the different portions of a circuitry – block interconnections, combinational logic and sequential logic – have a different susceptibility to the token classes as sown in Table 3.6. For instance, combinational logic with redundant gates as well as sequential logic may generate inhibited transitions described by $T^f(-1)$. On the other hand, inhibited transitions may not occur in block interconnections.

3.6. Summary

Table 3.6: Applicable Fault Sets

Circuit Type	Fault location (Fig. 3.8)	Applicable fault set T^f
Block interconnections – handshake path	(1)	$T^f(+0)$
Block interconnections – data path	(2)	$T^f(+1)$
Combinational logic without redundant gates	(3), (4)	$T^f(+0), T^f(+1)$
Combinational logic with redundant gates	(3), (4)	$T^f(-1), T^f(+0), T^f(+1)$
Sequential logic	(5), (6)	$T^f(-1), T^f(+0), T^f(+1)$

The class fault sets will be applied in the next chapter to evaluate the inherent robustness of QDI circuits as well as the robustness of fault mitigation strategies.

A short summary of the introduced terms is presented in Table 3.7. It describes a 2-bit QDI register with the expected input trace $t_e = \{13\}$ and depicts the various traces and trace sets that emerge from single faults.

3. Fault Description

Table 3.7: Summary of trace based fault model with example

Item	Abbr.	Description	Example ($n = 2$)
Expected trace	t_e	example of an expected trace	$\{13\}$
Expected trace set	T^e	Set of all expected traces	$\{13, 31\}$
Code Phase Set	T^φ	all traces that lead from one code phase to the next phase	$\{13, 31, 23, 32, 24, 42, 14, 41\}$
Single fault trace	t_{xx}	transient fault on rail x	$\{11\}$
Single fault set	T^{sf}	all possible transient faults	$\{11, 22, 33, 44\}$
Unexpected single fault set	T^{usf}	all transient faults on unexpected rails	$\{22, 44\}$
Simple fault set	T_y^{xx}	fault trace t_{xx} applied to trace t_y	$t_{xx} = \{22\}$, $t_y = \{13\}$: $\{2213, 2123, 2132, 1223, 1232, 1322\}$
Phase fault set	T_φ^f	all traces when T^{sf} is applied to T^φ	see Table 3.3
Class fault set $T(-1)$	$T^f(-1)$	traces derived from T^e with an inhibited transition	$\{1, 3\}$
Class fault set $T(+0)$	$T^f(+0)$	traces derived from T^e with one expected transition replaced by an unexpected one	$\{\overline{2}3, 3\overline{2}, \overline{1}4, 4\overline{1}\}$
Class fault set $T(+1)$	$T^f(+1)$	traces derived from T^e with one unexpected excited rail	$\{\overline{22}13, \overline{21}23, \overline{21}32, 1\overline{22}3, 1\overline{23}2, 13\overline{22},$ $\overline{44}13, \overline{41}43, \overline{41}34, 1\overline{44}3, 1\overline{43}4, 13\overline{44},$ $\overline{22}31, \overline{23}21, \overline{23}12, 3\overline{22}1, 3\overline{21}2, 31\overline{22},$ $\overline{44}31, \overline{43}41, \overline{43}14, 3\overline{44}1, 3\overline{41}4, 31\overline{44}\}$

4

Fault Mitigation

This chapter takes a closer look at the mitigation of faults in QDI circuits using the trace based model developed in the previous chapter. First an overview of different mitigation methods is given. Then a new method based on cross-coupled signal rails is presented. Thereby a fault provokes an inconsistent token that is inherently blocked by QDI logic.

4.1 Introduction

This work investigates the mitigation of transient fault effects in asynchronous QDI logic. Thereby the word *mitigation* is understood as follows:

Definition 4.1.1. Fault mitigation aims to reduce or eliminate the frequency, impact and effect of harmful errors in a system.

According to this definition, the mitigation of faults is a rather general term. In principle, two strategies can be applied to mitigate the effect of a transient fault:

1. *Fault prevention* deals with the reduction of the fault cause. It is often associated with removing external sources of faults. For instance, the operation of a circuit is only allowed in a less harsh environment or the environmental are reduced by e.g. shielding.

2. *Fault tolerance* deals with the reduction of errors while faults are assumed to occur. In fault-tolerant systems, the internal structure is hardened by various techniques to reduce the generation of errors. The faulty environment is accepted.

This thesis is only concerned with the second methodology, the application of fault tolerance mechanisms, so a system will meet its specification despite the presence of faults.

4. Fault Mitigation

Therefore within this work the term fault mitigation is equivalent to fault tolerance. Any fault mitigation strategy must adhere to certain boundary conditions. If these boundaries are violated, e.g. another fault model is applied, the fault tolerance properties may change. Therefore, whenever defining fault tolerance or fault mitigation, the underlying boundary conditions must be known as well.

Another term that is often used in this context is *robustness*: A system is called robust if it is able to tolerate some unspecified behaviors, such as faults but also unspecified operating conditions such as ambient temperature or the speed of the environment. A robust system may not tolerate all abnormalities. In a more formal way, robustness can be understood as continuous property: If the operating conditions (which includes the presence of faults) are changed by a positive real epsilon, a robust system will respond at most with some finite delta change [82]. Thus the system's response is bounded and will not be totally wrong. This definition primarily applies to embedded systems that interact with a physical environment. For an abstract digital system the term robustness can hardly be applied as the response is discrete: A boolean result is either true or false. For this work, robustness is understood as the quality of fault-tolerance as no connection to physical effects are considered. A circuit's robustness depends on many parameters such as the data content, the moment of fault occurrence, the fault duration, the speed of the circuit, the current state of the circuit, the application, etc. [15, 63, 83].

The mitigation of faults can be related to different abstraction levels. Within this thesis, it is applied to the register level, which is the same abstraction as the fault model, see 2.2.5. Mitigating a fault at the register level also means that this abstraction level is aimed to be fault-free, or more simply, no wrong result shall be stored in a register. Other possibilities may be to mitigate faults at lower levels, e.g. by hardening a transistor circuitry using an adequate semiconductor process or at higher levels, e.g. by inserting checksums into a data stream, which is a common technique in communication engineering.

4.1.1 Soft Error Rate

Soft errors arise from *Single Event Transients* (SET), which become memorized. A soft error is not permanent and can be removed by restoring the correct data. Permanent or hard errors are not treated in this thesis, i.e. only soft errors are considered in the assessment of the circuit's robustness.

The *Soft Error Rate* (SER) defines how often soft errors occur per time. It depends on both external parameters such as the particle flux as well as on internal parameters such as the circuit design. The SER has been intensively investigated in synchronous circuits [5, 84, 85]. In general, the soft error susceptibility of a circuit node n with respect to a latch l can be described by three factors [86]:

4.1. Introduction

1. $R_{SET}(n)$ is the rate of SETs at node n that have sufficient energy to generate a logic glitch. This parameter depends on the device characteristics (sensitive area, capacitance, etc.) as well as the energy distribution of the external particle flux.

2. $P_{sens}(n,l)$ is the probability that node n is functionally sensitized to propagate a transient fault to the latch l. This parameter depends on the input data and the logic function between n and l but also on the electrical properties on that path, which define the propagation of a logic glitch.

3. $P_{latched}(n,l)$ describes the probability that a logic glitch created at node n is captured in the latch l. In such a case the fault must have a sufficient duration and it must arrive during the sensitive timing window of the latch.

The above terminology differs slightly from [86] where the authors use the term *Single Event Upset* (SEU) rate $R_{SEU}(n)$ to describe the transient fault rate. There is no generally accepted naming convention and the term SEU is often used to describe a single event effect in general. In this thesis, the terminology as commonly used in space engineering is applied. An SEU describes a transient fault that has already been stored and become a soft error [59]. An SET describes a logic glitch that may become an SEU if it is captured in a memory cell. So the terminology $R_{SET}(n)$ is used instead, although the origin and effect are identical.

To compute the soft error rate of an arbitrary node-latch pair $SER(n,l)$, these three factors have to be multiplied:

$$SER(n,l) = R_{SET}(n) \cdot P_{sens}(n,l) \cdot P_{latched}(n,l). \tag{4.1}$$

The soft error rate of a particular latch l is defined by adding the soft error rates from all nodes in the circuit

$$SER(l) = \sum_{i=1}^{N} SER(n_i, l) \tag{4.2}$$

with $\{n_1, n_2, ..., n_N\}$ being the node set of the circuit. In principle that sum can be simplified by only taking into account those nodes that are functionally sensitized to the latch l. Finally, the soft error rate of a circuit $\mathcal{C}$ can be computed by adding the soft error rates from each particular latch:

$$SER(\mathcal{C}) = \sum_{i=1}^{L} SER(l_i) \tag{4.3}$$

with $\{l_1, l_2, ..., l_L\}$ being the latch set of the circuit.

This thesis does not cover the analysis of the SET rate $R_{SET}(n)$, as there is a lot of research available on that topic e.g. [8, 55, 87]. Especially for the space industry, the calculation of the SET/SEU rate is supported by tools such as GEANT4 [88] or

4. Fault Mitigation

CREME [89]. These tools allow to specify a radiation environment and to input radiation test data from components to calculate the soft error rate for a specific mission. In principle, $R_{SET}(n)$ is also more a technological problem. It does not distinguish between synchronous and asynchronous circuits with one exception: Since asynchronous circuits generally require more area they contain more radiation sensitive nodes.

This thesis focuses on the last two terms in (4.1), which describe the masking effects that prevent a transient fault to be captured in a latch. As already introduced, one has to consider electrical, logical, temporal and code masking. Omitting electrical masking as stated in 2.2.4 and setting $R_{SET}(n) = 1$ as described above, modifies (4.1) to

$$P_f(n,l) = \underbrace{[1 - Q_{log}(n,l)] \cdot [1 - Q_{code}(n,l)]}_{=P_{sens}(n,l)} \cdot \underbrace{[1 - Q_{temp}(n,l)]}_{=P_{latched}(n,l)} \quad (4.4)$$

where $P_f(n,l)$ expresses the overall probability that a transient fault leads to a soft error.

Logical ($Q_{log}(n,l)$) and code masking ($Q_{code}(n,l)$) determine the prevention of a sensitized path to a memory element and temporal masking ($Q_{temp}(n,l)$) determines the rejection of an applied fault. In the following, these masking effects are assessed in conjunction with the trace based fault description from 3.4.

4.1.2 Fault Trace Propagation

As defined in 3.4.3, a transient fault may disturb an expected trace and generate a fault trace that can be separated by the three token classes $T(-1)$, $T(+0)$ and $T(+1)$. Thereby the classes $T(+0)$ and $T(+1)$ may lead to a token error if they are captured in a memory element. It was shown that a $T(-1)$ token can only lead to a deadlock, which does not directly contribute to the SER. Although a deadlock contributes to the overall failure rate of a circuitry, it's nature is not considered as soft error. A deadlock cannot be recovered by non-redundant QDI circuit. It requires some kind of redundancy to remove the cause of the deadlock either by (i) initiating a reset after a time-out has been expired [17] or by (ii) bypassing the source of the deadlock via a redundant path [66, 90]. The latter methods can be deployed to even mitigate from permanent faults that trigger a deadlock in a QDI circuit. This thesis focuses on the mitigation of soft errors or token errors that are caused by transient faults. Therefore, the mitigation of $T(-1)$ tokens is not further treated.

In a first assessment, no explicit redundancy is assumed, which means an unprotected QDI circuit is subjected to transient faults. To have an application independent investigation, the implicit logical masking is also excluded, i.e. the masking properties of the logic function and the impact of the input value are not considered. Finally, temporal masking is also not taken into account, since it is also related to implementation properties such as the used logic family or the complexity of the logic function that determines the processing speed and therefore the handshake period.

4.1. Introduction

These prerequisites constitute a worst case boundary and mean that a transient fault, provided it arrives at the input of a memory element will be latched and trigger a soft error or token error. The only masking terms that may prevent such a scenario is code masking. This kind of masking helps to reduce the SER in QDI circuits, without adding explicit redundancy. So (4.4) is further simplified to

$$P_c(T^f, l) = 1 - Q_{code}(T^f, l). \qquad (4.5)$$

Thereby the node n in the parameter list has been replaced by the applicable fault set, since the error probability is now based on the input trace of latch l. It should be clarified that although no explicit redundancy is needed to prevent a transient fault from propagating in a QDI circuit, that (information) redundancy is implicitly added via the delay-insensitive encoding, which is the reason for the code masking property.

To asses the code masking, it must be investigated under which conditions a fault trace t_f will be processed by a memory element, without taking into account any other masking effects. Thereby the *fault propagation possibility* is introduced:

Definition 4.1.2. The *fault propagation possibility* $Pb(t_f) = \{0, 1\}$ describes whether a faulty trace t_f will be received by a latch l and manifest as token error.

Instead of using a probability figure, the term propagation possibility is used. Since all masking effects except code masking have been excluded, it implies that any fault trace that is received by a latch will also propagate as token error. The possibility that a fault trace is received is a boolean decision, either 0 (the trace is masked) or 1 (the trace propagates).

Applied to a trace set, such as the class fault sets $T^f(+0)$, $T^f(+1)$ as defined in 3.4.3, the fault propagation possibility is converted to a probability figure. That probability largely depends on the actual fault trace distribution within the trace set. To compare the inherent fault tolerance of QDI circuits as well as to compare different hardening methods on a fair base, a uniform fault trace distribution is assumed, which is described by the *fault propagation probability* (FPP):

Definition 4.1.3. The *fault propagation probability* $0 \leq FPP(T^f) \leq 1$ describes the soft error probability $P_c(T^f, l)$ of a latch l when all traces within T^f are uniformly distributed and only code masking is considered.

The fault propagation probability can be calculated by relating all fault traces to the size of the applicable fault set:

$$FPP(T^f) = \frac{1}{|T^f|} \cdot \sum_{i=1}^{|T^f|} Pb(t_i); \ \forall t_i \in T^f. \qquad (4.6)$$

If $FPP(T^f) = 0$, it means that no fault trace will propagate under the agreed boundary conditions of the fault hypothesis. If $FPP(T^f) = 1$, every trace in T^f will propagate as error. Both cases are rather theoretic.

4.1.3 Assessment of Soft Error Probability

To obtain a realistic soft error probability $P_f(n,l)$ according to (4.4) all masking effects as well as the probability of each faulty trace within the phase fault set T_φ^f have to be considered. In a real circuit, a uniform trace distribution is unlikely. In such a case, the real trace distribution in T_φ^f has to be determined. A weighting factor $0 \leq w_{i,k}(l) \leq 1$ is derived for each trace $t_i \in T_\varphi^f$ a latch l receives, which describes how often the trace t_i occurs within k handshake cycles:

$$w_{i,k}(l) = \frac{1}{k} \cdot \sum_{j=1}^{k}(t_j = t_i) \qquad (4.7)$$

with t_j being the trace of the jth handshake cycle. Thereby only those handshake cycles are counted where a fault is applied.

To get a confident statistical weighting factor, k has to be selected large enough, at least $k \gg |T_\varphi^f|$ or ideally $k \to \infty$. In that case the probability distribution of each t_i within T_φ^f is found and the index k can be omitted. Eventually, the reduced soft error probability of a latch l taking into account all applicable masking effects can be calculated as

$$P_f(l) = [1 - Q_{log}(l)] \cdot [1 - Q_{temp}(l)] \cdot \sum_{i=1}^{|T_\varphi^f|} Pb(t_i) \cdot w_i(l); \; \forall t_i \in T_\varphi^f. \qquad (4.8)$$

To calculate the SER of a circuit $\mathcal{C}$, the SER of all included latches l have to be added according to (4.3). Thereby the transient fault rate $R_{SET}(n)$ has to be taken into account to convert the probability figure into errors per time.

Since the weighting factor considers the real fault trace distribution of a circuit, it actually describes the amount of code masking. Neglecting the input data distribution and the inherent logic function of a circuit, the fault trace distribution depends on factors that are generally not affected by the user, such as the supply voltage, the temperature or inherent delay settings due to process variations in different implementations.

Example 4.1.1: Let's regard a 2-bit ripple carry adder, which has the output $z = \langle s(1)_a, s(1)_b, s(0)_a, s(0)_b, co_a, co_b \rangle = \langle 1, 2, \ldots, 6 \rangle$. Due to its design, the adder generates an output sequence $\{s(0); s(1); co\}$, i.e. starting with the least significant bit $s(0)$ and ending with the carry output co. Provided the skew on the path to the receiving latch is moderate, this order will also be observed by that latch. Using index notation, the trace $t_1 = \{236\}$ is more likely to be received at the successor than e.g. $t_2 = \{632\}$, which requires that the last generated co rail transition will be received first.

The logical masking in (4.8) takes care about the rejection of faults by means of the implemented logic function itself, which also depends on the input distribution. In principle, code and logical masking are closely related, however, they are treated separately in this work.

4.1. Introduction

Example 4.1.2: Let's take the 2-bit adder from the previous example. Under nominal input conditions, no overflow may occur. Thus the carry output should be logic 0 most of the time: $\langle co \rangle = \{00, 01\}$, i.e. the a-rail will remain at logic 0, while the b-rail toggles with each new code phase. So a trace with a transition on co_a (= rail index 5) is rather seldom. So the trace $t_1 = \{135\}$, is assumed to occur less frequently in the circuit's trace set than $t_1 = \{136\}$, which marks the code phase transition on co.

Temporal masking describes the probability that a faulty trace received at the primary input of a latch will be captured, e.g. a latch that is not ready to receive a new token will reject any faults applied to its input. The probability to temporary mask a faulty trace depends on the fault duration, the duration of a sensitive state within the actual handshake cycle and the critical window of the latch. The latter defines how long a fault must persist until it can be captured. That parameter is also strongly related to electrical masking, which is however, not considered in this work.

Example 4.1.3: The expected trace of a 2-bit QDI register may be $t_e = \{13\}$. Due to a $T^f(+1)$ fault the register receives the wrong trace $t_f = \{1\overline{43}4\}$, where the first two transitions describe a token error. If the latch is in an insensitive state until the last transition $\{\overline{4}\}$ is received, the token error is rejected.

The previous examples have shown how the particular masking effects will contribute to the overall soft error probability of a latch. A theoretic assessment how to calculate these masking factors goes beyond the scope of this thesis. Their practical evaluation is limited to experiments by means of simulation in chapter 5.

4.1.4 Principle of Redundancy

To mitigate faults that are not inherently masked some kind of redundancy has to be added to the system, which inevitably decreases the efficiency. In general, redundancy can be applied at three different areas [91]:

- **Hardware redundancy:** The hardware needed to perform an operation is replicated. A popular representative of this method is *Triple Modular Redundancy* (TMR), which triplicates a function and assigns the overall output to the majority of the three individual results. Other popular methods are "duplication and comparison" or short *duplex*, where only two instances of a function are generated. Often this method is just used to detect an error.

- **Temporal redundancy:** The function is calculated several times. This method requires additional hardware or computation time to compare the results of the replicated calculations and to determine the final output.

4. Fault Mitigation

- **Information redundancy:** Redundant data is added to the information to be conveyed. Based on this information, integrity checks on the data (and the results produced thereof) can be performed. This type of redundancy is often found in broadcast systems and for memory protection. A well known implementation is the simple parity, which allows to detect a single error. More sophisticated schemes allow to detect multiple errors or even correct them.

This thesis focuses on hardware redundancy, which is commonly used to protect the core functions of processors or signal processing applications. Temporal redundancy may also be applied in that area but it has a significant drawback in terms of throughput. Information redundancy is rarely used for such applications. Further, hardware redundancy is the only method that allows to mitigate permanent faults and static errors because in this case parallel, redundant data is needed to replace the erroneous information. Although only transient faults are treated in this thesis, it is considered as framework to generally improve the fault tolerance of QDI logic for both, transient and permanent faults [90].

4.2 Related Work

4.2.1 Hardware redundancy methods

Comparing several replicas of an asynchronous circuit is not that easy as in synchronous systems. Especially the handshaking protocol used in asynchronous circuits makes it difficult to apply any *N-modular redundancy* (NMR) scheme. It implies a "wait-for-all" strategy, and thus a soft error in the handshake of one replica might lead to a deadlock of the complete system because the voter indefinitely waits for the next token. Although the majority of the replicas is correct, the erroneous replica blocks any further processing so the complete system fails. NMR generates an increased hardware effort due to the replication. QDI logic anyhow has a bad hardware efficiency as it requires more resources to implement the DI encoding and the handshake protocol. Installing a QDI-NMR scheme would further degrade the overall resource efficiency. It has also been shown that NMR reduces the throughput depending on the fault rate [92]. Due to these disadvantages an NMR approach doesn't seem to be well suited for QDI logic.

4.2.2 Duplication

A hazard-free comparison by means of *duplication and double-checking* (DD) is presented in [93]. The logic functions are duplicated and the associated rails are synchronized via C-elements. Fig. 4.1 shows a normal AND gate and its duplicated soft error tolerant version. The double-checking C-elements only pass a token if both paths agree. If a soft error corrupts one path the circuit is halted until the soft error is removed. To prevent

4.2. Related Work

a corruption if a second soft error occurs on the other path and leads to an agreement, additional "weak" feedback C-elements can be added to the synchronized outputs that tend to restore the inputs in case they differ [93]. The hardware overhead of this method is slightly higher than 100% due to the synchronizing C-gates in addition to the duplication. A simple, one-bit wide comparator implemented using a standard *Pre-Charged Half Buffer* (PCHB) design is compared with the duplicated double-checking version in [18]. The hardware effort of the soft error tolerant comparator is three times larger and the circuit ran only with half the speed of the standard implementation.

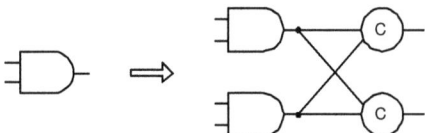

Figure 4.1: Duplicated Double-Checking Gate [93]

The duplicated double-checking architecture was used to design a soft-error tolerant asynchronous microprocessor (STAM) [94]. The STAM was simulated in TSMC.SCN 0.18 μm using SPICE. It runs at 170 MHz with a cost in through-put of 30 to 40% compared to a non-error tolerant version. The area penalty is between a factor 2 and 3.

In [95], QDI circuit elements are decomposed into a computational part that implements the logical function and a memory part (registers) that implements the handshake protocol between the consecutive asynchronous stages. The computational part is *duplicated and hardened*, using modified Muller gates in the memory part, see Fig. 4.2. The technique is similar to the previously described double-checking, except that it applies the synchronizing C-gates only within the registers. Thereby the C-gates are not doubled on gate level but their transistor level design is altered and the duplicate computational result is also received. The circuit will prevent any different results from the duplicated computational logic, as the received inputs of the hardened C-gates do not agree. The circuit requires about twice the area compared to the initial design and the speed is only marginally affected as the C-gate synchronization takes place on transistor level, which improves the throughput.

4.2.3 Rail synchronization

The rail synchronization techniques in [96] uses synchronized, cross-coupled channels in a pipeline stage as shown in Fig. 4.3(a). The method uses 4-phase dual-rail logic. A common implementation of this design style is that each particular bit of a register is individually controlled by its own C-gate (see Fig. 3.21), which reduces the hardware overhead especially for smaller register widths. The drawback is the reduced inherent code masking, since a single dual-rail cannot mask a false rail transitions (mapped to

4. Fault Mitigation

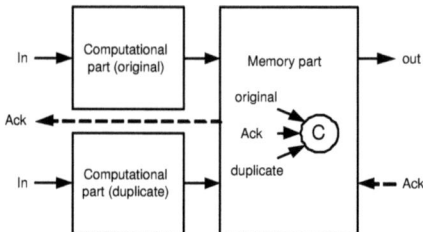

Figure 4.2: Asynchronous stage hardened by duplication [95]

the trace based model, any fault trace on a 1-bit dual-rail signal will generate a soft error provided the receiving register is ready for new data). The code masking can be improved by synchronizing two bits in an N-bit pipeline. Thereby only the presence of data is synchronized not their content. Thus as soon as both channels sense the reception of a new token, both will initiate its capturing without evaluating its content. The method is based on the timing assumption that a correct and faulty transition are not much separated in time. If the faulty transition occurs first, the circuit will wait until the coupled channel receives its expected transition. In the meantime the faulty channel will also receive its expected transition, which generates the illegal code '11' in the 4-phase dual-rail protocol. In case of a single-bit register, an artificial redundant control circuit is proposed as depicted in Fig. 4.3(b).

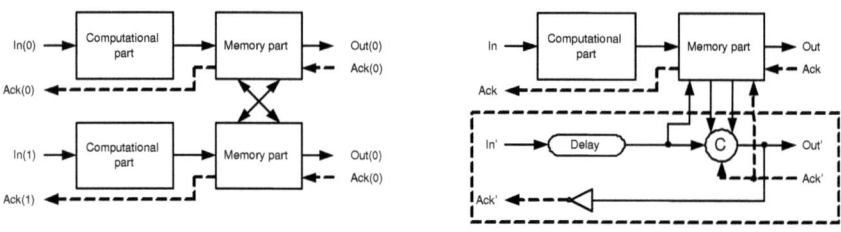

Figure 4.3: Asynchronous stage hardened by rail synchronization [96]

The advantage of this method is the reduced hardware overhead as no literal duplicated items are necessary and the speed of the circuit is only slightly decreased. However, the fault tolerance is by far not as good as for the previously mentioned duplication-based methods. The fault tolerance of a Data Encryption Standard (DES) crypto-processor using the rail synchronization method is investigated in [96]. The fault resistance of an unprotected reference design was found as 17%, while the rail-synchronized design had only 7% faults. The area overhead of the rail synchronization was 8% and the computation speed was only 82% of the unprotected design.

4.2. Related Work

In principle, the rail synchronization technique is very similar to one possible basic implementation style of QDI registers when LEDR is applied (see Fig. 3.20) [36,47]. Here, the presence of a valid token at the input of a register is determined by a completion detector that monitors all bits of the input. So essentially, the difference to the rail synchronization is that ALL channels of a pipeline stage are synchronized and not only two coupled channels and that the channel synchronization is already an inherent, mandatory function and not added to improve the robustness. The error detection capability of these FSL registers is investigated in [15, 63].

4.2.4 Re-calculation

A research focusing on soft errors in combinational circuits by simple *recalculation without duplicating* the hardware is presented in [79]. First, the gate structure is modified on transistor level to harden the logic cells against soft errors. Second, the probability of storing a soft error is reduced by introducing additional latches as well as a reset circuit that resets the combinational functions in case of erroneous transitions. The circuit requires a delay element to mitigate some fault classes as well as assumes the registers and the reset circuit are error-free.

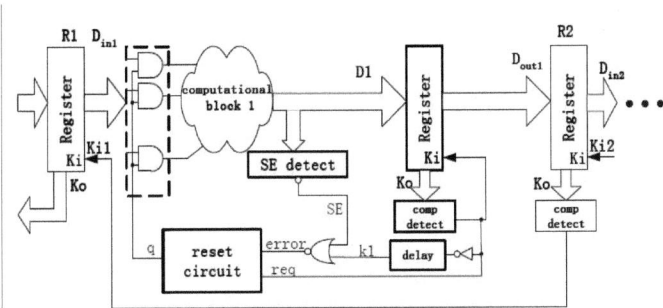

Figure 4.4: Soft error detection and detection scheme [79]

The method in [97] uses *duplication and recalculation*. A checker compares the output of two redundant circuits as depicted in Fig. 4.5. In case of a mismatch, the affected circuit parts are reset and the corrupted data is re-calculated until the results agree. Thereby the handshake protocol of QDI logic ensures that the correct inputs are still kept in the preceding pipeline stage. This method combines hardware and temporal redundancy, although the latter is only applied in case of a mismatch. The addition of a checker as well as the modification of the circuit parts to make them resetable generates considerable hardware overhead. An experimental evaluation of the method has not been presented.

4. Fault Mitigation

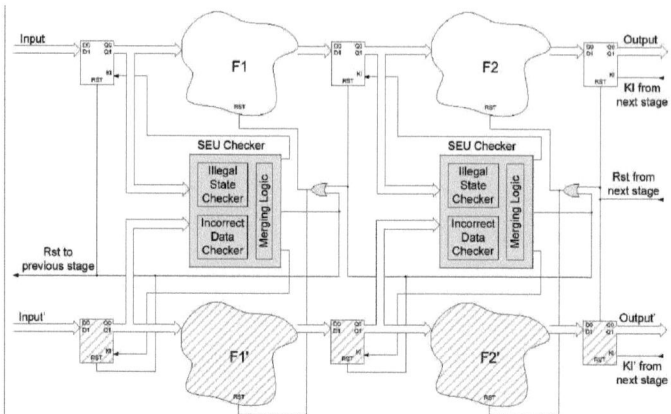

Figure 4.5: Duplication and recalculation method [97]

4.2.5 Forcing deadlocks

In [98], pipelined QDI circuits are modified in such a way to achieve a *fail-stop behavior* in the presence of permanent and transient faults. The authors limit their investigation on the *Pre-Charged Half Buffer* (PCHB) depicted in Fig. 4.6, which is an important building block for QDI circuits. An important property of the PCHB is its fail-stop behavior with respect to permanent stuck-at faults. The circuit either produces a deadlock or it returns the illegal dual-rail code '11'.

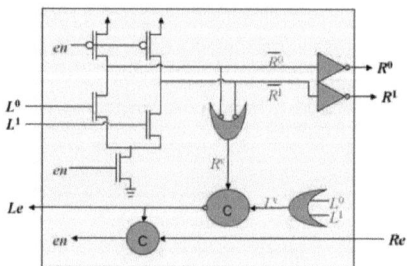

Figure 4.6: Pre-charged half buffer [98]

That fail-stop property can also be applied to soft errors. However, a soft error may lead to premature firings that generates a wrong computation or an illegal event-ordering. By adding extra rails and logic a *Fail-Stop Pre-charge Half Buffer* (FS-PCHB) is created as shown in Fig. 4.7. One additional rail L^v, R^v is added to cross-check each dual-rail encoded input (L^t, L^f) and output (R^t, R^f). The acknowledge rail is duplicated, L_1^a, L_2^a

and R_1^a, R_2^a, cross-checking each other. Any soft error as well as any single stuck-at fault leads to a deadlock in the FS-PHCB. The advantage of this method compared to the duplication-based error detection is that no timing assumptions are necessary and that no component has to be fault-free. The drawback is the mandatory deadlock detector, usually formed by some kind of delay line, and the limitation to the PCHB architecture. Thus the method cannot be applied to commonly available prototyping platforms such as FPGAs. Several adder circuits where evaluated in terms of hardware overhead, data throughput and power consumption in [98]. The result was nearly independent of the adder size and gave a hardware overhead of 92%, a throughput reduction of 30% and an increase in power consumption of 80%. These figures are getting better with more complex circuits. As an example, a 6-input FS-PCHB block shows a hardware overhead of 54%, a throughput reduction of 35% and a power increase of 50%.

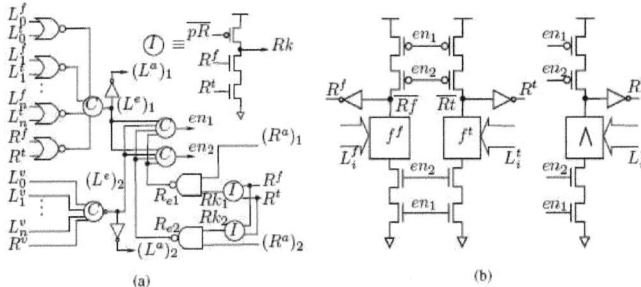

Figure 4.7: Fail stop pre-charged half buffer [98]

A similar approach is presented in [99] and applied on self-timed VLSI pipelines. An asynchronous circuit is constructed in *Differential Cascode Voltage Switch Logic* (DCVSL), which has nearly the same topology as a PCHB. A checker circuit is added that raises a completion signal only in the case all dual-rail encoded bits are complementary. If one or more signal pairs have the value '00' or '11' the circuit is halted. A simple RC timer is suggested that will detect such a condition. The authors simulated various transient errors on net list level, where all errors were detected. No indication about the additional hardware effort and performance impact was presented.

4.2.6 Concurrent error detection

A concurrent error detection method in a QDI security application by means of minimum distance robust error-detecting codes is presented in [100]. The technique is investigated on the example of an Advanced Encryption Standard (AES) circuitry but may be applicable for general QDI designs as well. Fig. 4.8 shows the basic architecture for the concurrent error detection. The 32-bit input of the linear portion of an AES round

4. Fault Mitigation

is in parallel fed to a predictor (P). The output of that predictor and the unprotected AES circuit are passed to an error detecting network (EDN), which compares the AES output with the prediction and raises an error flag if an unpredicted result is encountered. The presented work aims on security applications, therefore it's scope is to detect errors but not to autonomously correct them.

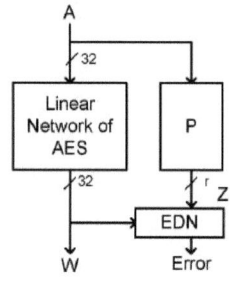

Figure 4.8: AES architecture for concurrent error detection [100]

Additional work in this field, such as asynchronous processors that use concurrent error detection based on Dong's code are presented in [91, 101]. An asynchronous burst-mode machine that uses a Berger code-base error detection is published in [102].

A comprehensive overview of concurrent error detection, such as duplication and comparison, block codes for error detection, parity and group parity checking, code-disjoint circuits, etc. is found in [103]. In principle, the methods described in this book could also be applied to QDI circuits, however, they may result in non-optimum results. Contrary to common single-rail logic, QDI logic already includes inherent checker circuits by means of the phase or code completion detectors. This thesis shows how these completion detectors can be utilized not only for error detection but also for error correction.

4.3 Trace Based Fault Assessment

This section shows how to generally derive the fault propagation probability as defined in 4.1.2 by using the trace based model developed in 3.4. The impact of the internal circuit design, which affects the trace re-ordering in a gate or register, the dependency on the encoding of the data and the handshake protocol are highlighted. Special care is also taken of multiple errors in QDI circuits.

4.3.1 Evaluation of Fault Propagation

In 4.1.2, the fault propagation probability (FPP) was introduced, which calculates the code masking of a certain latch l, assuming a uniform fault trace distribution. Thereby, the masking effects are reduced to the fundamental property of QDI circuits to reject inconsistent data. This approach allows to assess the fault tolerance of a circuit independently of application dependent effects and allows a more transparent comparison of the inherent robustness of QDI circuits as well as the robustness of explicit hardening methods. To calculated the FPP of a given latch a general procedure has been developed:

1. Select an expected trace t_e from the code phase set T^φ and build the expected trace set T^e as well as the unexpected trace set T^u.

2. Derive the applicable fault set T^f as shown in Table 3.6.

3. Determine the wrong prefix set $T^{pf} = \{t \in T^f | \text{pref}(t) \in T^u\}$.

4. Calculate
$$FPP(T^f) = \frac{|T^{pf}|}{|T^f|} \qquad (4.9)$$

The first two points of the above list construct the faulty traces starting from the expected trace set. Thereby the applicable class fault set $T^f(-1)$, $T^f(+0)$ or $T^f(+1)$, depend on the type of circuit and the fault location, see also 3.5. The remaining points describe the migration of code masking: A fault must (i) complete the code phase transition (2.1) to be received by a QDI circuit and (ii) generate unexpected data. All traces that fulfill these two conditions are collected in the *wrong prefix set*.

Definition 4.3.1. The *wrong prefix set* T^{pf} of a trace set T^f is the subset of T^f containing all traces for which the prefix is a member of the unexpected code set $T^u = T^\varphi \setminus T^e$: $T^{pf} \subseteq T^f$ and $T^{pf} = \{t \in T^f | \text{pref}(t) \in T^u\}$.

If a trace $t \in T^f$ contains a prefix that is a member of the unexpected code set T^u, it will complete the code phase and trigger the capture of wrong data as $Pb(T^u) = 1$. That statement holds if the receiving register is ready for new data – which has been defined as a boundary condition for this fault assessment. Contrary, a fault trace will be code masked if all its prefixes solely contain expected traces, i.e. $T^{pf} = \emptyset$.

Example 4.3.1: Let's calculate the fault propagation probability of a 2-input QDI register and let's assume, the faults are directly applied to the inputs of the register, which corresponds to location (2) in Fig. 3.8. According to Table 3.6, the applicable fault set becomes $T^f(+1)$. The expected trace may be $t_e = \{13\}$ and the expected

4. Fault Mitigation

trace set $T^e = \{13, 31\}$. The class fault set $T^f(+1)$ comprises the following 24 entries (which are repeated from Table 3.7 for convenience):

$$T^f(+1) = \{\overline{22}13, \overline{21}\overline{2}3, \overline{21}3\overline{2}, 1\overline{22}3, 1\overline{2}3\overline{2}, 13\overline{22}, \overline{44}13, \overline{41}\overline{4}3, \overline{41}3\overline{4}, 1\overline{44}3, 1\overline{4}3\overline{4}, 13\overline{44},$$
$$\overline{22}31, \overline{23}\overline{2}1, \overline{23}1\overline{2}, 3\overline{22}1, 3\overline{2}1\overline{2}, 31\overline{22}, \overline{44}31, \overline{43}\overline{4}1, \overline{43}1\overline{4}, 3\overline{44}1, 3\overline{4}1\overline{4}, 31\overline{44}\}$$

From these 24 traces, the wrong phase prefix set is calculated. A 2-input QDI register will complete its code phase, if a single rail transition is received at each of the two dual-rail inputs. Scanning the class fault set for traces that complete the phase with an unexpected trace leaves the following 8 traces in the wrong prefix set:

$$T^{pf} = \{3\overline{22}1, 3\overline{2}1\overline{2}, \overline{23}\overline{2}1, \overline{23}1\overline{2}, \overline{41}\overline{4}3, \overline{41}3\overline{4}, 1\overline{44}3, 1\overline{4}3\overline{4}\}$$

The fault propagation probability is found as

$$FPP(T^f(+1)) = \frac{|T^{pf}|}{|T^f(+1)|} = \frac{8}{24} = 33.33\%$$

i.e. 33.33% of all traces in $T^f(+1)$ will be received as wrong data.

That example shows how to determine the fault propagation probability in a simple, non-redundant QDI circuit that is exposed to single rail faults. The example and its formatted output have been generated using Matlab. Although a numerical method is a handy tool to check whether the assumptions being made are correct, it soon runs into limitations even at moderate number of bits as the number of permutations grows very rapidly. There is also an analytical solution to the prefix problem, which depends on the class fault set.

First, the wrong prefix set is derived for $T^f(+1)$, which is the more complicated task. Fig. 4.9 shows how to define a wrong prefix in a 4-bit circuit. Both traces convey the information $\{1357\}$, i.e. there is a transition on every a-rail. The definition of the $T^f(+1)$ set requires that a fault excites one additional rail, i.e. injecting a transient fault generates $n+2 = 6$ transitions. Fig. 4.9(a) depicts such a trace with two additional events on the unexpected rail 4. The trace $\{1\overline{4}5\overline{4}37\}$ is one possible result from the $|T_e^{44}|$ = $(n+2)!/2 = 360$ possibilities. To complete the code phase, the first n transitions must be a member of the phase set, which is not the case for $\{1\overline{4}5\overline{4}\}$. In this trace, the code phase will be completed only after the last transition so the fault is masked. Another scenario is shown in Fig. 4.9(b) with the trace $\{1\overline{4}57\overline{4}3\}$. Here, the first n transitions complete the code phase and the token error $\{1\overline{4}57\}$ is received.

Looking at this simple example, three prerequisites have to be fulfilled to generate a wrong prefix $T^{pf}(+1)$:

1. The fault must affect an unexpected rail, otherwise it has no effect at all.

4.3. Trace Based Fault Assessment

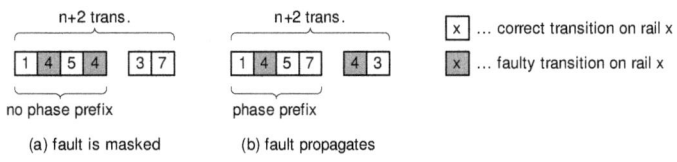

Figure 4.9: Definition of sensitive prefixes in single fault trace

2. The last two transitions must contain one faulty transition, while the other faulty transition occurs in the phase prefix.

3. The last two transitions must take place on the same (dual-rail) signal, which ensures that an expected transition is replaced by a faulty transition in the phase prefix. The dual-rail expression has been put into parentheses, as this statement is applicable for all types of delay-insensitive codes.

In simple words, the first n rail transitions must complete the code phase with an unexpected trace. The number of traces in $T^{pf}(+1)$ can be calculated by the following approach. From Fig. 4.9, a single transient fault generates two additional transitions, i.e. the total number of transitions in the trace is $n+2$. If the first n transitions shall complete the code phase, the last two transitions must take place on the same signal. These two transitions offer two possible arrangements, while the preceding n transitions contain $n!$ arrangements. From the $2n$ single faults in T^{sf}, exactly n affect an unexpected rail, thus the wrong phase prefix set comprises

$$|T^{pf}(+1)| = 2n \cdot n! \qquad (4.10)$$

entries and the fault propagation probability is given by

$$FPP(T^f(+1)) = \frac{|T^{pf}(+1)|}{|T^f(+1)|} = \frac{2n \cdot n!}{\frac{n \cdot (n+2)!}{2}} = \frac{4}{(n+1) \cdot (n+2)}. \qquad (4.11)$$

Example 4.3.2: The fault propagation probability $FPP(T^f(+1))$ from Example 4.3.1 can be calculated analytically using (4.10) and (4.11):

$$FPP(T^f(+1)) = \frac{4}{(n+1) \cdot (n+2)} = \frac{4}{3 \cdot 4} = 33.33\%.$$

The number of wrong phase prefixes and the fault propagation probability for the remaining class fault sets could be also derived by this method, however, they are much more simpler to obtain. The inhibited class fault set $T^f(-1)$ cannot complete a code phase so it cannot contain any phase traces, i.e. $T^{pf}(-1) = \emptyset$. The $T^f(+0)$ set contains

4. Fault Mitigation

exactly as much transitions as expected by the encoding. Thus every member of $T^f(+0)$ will hold a wrong phase prefix, i.e. $T^{pf}(+0) \equiv T^f(+0)$. Taking these properties into account, the fault propagation probability according to (4.9) will be:

$$FPP(T^f(-1)) = 0$$
$$FPP(T^f(+0)) = 1$$
$$FPP(T^f(+1)) = 0 \leq x \leq 1 \quad (4.12)$$

From (4.12), some important properties can be derived:

1. The set $T^f(-1)$ does not contain any wrong phase prefixes, i.e. the fault propagation is zero. Inhibited transitions cannot propagate wrong data, although they will always lead to a deadlock independent of the trace distribution.

2. All traces in $T^f(+0)$ hold wrong phase prefixes, i.e. every trace of that set will generate wrong data due to a token or synchronization error, independent of the fault trace distribution. A non-hardened QDI circuit cannot mask a $T^f(+0)$ trace.

3. In $T^f(+1)$, not all traces will propagate an error. There exist traces within this class that will not complete the code phase with an unexpected trace and it depends on the actual fault trace distribution how the class fault set $T^f(+1)$ eventually contributes to the soft error rate. The impact of the fault trace distribution is investigated in chapter 5.

Table 4.1 presents an overview of the fault propagation probability of the different class fault sets versus the number of bits n of a simple, non-redundant QDI function. Due to the nonlinear relation, the fault propagation drops rapidly at large n.

Table 4.1: Fault propagation probability of a simple, non-redundant n-bit QDI function

n	$FPP(T^f(-1))$	$FPP(T^f(+0))$	$FPP(T^f(+1))$
1	0%	100%	66.67%
2	0%	100%	33.33%
4	0%	100%	13.33%
8	0%	100%	4.44%
16	0%	100%	1.31%
32	0%	100%	0.36%

The definition of the fault propagation probability requires that all wrong phase prefixes will capture an error while all correct phase prefixes, independent whether there are faulty transitions appended or not, will be received as correct token. That model is based on two important constraints:

1. The design of the receiving QDI register includes an input completion detector that will only enable the capture of new data if all n inputs are in the same code phase, see [36, 47].

2. The method assumes that a trace, once it has been received will not alter its sequence anymore. This constraint prohibits the re-ordering of traces within basic gates and registers.

While the first constraint can be fulfilled by means of a proper implementation, the latter one requires to accept certain timing assumptions.

4.3.2 Trace Re-ordering

An important constraint for this thesis deals with the re-ordering of traces. Fig. 4.10 shows the preferred implementation of an n-bit QDI register in FSL as it is used in this work. The principle of operation has already been illustrated in Fig. 3.20. The register timing can be described via 10 delay elements $d1 \ldots d10$ that not only define the propagation speed of the signals but also their skew and therefore the internal signal trace. Each delay element is actually a vector $d_i = \{d_{i,1}, d_{i,2}, \ldots, d_{i,2n}\}$ where each entry defines the propagation delay of its associated rail and thereby the trace of rail transitions. For single-rail signals, the vector contains only one entry. The propagation delay of a $2n$-rail wide signal is defined by $\Delta d = \max(d)$.

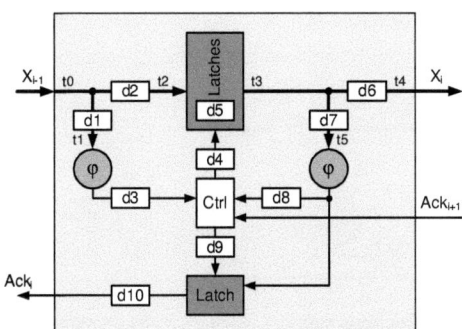

Figure 4.10: Different inherent delays and traces in a QDI register

New data is received as trace t_0 at the primary input X_{i-1}. The trace t_1 received by the input phase detector after $\Delta d1$ determines whether a token is recognized or not. If a new token is sensed, the latches will be enabled after $\Delta d3 + \Delta d4$, provided the register is ready for new data. At the same time, the input data propagates as trace t_2 via $\Delta d2$ to the latch input. Actually the register input forms a fork as displayed in Fig. 4.11(a) with the input enable time $t_{en} = \max(\Delta d1 + \Delta d3 + \Delta d4, \Delta d2)$.

4. Fault Mitigation

This fork may be isochronic, but since all internal blocks of the register are located close together, the path via the phase detector is assumed to be the longer one in practice. In Fig. 4.11(b) the corresponding delay graph is depicted. Assuming $(\Delta d1 + \Delta d3 + \Delta d4) > \Delta d2$ holds in practical circuits, the partial order of t_2 at the latch inputs is destroyed as all transitions of t_2 have already taken place when the latches are enabled. Thus the trace t_3 at the latch output may differ from t_2 at the latch input.

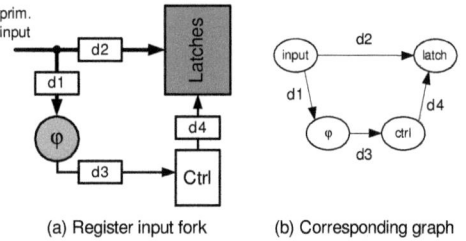

(a) Register input fork (b) Corresponding graph

Figure 4.11: Input delay graph of a real FSL register design

At the output, another fork becomes evident as given in Fig. 4.12. Again, a practical implementation leads to the constraint $(\Delta d7 + \Delta d8 + \Delta d4) > \Delta d6$. That fork will not have an impact on the output trace but defines how long the register remains in a transparent state after providing a new output. The asymmetric fork in conjunction with the dedicated acknowledge latch also ensures that a new token becomes visible at the register output before it is acknowledged, see also [47].

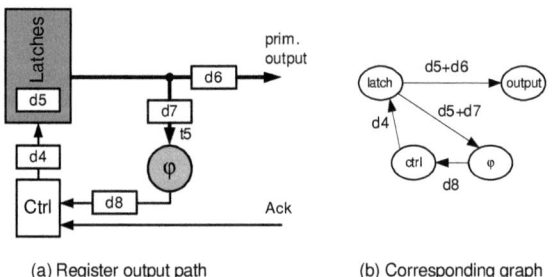

(a) Register output path (b) Corresponding graph

Figure 4.12: Output delay graph of a real FSL register design

Without faults, these practical constraints do not affect the operation of a QDI register. The same applies to $T(-1)$ and $T(+0)$ tokens as well. On the other hand, the input and output forks influence the handling of $T(+1)$ tokens. The additional rail transition(s) lead to prefixes that may be correct or wrong. The various delays and skews in the receiving QDI register may e.g. prevent a wrong phase prefix from propagating to the output although it was been captured by the input or they may output a wrong

4.3. Trace Based Fault Assessment

phase prefix if a correct prefix trace is re-ordered on its journey through the register. The probability of such effects depends on various parameters such as the actual timing, the semiconductor process, the environmental conditions, the implementation, etc. To simplify the treatment of all these internal traces but also to be independent of the actual implementation, *fixed trace circuits* are introduced:

Definition 4.3.2. In a *fixed trace circuit* all internal gates see the same trace as the primary inputs, provided the circuit is ready to receive new data.

Applying that definition to Fig. 4.10, means $t_0 \equiv t_1 \equiv t_2 \equiv t_3 \equiv t_4 \equiv t_5$. Hence the internal skew defined by the delay vectors $d1, d2, d5, d6, d7$ is small enough so no internal re-ordering of the traces occurs. Thereby only the constant ordering of the rail transitions is of interest, the time between the particular transitions is irrelevant. The benefit of a fixed trace circuit is that the traces are all well defined. A correctly received trace is not re-ordered and cannot produce a wrong output. Similarly, a wrong phase prefix at the input will generate a wrong output.

Example 4.3.3: Let's assume the faulty trace $t_0 = t_1 = \{13\overline{22}\}$ is received. That trace has an expected phase prefix followed by a transient fault on rail index 2. Consequently, the input phase detector will enable the capture of this trace. Allowing an unbounded delay, the trace may be re-ordered by $d2$ and turned into $t_2 = \{\overline{23}\overline{2}1\}$. This trace has a wrong phase prefix $\{\overline{23}\}$ that enters the latch and may be captured. In a fixed trace circuit, $t_2 = t_1$ and the correctly received trace will enter the latch.

The processing of erroneous tokens in a QDI register is considered in the temporal masking factor $P_{latched}(n, l)$ of (4.1). A fixed trace circuit excludes that masking term at first glance and only takes code masking into account. So a token error is assumed if a wrong phase prefix is received and the correct token is assumed if a correct phase prefix is received. Thereby different implementations of circuits can be compared on a fair base. In real circuits, temporal masking will additionally affect the processing of both correct or erroneous tokens.

Example 4.3.4: From the previous example, the fault trace $t_0 = \{13\overline{22}\}$ is received. Provided the register is ready for new data, the input phase detector will initiate the capturing as it receives the prefix $\text{pref}(t_1) = \{13\}$. During the storage process, the first faulty transition reaches the latches and when the control circuitry switches the latches opaque, an inconsistent token described by the trace $t_4 = \{13\overline{2}\}$ is stored.

Fixed trace circuits cannot adhere to the unbounded delay model. Therefore, this restriction is only applied to the internal design of the basic building blocks of a circuit, such as registers and simple gates. A more complex logic function that is composed of several (non-DI) gates and registers still follows an unbounded delay model on the

4. Fault Mitigation

macroscopic level. That assumption is similar to the practical design constraint of QDI circuits that makes realistic timing assumptions for the internal design of a gate, see 2.1.5. For the remainder of this thesis, all internal designs of registers as well as gates are assumed to be fixed trace circuits.

4.3.3 Dependency on the encoding

In QDI circuits, data is transmitted with a delay-insensitive code. There exist various coding schemes such as the dual-rail code (also called 1-of-2 or length-two one hot code), the 1-of-m code or the k-of-m code, to name some popular representatives. The dual-rail code is typically used in logic functions, while for data transmission channels other codes provide higher throughput and power savings potential. Although these codes look different, their nominal behavior is identical as they all must adhere to the principles of delay-insensitive communication.

In [20], the susceptibility of interconnection buses in network-on-chip structures is investigated on rail level. The authors examined various 4-phase k-of-m protocols, such as the a 1-of-3 code. This code is used to show the application of the trace based model.

Example 4.3.5: Let's assume an arbitrary 2-input function $X = \langle x_0 x_1 \rangle$ with a 1-of-3 code. The $3n = 6$ rails are assigned to rail indices from 1 to 6. The expected trace is $t_e = \{15\}$, i.e. rail 1 of x_0 and rail 2 of x_1 are excited. The expected trace set becomes $T^e = \{15, 51\}$. The size of e.g. the class fault set $|T^f(+1)|$ can be derived from (3.11) by taking into account that each of the n bits in a 1-of-3 code contains $3 - 1 = 2$ unexpected rails:

$$|T^f(+1)_{1-3}| = 2n \cdot \frac{(n+2)!}{2}. \tag{4.13}$$

The number of wrong prefixes in $T^f(+1)$ is found by adapting (4.10) in a similar way. Each of the $2n$ unexpected rails contains $2n!$ wrong prefixes:

$$|T^{pf}(+1)_{1-3}| = 4n \cdot n!. \tag{4.14}$$

The fault propagation probability is then

$$FPP(T^f(+1))_{1-3} = \frac{|T^{pf}(+1)_{1-3}|}{|T^f(+1)_{1-3}|} = \frac{4n \cdot n!}{\frac{2n(n+2)!}{2}} = \frac{4}{(n+1) \cdot (n+2)}. \tag{4.15}$$

The code masking in a 1-of-3 circuit is the same as in a dual-rail code circuit, see (4.11). That statement holds for any 1-of-m code, which can be shown by considering

4.3. Trace Based Fault Assessment

$m \cdot n$ expected rails and $(m - 1) \cdot n$ unexpected rails in (4.13) and (4.14), respectively:

$$|T^f(+1)_{1-m}| = (m - 1) \cdot n \cdot \frac{(n + 2)!}{2}$$

$$|T^{pf}(+1)_{1-m}| = (m - 1) \cdot n \cdot 2 \cdot n!$$

$$FPP(T^f(+1))_{1-m} = \frac{|T^{pf}(+1)_{1-m}|}{|T^f(+1)_{1-m}|} = \frac{(m - 1) \cdot n \cdot 2 \cdot n!}{(m - 1) \cdot n \cdot \frac{(n+2)!}{2}} = \frac{4}{(n + 1) \cdot (n + 2)} \quad (4.16)$$

However, the dual-rail code is the optimum 1-of-m code if the probability of hitting an unexpected rail is considered and a uniform fault probability is assumed. The chance that the fault hits an unexpected rail in a 1-of-m code is $(m - 1)/m$, since each bit has m expected rails opposed to $m - 1$ unexpected rails. In the dual-rail code, the probability to hit an unexpected rail is $1/2$ per bit, while the probability is increasing for higher numbers of m. For instance, in a 1-of-3 code the probability that a fault hits an unexpected rail is $2/3$. Thus the error probability of the dual-rail code is only $3/4$ compared to the 1-of-3 code, provided all other masking effects have an equal impact on both codes.

Since the fault propagation probability decreases at larger bit widths n, a 1-of-m code performs even worse as it requires fewer signals to transmit the same information.

Example 4.3.6: Let's assume a 1-of-4 code with n_{14} bits. That code conveys $4^{n_{14}}$ symbols, while an n_{dr}-bit dual-rail code only conveys $2^{n_{dr}}$ symbols. An 8-bit data bus shall be implemented, which requires 16 rails in a dual-rail system. A 1-of-4 code only requires 4 bits due to its more efficient encoding. However, in terms of signal rails the same effort is required, i.e. 16 rails are needed.

The fault propagation of the 1-of-4 code is worse. Applying (4.16), a dual-rail system ends up with $FPP(T^f(+1)_{dr}) = 4.44\%$, while the 1-of-4 code yields $FPP(T^f(+1)_{dr}) = 13.33\%$. Taking into account the probability to hit an unexpected rail, is $p_{dr} = 0.5$ in the dual-rail code, while it is $p_{14} = 0.75$ in the 1-of-4 code. That higher chance to hit an unexpected rail further degrades the robustness of the 1-of-4 code.

General k-of-m codes can be treated in a similar fashion. There are k rail transition on each bit, i.e. an n-bit code word comprises $(k \cdot n)!$ permutations. There are $(m - k)$ unexpected rails per bit. A fault may replace any of the k expected rails in the phase prefix, leaving $2k$ rail transitions that complete the trace, provided the fault manifests as logic glitch with two transitions. The number of wrong prefixes is

$$|T^{pf}(+1)_{k-m}| = (m - k) \cdot n \cdot 2k \cdot (k \cdot n)!. \quad (4.17)$$

The class fault set for a k-of-m code is derived from (3.11) by taking into account $(m - k)$ unexpected rails per bit and $(k \cdot n + 2)!$ permutations on each fault trace

$$|T^f(+1)_{k-m}| = (m - k) \cdot n \cdot \frac{(k \cdot n + 2)!}{2}. \quad (4.18)$$

87

4. Fault Mitigation

The fault propagation probability of an k-of-m code is then:

$$FPP(T^f(+1))_{k-m} = \frac{|T^{pf}(+1)_{k-m}|}{|T^f(+1)_{k-m}|} = \frac{(m-k) \cdot n \cdot 2k \cdot (kn)!}{(m-k) \cdot n \cdot \frac{(kn+2)!}{2}} = \frac{4k}{(kn+1) \cdot (kn+2)}. \tag{4.19}$$

Example 4.3.7: The implementation of an 8-bit data bus using a 2-of-7 code is compared with a dual-rail code. The FPP of the dual-rail is $FPP(T^f(+1)_{dr}) = 4.44\%$ as shown in the previous example. The 2-of-7 code can transmit 21 symbols per bit, i.e. it only requires 2 signals or 14 rails to transmit an 8-bit message. Regarding (4.19), the FPP of such an interconnection is $FPP(T^f(+1)_{2-7}) = 26.67\%$. Again, the example assumes equally distributed faults. As the circuits are nearly of the same size, the fault rate can be assumed equal as well.

This subsection has shown that the coding scheme has a significant impact on the fault propagation in a QDI circuit and that a dual-rail code is the optimum choice in terms of robustness provided the fault rate and fault distribution is identical. This preconditions may not hold in practical cases, thus a general statement which encoding scheme is the most robust one cannot be given without further investigations, which goes beyond the scope of this thesis.

4.3.4 Impact of the handshake protocol

So far the traces in this work are understood as the change between two consecutive code phases. If more consecutive code phases shall be examined, the handshake protocol must be considered. For a 2-phase protocol such as used in FSL, a sequence of code phases can be described by lining up arbitrary traces from the code phase set:

$$t_{2ph} = t_1 t_2 ... t_n : t_1, t_2, ..., t_n \in T^\varphi. \tag{4.20}$$

Regarding the 4-phase protocol, only one code phase holds a valid token. The next code phase holds an invalid token or spacer, see 2.1.4. Again, all traces must be selected from the code phase set. However, all transitions that have been received in the valid code phase must be removed in the invalid code phase to generate the all-zero spacer:

$$t_{4ph} = t_1 \; (t \in t_1!) \; t_2 \; (t \in t_2!) \; ... \; t_n \; (t \in t_n!) : t_1, t_2, ..., t_n \in T^\varphi \tag{4.21}$$

with the expression $t_n!$ meaning all permutations of t_n. Thus during the invalid code phase, any permutation of the previous trace will be applied.

Example 4.3.8: Let's assume a 2-bit QDI function with the trace $t_1 = \{13\}$ in the first code phase. The next code phase depends on the handshake protocol. In case of a 2-phase protocol, the next trace t_2 can be arbitrarily selected from the code phase set $T^\varphi = \{13, 31, 23, 32, 14, 41, 24, 42\}$. In case of a 4-phase protocol, the next code trace t_2 must be selected from $t_1! = \{13, 31\}$.

Assuming the 2-bit binary series $\{00, 11, 00, 11, ...\}$ shall be transmitted with a dual-rail code. Each bit requires two rails, e.g. $0 \mapsto \langle 01 \rangle, \langle 00 \rangle \mapsto \langle 0101 \rangle$ depending on the code phase, see Table 2.1. The initial trace may be $t_1 = \{24\}$, which can occur with both handshake protocols. Applying a 2-phase protocol, that series is translated to $\{0101; 1111; 0101; 1111, ...\}$ described by the trace $\{24; 13; 24; 13; ...\}$. When a 4-phase protocol is used, the series can be written as $\{0101; 0000; 1010; 0000; 0101; 0000, ...\}$ taking into account the alternating valid and invalid tokens. A corresponding trace would be $\{24; 24; 13; 31; 24; 42; 13; 13; ...\}$.

These different handshake protocols have a significant impact on the fault sensitivity. The 2-phase protocol has already been described extensively, therefore the 4-phase protocol shall be examined more closely. In general, 4-phase QDI circuits are not fully encoded in the valid code phase, i.e. they wait for a transition on any of the two rails. If a fault hits an unexpected rail it generates a $T(+1)$ token. If the wrong rail transition is detected first, it will propagate a token error provided the receiving QDI register is ready for new data. Depending on the implementation, if a transition on both rails occurs nearly simultaneously, an illegal token '11' will propagate. This state can be used to trigger an alarm [104, 105]. In conclusion, the valid code phase, a 4-phase QDI circuit behaves identically as a 2-phase circuit.

In the invalid code phase, a 4-phase QDI circuit is fully encoded, i.e. all rails have to go to logic zero to acknowledge an invalid token. The invalid code phase only contains falling transitions. A rising transition in this phase may lead to an illegal token '11' but it will not lead to wrong data. Thus the token class $T(+1)$ cannot occur in that phase. A falling transition will lead to a premature completion of the invalid token, which is generally not a problem. Thus the invalid code phase is more robust to transient faults. That is another advantage of the 4-phase protocol in addition to the (general) more simple circuit design. With respect to fault tolerance that does not help, as the invalid code phase is solely used for the handshaking but does not convey data tokens. Therefore, although the 4-phase protocol seems to be more robust it eventually behaves identically as the 2-phase protocol as only the valid code phase must be counted.

4.3.5 Multiple rail transitions

As shown in 3.5.2, a single fault applied to the primary inputs or to an internal node of a combinational QDI function may lead to multiple errors at the primary outputs due to some internal forks. As shown by Fig. 3.19, a single fault at the input of a 2-bit adder leads to multiple transient errors on its 3-bit output. The adder first produces the wrong result $\langle z_2, z_1, z_0 \rangle = \langle 10, 01, 01 \rangle = 4$. After the input fault has gone, the correct

4. Fault Mitigation

result $\langle 01, 10, 10 \rangle = 3$ is established. The transition $4 \rightarrow 3$ is accompanied by transitions on all rails, which violates the single event property of dual-rail codes, see 2.1.5. That descriptive example leads to a more general conclusion:

1. A single fault at the primary inputs of a QDI network or a single internal fault in such a network may lead to a consistent output where 1 to n bits are wrong, with n being the total width of the output. That initial token can be described by the class $T(+0)$, since exactly the expected number of rail transitions are generated on each primary output bit.

2. Once the wrong output has been generated, it may be maintained for the complete duration of the transient fault, even if the expected transition arrives in the meantime (in case of a strongly indicating QDI circuit, see 2.1.5). The expected transition leads to an inconsistent state, either at the primary input or at least at some internal node. The basic properties of QDI logic will prevent that the current output reacts to such an inconsistent state.

3. This thesis only considers non-redundant logic functions, i.e. a transient fault cannot be memorized in a combinational function as long as the primary inputs are driven. So the fault will eventually disappear and the correct input will re-calculate the primary output. That re-calculation means that there must be transitions on both rails at least on one output: One transition to remove the faulty rail and one to restore the correct result. This sequence can be described by the class $T(+1)$.

That sequence is important for the fault mitigation. The class $T(+0)$ and its associated fault set $T^f(+0)$, which describes the initial token error is hazard-free. Thus it is possible to detect by comparison that error on token level and to prevent it from being further processed. On the other hand, being free of hazards also means no code masking will prevent a token being captured – independent whether correct or erroneous. Thus a hardening method becomes mandatory to mitigate the class fault set $T^f(+0)$. The transfer to the token class $T(+1)$, when the correct result is re-calculated, is problematic as well because that process may involve hazards. At first glance, that partial order of the token classes $T(+0) \prec T(+1)$ will be considered when the code masking of multiple rail faults is calculated.

Example 4.3.9: A single fault at the input of the 2-bit adder in Fig. 3.19 results in the faulty trace set $T_1 = \{\overline{146}\}!$ instead of the expected trace set $T^e = \{235\}!$. When the correct output is re-established, the trace set $T_2 = \{\overline{146}235\}!$ has to be appended. The total number of traces considering $T_1 \prec T_2$ is $3! \cdot 6! = 6 \cdot 720 = 4320$. Fig. 4.13(a) shows an expected trace modeled by the class $T(+0)$. Fig. 4.13(b) depicts one possible fault trace that obeys $T_1 \prec T_2$.

4.3. Trace Based Fault Assessment

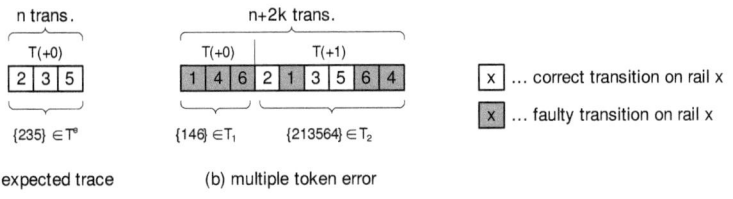

Figure 4.13: Possible trace description of the fault in Fig. 3.19

More generally, a single fault in an n-bit circuit is able to trigger $k \leq n$ errors. The fault model in this thesis assumes all faulty transitions will eventually take place, which is practically achieved by assuming the duration of the fault and its effect is shorter than the handshake period. This assumption seems to be legitimate by taking into account the typical fault durations that are caused by radiation or EMI, see 2.2.2, compared to handshake periods that are an order of magnitude longer, see chapter 5. Since the preceding $T(+0)$ token will complete the phase it might happen that the last 6 transitions in Fig. 4.13(b) that form the $T(+1)$ postfix will not be completed as the next token is requested, which depends on the handshake cycle time, the propagation delay of the predecessor circuit stage, etc. For the assessment of the code masking of multiple errors, it is assumed that all transitions in the $T(+1)$ postfix take place. In this case, the complete faulty trace is described by

$$t_f = t_{f1} \prec t_{f2} \qquad (4.22)$$

with $t_{f1} \in T(+0)$ and $t_{f2} \in T(+1)$. Due to the partial order of these two traces, the fault propagation probability becomes

$$FPP(T^f(+1)_{n,k}) = 1 \qquad (4.23)$$

as the preceding $T(+0)$ trace completes the code phase with an error. Thus no code masking applies in this case.

Although that pre-defined order is generated at the primary outputs of the erroneous combinational function, it does not necessarily arrive at the primary inputs of the receiving logic as depicted by Fig. 4.14. A single transient fault at locations (1) or (2) leads to multiple errors at location (3) that can be described with (4.22). While the transitions travel to the receiving register (4), the trace may be re-ordered. The trace t_1 generated at location (3) eventually is received as t_2 at location (4). The change of the trace on its travel path is described by a trace sequence, e.g. $\{t_1; t_4; t_8; t_2\}$. Each of these traces can be received at (4).

Taking into account an unbounded delay on the received path between locations (3) and (4) in Fig. 4.14, (4.22) is modified to

$$t_f = t_{f1} \cup t_{f2} \qquad (4.24)$$

4. Fault Mitigation

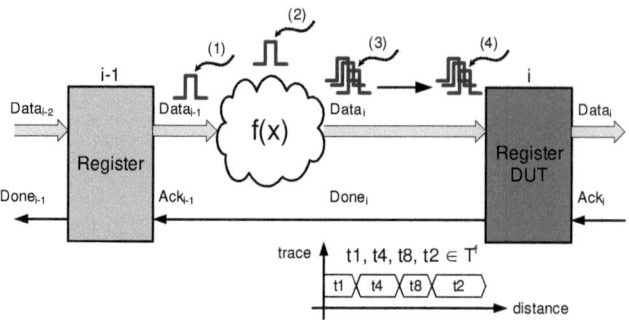

Figure 4.14: Trace Re-ordering in the data path

and the partial order at the receiver is resolved and replaced by the merged trace $t_{f1} \cup t_{f2} \in T^f(+1)$.

While the precedence order described in (4.22) inhibits code masking, the arbitrary order described by (4.24) has a certain code masking capability that can be assessed by a similar 3-step approach as already shown for single faults in 4.3.1. The calculation of the fault propagation probability is similar to the approach for single faults in $T^f(+1)$. To generate a wrong prefix $T^{pf}(+1)$ taking into account k faults, the following prerequisites have to be fulfilled:

1. At least one fault must affect an unexpected rail.

2. The last $2k$ transitions must contain at least k faulty transitions.

3. At least one pair within the last $2k$ transitions must take place on both rails of a (dual-rail) signal.

The first n transitions have to trigger a new code phase, thereby expected transitions in the first n events are replaced by faults and shifted to the last $2k$ transitions of the trace. Therefore each multiple fault trace has $(2k)! \cdot n!$ permutations. The wrong prefix may contain one to k faults, thus all combinations to select up to k faults have to be considered. Finally, the result has to be multiplied by the number of combinations to select k faults out of n unexpected rail transitions. Fig. 4.15 depicts the calculation of such a wrong prefix for $n = 3$ and $k = 2$.

$$|T^{pf}(+1)_{n,k}| = \binom{n}{k} \cdot (2k)! \cdot n! \cdot \sum_{j=1}^{k} \binom{k}{j}. \qquad (4.25)$$

The size of the class fault set $T^f(+1)$ for k faults is also derived from the single fault case in (3.11). A fault trace comprises $(n + 2k)$ transitions. As the order of the

4.3. Trace Based Fault Assessment

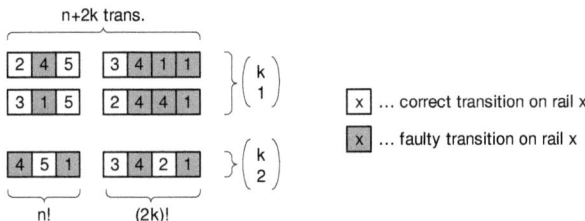

Figure 4.15: Calculation of $T^{pf}(+1)$ for $n = 3$ and $k = 2$

k faulty transitions is arbitrary, a multiple fault generates $(n+2k)!/2^k$ possible traces, which can be derived from a simple variation with k identical elements. To complete the class fault set, all combinations to select exactly k faults within n unexpected rails have to be considered:

$$|T^f(+1)_{n,k}| = \binom{n}{k} \cdot \frac{(n+2k)!}{2^k}. \tag{4.26}$$

The fault propagation probability due to multiple faults becomes

$$FPP(T^f(+1)_{n,k}) = \frac{|T^{pf}(+1)_{n,k}|}{|T^f(+1)_{n,k}|} = \frac{\binom{n}{k} \cdot (2k)! \cdot n! \cdot \sum_{j=1}^{k}\binom{k}{j}}{\binom{n}{k} \cdot \frac{(n+2k)!}{2^k}} = \frac{2^k \cdot (2k)! \cdot \sum_{j=1}^{k}\binom{k}{j}}{\prod_{i=1}^{2k}(n+i)} \tag{4.27}$$

for $k = 1$, (4.27) is getting equal to (4.11)

$$FPP(T^f(+1)_{n,1}) = \frac{2 \cdot 2!}{\prod_{i=1}^{2}(n+1)} = \frac{4}{(n+1)(n+2)} \tag{4.28}$$

and for the worst case $k = n$, (4.27) becomes

$$FPP(T^f(+1)_{n,n}) = \frac{2^n \cdot (2n)! \cdot \sum_{j=1}^{n}\binom{n}{j}}{\prod_{i=1}^{2n}(n+1)}. \tag{4.29}$$

Table 4.2 summarizes the *FPP* for $k = n$, $k = 1$ faults versus n dual-rail signals and the type of re-ordering. The first two columns show an arbitrary re-ordering according to (4.24). For $n \leq 8$, the fault propagation when $k = n$ faults occur is higher than for single faults, as the number of wrong prefixes is larger. To generate a token error, one fault in the phase prefix is already sufficient. For larger n, the fault propagation drops, as the class fault set grows faster than the wrong prefix set when the number of faults k increases. The rightmost column shows a fault propagation of 100% for the fixed partial order given by (4.22).

4. Fault Mitigation

Assuming a practical circuit, that fixed order as it is produced by the faulty circuit, is unlikely to be disturbed on its journey towards the receiver. Although the unbounded delay model allows an arbitrary re-ordering, it would rather highlight a bad chip design or bad routing if the skew on an interconnection bus completely re-arranges the rail transitions. Thus under practical circumstances, a fixed partial order can be expected due to transient faults and has to be considered in the evaluation of a circuit's robustness. In this case, some kind of fault mitigation method is mandatory to prevent a token error.

Table 4.2: Multiple fault propagation probability versus re-ordering for k faults

	$t_f = t_1 \cup t_2$		$t_f = t_1 \prec t_2$
n	$FPP(T^f(+1)_{n,1})$	$FPP(T^f(+1)_{n,n})$	$FPP(T^f(+1))$
1	66.67%	66.67%	100%
2	33.33%	80.00%	100%
4	16.67%	48.48%	100%
8	6.67%	8.88%	100%
16	2.22%	0.20%	100%
32	0.65%	6.2e-05%	100%

4.4 Duplication and Rail Cross-coupling

4.4.1 Principle

To mitigate a transient fault it must not be stored in a sequential element (register, latch) and become a soft error. Keeping this in mind, a new duplication based method with minimal additional hardware overhead has been developed. A dual-rail pipeline is duplicated and the rails of the redundant register inputs are cross-coupled. While the a-rails are used from their associated path, the b-rails are connected to the redundant path as shown in Fig. 4.16. This original concept is called *Duplication and Rail Cross-Coupling* (DRXC).

The idea is that a single fault, even a token error, will eventually lead to an inconsistent codeword, which will stop the circuit operation as long as the fault persists. Due to the unbounded delay model, any QDI circuit may be stopped for an arbitrary time without violating the circuit's specification. The cross-coupling serves as both completion detector and comparator at the same time. Thereby, a *rail cross-coupled* signal is defined as follows:

Definition 4.4.1. Assuming two dual-rail signals $X = \langle x_a x_b \rangle$ and $Y = \langle y_a y_b \rangle$, the *rail cross-coupled* signals $X_c = \langle x_a y_b \rangle$ and $Y_c = \langle y_a x_b \rangle$ are obtained by swapping the b-rails between X and Y. This property can be extended to n-bit signals $X = \langle x_{1,a} x_{1,b} ... x_{n,a} x_{n,b} \rangle$

4.4. Duplication and Rail Cross-coupling

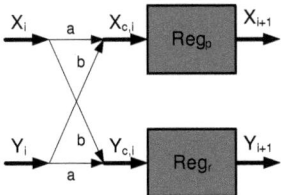

Figure 4.16: Simple rail cross-coupling

and $Y = \langle y_{1,a}y_{1,b}...y_{n,a}y_{n,b}\rangle$ accordingly. The rail cross-coupled n-bit signals are then $X_c = \langle x_{1,a}y_{1,b}...x_{n,a}y_{n,b}\rangle$ and $Y_c = \langle y_{1,a}x_{1,b}...y_{n,a}x_{n,b}\rangle$, respectively.

The following subsections investigate the properties of rail cross-coupled QDI circuits. Thereby the nominal path is denoted X and the redundant path is denoted Y.

4.4.2 Evaluation of Fault Masking

The tokens on two redundant pipelines are equal if all associated rails match:

Definition 4.4.2. Two dual-rail signals x, y are equal if and only if each rail a, b is equal: $\{x_a = y_a \wedge x_b = y_b\}$. Two dual-rail tokens $X = \langle x_i\rangle^n, Y = \langle y_i\rangle^n$ are equal if and only if all signals x_i, y_i in the token are equal: $\{\forall i \in \{1...n\} : x_i = y_i\}$.

These two conditions can be summarized in the checker function

$$X = Y \Leftrightarrow \{\forall i \in \{1...n\} : (x_{i,a} = y_{i,a}) \wedge (x_{i,b} = y_{i,b})\}. \tag{4.30}$$

The checker function is adapted to rail cross-coupled tokens:

$$X_c = Y_c \Leftrightarrow \{\forall i \in \{1...n\} : (x_{i,a} = y_{i,a}) \wedge (y_{i,b} = x_{i,b})\} \tag{4.31}$$

which is nothing but the operands of the second equation in (4.30) swapped, so

$$X = Y \Leftrightarrow X_c = Y_c. \tag{4.32}$$

To compare dual-rail signals as well as tokens, they must be in the same code phase. If two tokens $x \neq y$ are received in the same code phase, they do not fulfill (4.30). If the rails are cross-coupled, (4.31) is not fulfilled either. However, the rail cross-coupling modifies the code phase of the faulty signal $x_c \neq y_c$ to the old code phase, which will stop the processing of the complete signal vector. A short example illustrates this property.

4. Fault Mitigation

Example 4.4.1: A duplicated single-bit pipeline holds the token $x = y = \langle 00 \rangle$, so the actual code phase is $\varphi 2 = \{00, 11\}$. The next token in phase $\varphi 1 = \{01, 10\}$ shall be $x = y = \langle 01 \rangle$. Due to a transient fault, the token error $\bar{y} = \langle 10 \rangle$ is produced. Fig. 4.17(a) shows a simple duplicated pipeline. Although $x \neq \bar{y}$, both tokens are received in the expected code phase $\varphi 1$ and the circuit proceeds with a token error. In Fig. 4.17(b) the rails are cross-coupled. Here, the same token error generates the cross-coupled signals $x_c = \langle 00 \rangle$ and $y_c = \langle 11 \rangle$. Again $x_c \neq y_c$ but now both tokens are from the old code phase $\varphi 2$, which will not be interpreted by the receiver. The circuit stops as long as the error persists.

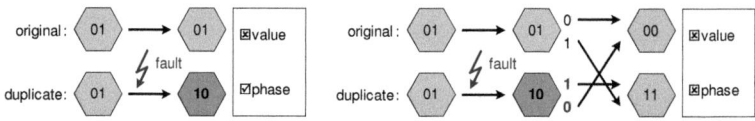

Figure 4.17: Blocking of a token error due to rail cross-coupling

The goal of the rail cross-coupling is to prevent that any faulty trace leads to a new, valid code phase. The properties of rail-cross coupling are investigated more formally. The code phase can be calculated with (2.1). In the special case of a dual-rail code, that equation can be further simplified to

$$\varphi(X) = 1 \Leftrightarrow (x_{1,a} \oplus x_{1,b}) \wedge ... \wedge (x_{n,a} \oplus x_{n,b}) = 1$$
$$\varphi(X) = 0 \Leftrightarrow (x_{1,a} \oplus x_{1,b}) \vee ... \vee (x_{n,a} \oplus x_{n,b}) = 0$$
$$\varphi(X) = \mathtt{X} \text{ otherwise} \tag{4.33}$$

and adapted to rail cross-coupled tokens

$$\varphi(X_c) = 1 \Leftrightarrow (x_{1,a} \oplus y_{1,b}) \wedge ... \wedge (x_{n,a} \oplus y_{n,b}) = 1$$
$$\varphi(X_c) = 0 \Leftrightarrow (x_{1,a} \oplus y_{1,b}) \vee ... \vee (x_{n,a} \oplus y_{n,b}) = 0$$
$$\varphi(X_c) = \mathtt{X} \text{ otherwise.} \tag{4.34}$$

The code phase will be logic 1(0) if and only if all XOR-terms ($\oplus$) in (4.33), (4.34) are logic 1(0). Otherwise the phase is undefined, which is marked by the X, and has the effect that the current phase is maintained. Thus the code phase will only change, when *each* XOR-term in (4.33) and (4.34) toggles the same way, respectively. To toggle a 2-input XOR term, exactly one input must be inverted – which has been described by the single-event property in 2.1.5.

To formulate the change of the code phase in a dual-rail QDI circuit, an artificial signal $e_i = \{0, 1\}$ is added to each dual-rail signal x_i, which describes the occurrence of

4.4. Duplication and Rail Cross-coupling

an event ($e_i = 1$) as well as its absence ($\neg e_i = 0$). The toggling of a logic state can be expressed by the function $\neg x = x \oplus 1$, thus the event signal is combined with the current code phase $\varphi(x_i)$ via an XOR-function to derive the next code phase $\varphi(x_i)'$. So the nominal change of the code phase for the X path can be described by (the Y path behaves accordingly)

$$\varphi(X)' = (x_{1,a} \oplus x_{1,b} \oplus e_1) \wedge ... \wedge (x_{n,a} \oplus x_{n,b} \oplus e_n) = \neg\varphi(X)$$
$$\varphi(X_c)' = (x_{1,a} \oplus y_{1,b} \oplus e_1) \wedge ... \wedge (x_{n,a} \oplus y_{n,b} \oplus e_n) = \neg\varphi(X_c). \qquad (4.35)$$

A single rail transition per dual-rail signal also ensures that the circuit operates hazard-free, see 2.1.5. The single-event ensures that the same data that is generated by the transmitter eventually arrives at the receiver, independent of the actual delay on the transmission path.

To show the impact of transient faults on that fundamental property of QDI logic, the token class model is utilized. Table 4.3 illustrates the code phase transition of one particular XOR-term x_i in an N-bit code word. The first row shows a nominal circuit operation, which is described by $T(+0)$. The next code phase $\varphi(x_i)'$ is the inverse of the current code phase $\varphi(x_i)$ according to (4.35). The class fault set $T^f(+0)$ excites an unexpected rail but has no impact on the code phase transition. The inhibited fault set $T^f(-1)$ does not change the code phase and (4.33) will maintain its current state. The fault class $T^f(+1)$ might have one additional transition or one additional glitch on an unexpected rail. The resulting trace sets do not follow the single-event property. If an additional transition occurs, the next code phase is the same as the current one. For an additional glitch, the next code phase is the inverse of the current one. Both statements only hold after all transitions, the expected and the unexpected ones, have taken place, which has been defined as boundary condition in this thesis.

Table 4.3: Code phase transitions on a simple dual-rail signal

Token class	Trace Set	Code Phase Transition
$T(+0)$	$\{1\}$	$\varphi(x_i)' = \varphi(x_i \oplus e_i) = \neg\varphi(x_i)$
$T^f(+0)$	$\{\overline{2}\}$	$\varphi(x_i)' = \varphi(x_i \oplus e_i) = \neg\varphi(x_i)$
$T^f(-1)$	$\{\epsilon\}$	$\varphi(x_i)' = \varphi(x_i \oplus \neg e_i) = \varphi(x_i)$
$T^f(+1)$	$\{1\overline{2}\}!$	$\varphi(x_i)' = \varphi(x_i \oplus e_i \oplus e_i) = \varphi(x_i)$
	$\{1\overline{22}\}!$	$\varphi(x_i)' = \varphi(x_i \oplus e_i \oplus e_i \oplus e_i) = \neg\varphi(x_i)$

Table 4.4 shows the code phase transitions of a rail cross-coupled signal. The fault is assumed to occur only on X, while the same result is obtained if it is applied on Y. The b-rails, which are expressed by the even rail indices are swapped between X and Y and the cross-coupled signals X_c and Y_c are generated. Once all transitions have occurred, only correct traces lead to a change of the code phase. That also applies to the trace

4. Fault Mitigation

$\{1\overline{22}\}! \in T^f(+1)$ where the glitch eventually removes the fault condition. The fault $\{\overline{2}\} \in T^f(+0)$ will not change the code phase anymore.

Table 4.4: Code phase transitions on a cross-coupled dual-rail signal

Token class	Trace set	Cross-coupled trace set	Code Phase Transition
$T(+0)$	$X = \{1\}$	$X_c = \{1\}$	$\varphi(x_i)' = \varphi(x_i \oplus e_i) = \neg\varphi(x_i)$
	$Y = \{1\}$	$Y_c = \{1\}$	$\varphi(y_i)' = \varphi(y_i \oplus e_i) = \neg\varphi(y_i)$
$T^f(+0)$	$X = \{\overline{2}\}$	$X_c = \{\epsilon\}$	$\varphi(x_i)' = \varphi(x_i \oplus \neg e_i) = \varphi(x_i)$
	$Y = \{1\}$	$Y_c = \{1\overline{2}\}!$	$\varphi(y_i)' = \varphi(y_i \oplus e_i \oplus e_i) = \varphi(y_i)$
$T^f(-1)$	$X = \{\epsilon\}$	$X_c = \{\epsilon\}$	$\varphi(x_i)' = \varphi(x_i \oplus \neg e_i) = \varphi(x_i)$
	$Y = \{1\}$	$Y_c = \{1\}$	$\varphi(y_i)' = \varphi(y_i \oplus e_i) = \neg\varphi(y_i)$
$T^f(+1)$	$X = \{1\overline{2}\}!$	$X_c = \{1\}$	$\varphi(x_i)' = \varphi(x_i \oplus e_i) = \neg\varphi(x_i)$
	$Y = \{1\}$	$Y_c = \{1\overline{2}\}!$	$\varphi(y_i)' = \varphi(y_i \oplus e_i \oplus e_i) = \varphi(y_i)$
	$X = \{1\overline{22}\}!$	$X_c = \{1\}$	$\varphi(x_i)' = \varphi(x_i \oplus e_i) = \neg\varphi(x_i)$
	$Y = \{1\}$	$Y_c = \{1\overline{22}\}!$	$\varphi(y_i)' = \varphi(y_i \oplus e_i \oplus e_i \oplus e_i) = \neg\varphi(y_i)$

Unfortunately, the concept of DRXC only prevents the propagation of faults in the steady state, provided all faulty transitions are allowed to take place before the receiving circuitry will evaluate them. Table 4.4 clearly shows that $T^f(+0)$ and $T^f(+1)$ do not comply with the single-event property of QDI logic as these classes comprise $\#e_i > 1$ events. The code phase transition is not monotonic and the phase toggles at least once before it settles to its final state. However, as the fault is masked in the steady state, DRXC should lead at least an improvement in the *FPP*, which will be calculated in the following.

First, a combined index notation is introduced. To describe the main and redundant path in one common trace, the Y path is offset by $2n$ and all even rail indices are swapped:

$$\forall y \in Y : y = x + 2n$$
$$\forall x_b \in X : y_b = x_b + 2n$$
$$\forall y_b \in Y : x_b = y_b - 2n \tag{4.36}$$

with $X = \langle x \rangle^n$ and $Y = \langle y \rangle^n$ being n-bit tokens in index notation. The concatenated token $\langle XY \rangle^{2n}$ is described by the indices 1 to $4n$. As there are two nominal and two cross-coupled circuit paths, there exist four possible end-effects a transient fault will have: The fault will generate

a) no wrong prefixes at all

b) a wrong prefix in both the nominal and cross-coupled circuit

4.4. Duplication and Rail Cross-coupling

c) a wrong prefix only in the cross-coupled circuit

d) a wrong prefix only in the nominal circuit

A simple example illustrates these different scenarios.

Example 4.4.2: Fig. 4.18 depicts a 3-bit DRXC pipeline, which conveys the expected trace set $T_x^e = \{1, 3, 6\}!$. The corresponding trace set for Y is $T_y^e = \{7, 9, 12\}!$. A single fault trace t_{44} is injected at X. Fig. 4.18(a) shows one possible fault trace, $t_1 = \{1, \overline{4}, 3, 6, \overline{4}, 7, 9, 12\}$ and its corresponding DRXC trace $t_{1c} = \{1, \overline{10}, 3, 12, \overline{10}, 7, 9, 6\}$ obtained via (4.36). Neither t_1 nor t_{1c} have a wrong prefix, so the fault will not propagate. Fig. 4.18(b) selects another trace from the trace set: $t_2 = \{1, \overline{4}, 6, 7, \overline{4}, 9, 3, 12\}$ and $t_{2c} = \{1, \overline{10}, 12, 7, \overline{10}, 9, 3, 6\}$, respectively. Here, a wrong phase prefix occurs on X as well as on Y_c. Fig. 4.18(c) shows the trace $t_3 = \{1, \overline{4}, 7, 9, \overline{4}, 6, 3, 12\}$ that is modified to $t_{3c} = \{1, \overline{10}, 7, 9, \overline{10}, 12, 3, 6\}$. Although t_3 is code masked, the cross-coupling generates a wrong prefix. Finally, Fig. 4.18(d) depicts the last possibility. The wrong prefix trace $t_4 = \{1, \overline{4}, 6, 12, \overline{4}, 7, 9, 3\}$ is modified to $t_{4c} = \{1, \overline{10}, 12, 6, \overline{10}, 7, 9, 3\}$. That last scenario constitutes the original idea of the cross-coupling: The wrong prefix is modified in such a way to be code masked in the other circuit path.

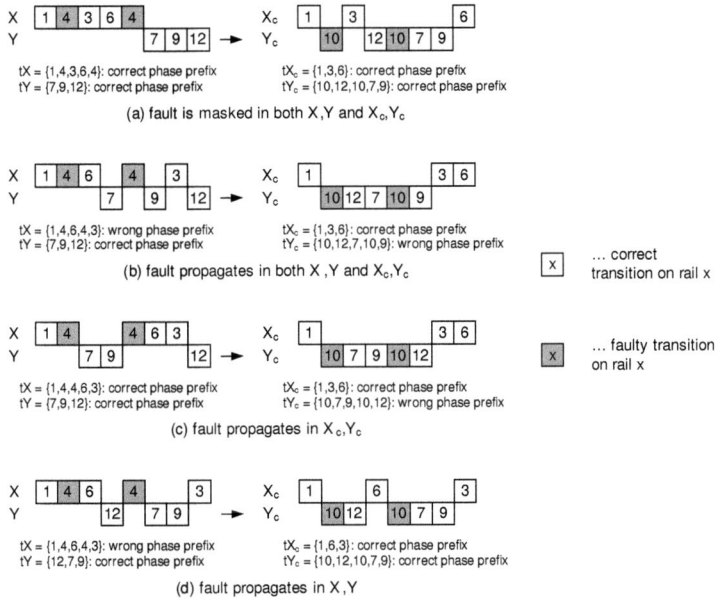

Figure 4.18: Wrong prefixes in a DRXC circuit subjected to $T^f(+1)$

4. Fault Mitigation

Regarding the above example, the calculation of the *FPP* for a DRXC circuit seems to be more complex. The extension to $2n$ rails, significantly increases the number of permutations that have to be scanned for wrong prefixes. Thus for the first assessment, a Matlab script was written that, based on a pre-defined expected trace, generates all possible single fault traces, their cross-coupled counterparts and eventually searches for wrong prefixes.

For the class $T^f(+1)$ the same result as for the original circuit was found. The reason for that result is that the phase prefixes of the two branches X and Y can be calculated independently from each other. All faults that affect an odd index are not affected by the cross-coupling at all, thus they contribute to the *FPP* as in a non cross-coupled pipeline. All faults that affect an even index are merely transferred to the other pipeline, where their contribution to the *FPP* is the same as no cross-coupling would have been applied at all. The DRXC scheme does not improve the *FPP* for the class $T(+1)$. Since there is no interaction between X_c and Y_c the *FPP* is identical to a non-redundant circuit, given by (4.11) and Table 4.1.

The class $T^f(+0)$ will have a 100% fault propagation, as each member constitutes a wrong prefix. Although that class was first only associated with redundant QDI gates (see 3.4.3), a fault that hits a combinational function may generate a fixed partial order on the fault trace, with the first token being a member of $T^f(+0)$ (see 4.3.5). If that fixed partial order is maintained at the receiver, the fault cannot be masked. However, when DRXC is applied the sensitivity against $T^f(+0)$ faults can be improved. A fault that hits an even rail is transferred to the other branch, while a fault that hits an odd rail is maintained on the same branch. Eventually, the rail cross-coupling transforms the $T^f(+0)$ token into a $T^f(+1)$ token that has $n+1$ rail transitions, as shown in Fig. 4.19. Such a token was excluded in this work, as it requires redundant QDI gates, see 3.4.3. The *FPP* for the class $T^f(+1)$ with $n+1$ can be calculated by taking into account that the fault must occur in the first n transitions while the last transition must occur on the same dual-rail signal as the fault. Thus the number of wrong prefixes is simply $n \cdot n!$ taking into account the n unexpected rails in the trace set

$$FPP(T^f(+0)_{n+1}) = \frac{n \cdot n!}{n \cdot (n+1)!} = \frac{1}{n+1} \qquad (4.37)$$

with the *FPP* related to the origin $T^f(+0)$ class fault set. Table 4.5 compares the *FPP* for the different class fault sets in an n-bit DRXC circuit.

Although the basic idea of token errors that force inconsistent tokens and prevent a fault from propagating looked quite promising in the beginning, a detailed investigation did not yield the expected reduction in terms of *FPP*. Fig. 4.20(a) depicts the propagation of a $T^f(+0)$ token error. The pair $T^f(+0)/T(+0)$ in the main and redundant path is separated into the pair $T^f(+1)/T^f(-1)$ due to the rail cross-coupling. While $T^f(-1)$ cannot propagate, $T^f(+1)$ may propagate an error depending on trace ordering. Similarly, a $T^f(+1)$ token error is separated into the pair $T^f(+1)/T^f(+0)$ as given in Fig. 4.20(b).

4.4. Duplication and Rail Cross-coupling

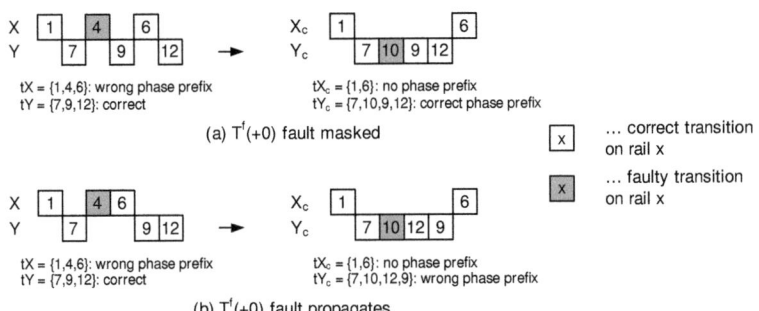

Figure 4.19: Wrong prefixes in a DRXC circuit subjected to $T^f(+0)$

Table 4.5: Fault propagation probability of an n-bit DRXC QDI function

n	$FPP(T^f(-1))$	$FPP(T^f(+0))$	$FPP(T^f(+1))$
1	0%	50.00%	66.67%
2	0%	33.33%	33.33%
4	0%	20.00%	13.33%
8	0%	11.11%	4.44%
16	0%	5.88%	1.31%
32	0%	3.03%	0.36%

The reason for the unexpected high *FPP* of a DRXC circuit is the missing correlation between the nominal and redundant path. Especially, the $T^f(-1)$ can be utilized to prevent a token error from propagating any further as this token class stops the operation of the circuit without producing any hazards. An improved, more robust version of DRXC is presented in the next subsection.

4.4.3 Synchronized rail cross-coupling

By means of a synchronization, as shown in Fig. 4.21, DRXC can be made more robust. The φ-detectors from the main and redundant path are synchronized and a token will only be received when both paths are in the same phase. As will be shown below, the *synchronized duplicated and rail cross-coupled* architecture (DRXS) is able to mask all $T^f(+0)$ faults and further improves the robustness against $T^f(+1)$ faults.

The synchronization of the two paths will mask all $T^f(+0)$ faults as illustrated by Fig. 4.22(a). The $T^f(-1)$ token that has been generated via the cross-coupling will block the hazardous $T^f(+1)$ token in the other path. Regarding $T^f(+1)$ faults, the synchronization cannot prevent this type of fault from propagating down a circuit. As shown in Fig. 4.22(b), no $T^f(-1)$ token is being generated due to the rail cross-coupling.

4. Fault Mitigation

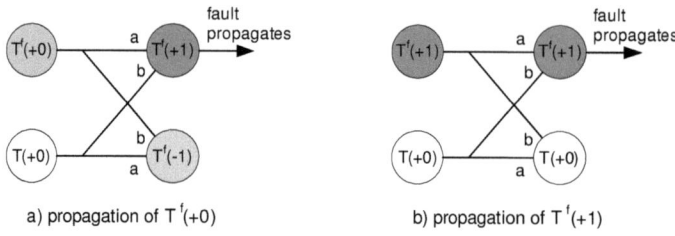

a) propagation of $T^f(+0)$ b) propagation of $T^f(+1)$

Figure 4.20: Principle of DRXC masking

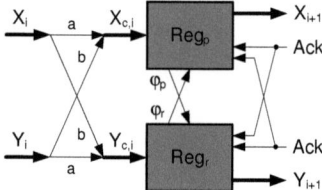

Figure 4.21: Rail cross-coupling with synchronized phase detectors

However, as the circuit must wait until both paths have reached the same phase, the propagation of a $T^f(+1)$ fault is reduced as it is less likely that a wrong prefix completes both code phases. In general, a $T^f(+1)$ fault cannot be mitigated on token level. In 4.4.6 it will be investigated whether that behavior is possible on rail level.

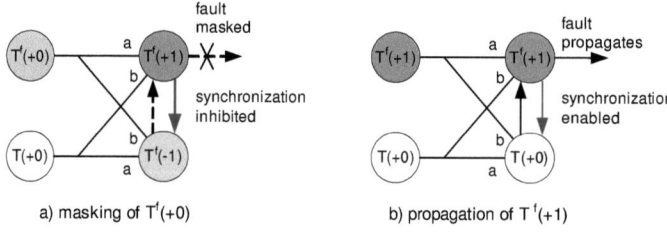

a) masking of $T^f(+0)$ b) propagation of $T^f(+1)$

Figure 4.22: Principle of simple versus synchronized rail cross-coupling

The code masking of all $T^f(+0)$ tokens in a DRXS can be proved by regarding Table 4.4. Due to the rail cross-coupling, at least one signal x_i of the token will not see an event e_i as the rail transition is transferred to the other path while no event is received in exchange. Thus the missing transition will (i) prevent the code phase completion on its own path and (ii) via the synchronization on the other path as well.

4.4. Duplication and Rail Cross-coupling

To propagate a $T^f(+1)$ token, the same prerequisites as derived in 4.3.1 apply: The fault must affect an unexpected rail and the last two transitions must take place on the same dual-rail signal. Due to the duplication, a faulty trace comprises $2n+2$ transitions. The FPP can be derived from (4.11) by substituting n with $2n$:

$$FPP(T^f(+1)_{DRXS}) = \frac{2 \cdot (2n) \cdot (2n)!}{\frac{(2n) \cdot (2n+2)!}{2}} = \frac{4}{(2n+1) \cdot (2n+2)}. \tag{4.38}$$

Table 4.6 presents the FPP for a DRXS pipeline versus the number of bits n. As for the non-redundant pipeline, the fault propagation decreases non-linear with the number of bits. So the code masking capability of DRXS is higher than just the factor of two that would have been expected due to the duplication. Nevertheless, it should be emphasized that the reduced FPP stems from an artificial duplication of the number of bits n. The robustness of a circuit also has to take into account the higher fault rate due to the increased circuit area, as described in 4.1.1.

Table 4.6: Fault propagation probability of an n-bit DRXS QDI function

n	$FPP(T^f(-1))$	$FPP(T^f(+0))$	$FPP(T^f(+1))$
1	0%	0%	33.33%
2	0%	0%	13.33%
4	0%	0%	4.44%
8	0%	0%	1.31%
16	0%	0%	0.36%
32	0%	0%	0.09%

Next, some physical implementations of a DRXS circuit are discussed. Fig. 4.23 shows two principal methods. In Fig. 4.23(a) the outputs of the input code phase detectors are fed to the latch control circuit, which enables / disables the register internal latches, see Fig. 3.20. The latches will only be enabled if the output of both input phase detectors are identical. The benefit of this implementation is the minimum amount of supplemental hardware in addition to the duplication. Only two additional AND-gates are needed. In Fig. 4.23(b) the phase detector inputs are synchronized. Therefore the set (Sx/Sy) and reset (Rx/Ry) signals of the input code phase detector are routed to the redundant register and combined via AND-gates. This implementation needs two more AND-gates as the previous architecture. The schematics also show that DRXS synchronizes the acknowledge signals as well, which is mandatory to mitigate synchronization errors that would otherwise unalign the two pipelines, see Fig. 3.14. Each of the two methods has its merits, which is shown by an example.

Example 4.4.3: A 3-bit DRXS pipeline according to Fig. 4.23(a) receives the $T^f(+1)$ fault trace $t_f = \{1, 3, \overline{6}, 7, 9, 5, 11, \overline{6}\}$. The first triple $t_1 = \{1, 3, \overline{6}\}$ toggles the in-

4. Fault Mitigation

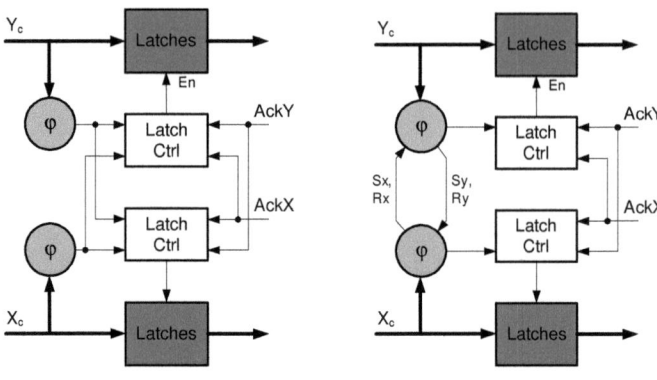

(a) DRXS with synchronized phase detector outputs

(b) DRXS with synchronized phase detector set/reset

Figure 4.23: Different methods how to synchronize a DRXS pipeline

puts phase detector X, but the latches are disabled until Y completes its phase after $t_2 = \{7, 9, 5, 11\}$ has arrived. When the Y phase is completed, the illegal trace $t_I = \{1, 3, \overline{6}, 5\}$ is applied to X as there must not be two transitions on the same dual-rail signal $\{\overline{6}, 5\}$. As the X phase detector maintains its state until the next code phase is applied, t_I is passed to the output.

The same trace t_f is applied to a DRXS pipeline according to Fig. 4.23(b). Here, the X phase detector will not be triggered by t_1. The circuit waits until the complete trace t_f has been received, as no intermediate trace stimulates both input phase detectors in the same way. Possibly, the fault is masked without passing a token error or inconsistent token to the output.

The synchronization of the set and reset signals presented in Fig. 4.23(b) has emerged as the more robust implementation and is used as preferred architecture for the DRXS designs in this thesis. The hardware overhead compared to Fig. 4.23(a) is negligible. Nevertheless, both implementations require timing assumptions if they are subjected to $T(+1)$ tokens. Otherwise, hazards may occur that lead to an unspecified metastable behavior. In Fig. 4.24(a) the previous example $\{1, 3, \overline{6}, 7, 9, 5, 11, \overline{6}\}$ is illustrated. The transition on rail 5 de-asserts the set input Sx, while the transition on rail 11 asserts the set input Sy. As long as these two events are sufficiently separated the synchronized set signal $Sx \cdot Sy$ will be hazard-free. Fig. 4.24(b) depicts another possible trace $\{1, 3, \overline{6}, 7, 9, 11, 5, \overline{6}\}$, where the transition sequence generates a glitch on the synchronized set signal. Such glitches may trigger a metastable behavior, which eventually results in a token or delay error, see 3.4.3.

In the next step, the overhead of DRXS is examined. The resources are analyzed

4.4. Duplication and Rail Cross-coupling

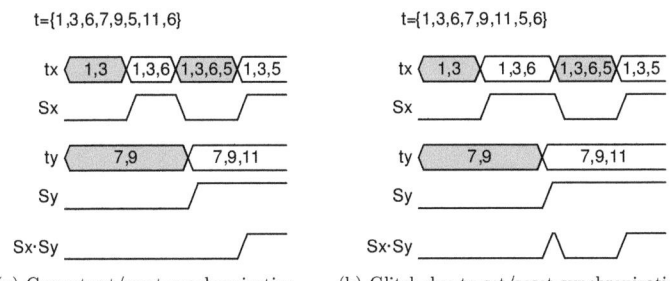

(a) Correct set/reset synchronization (b) Glitch due to set/reset synchronization

Figure 4.24: Race condition on synchronized set/reset signals of DRXS pipeline

in a general fashion by counting the number of 2-input gates and latches. Thereby the register design is based on Fig. 4.25.

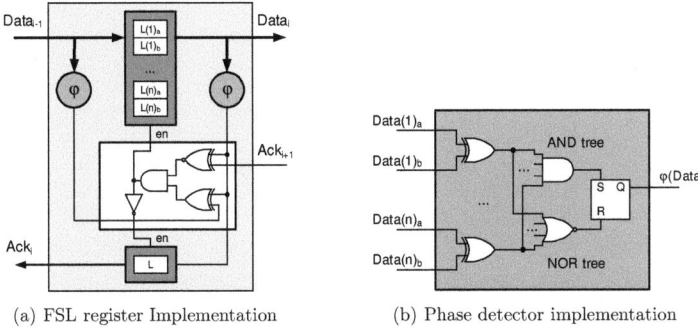

(a) FSL register Implementation (b) Phase detector implementation

Figure 4.25: Hardware resources of an FSL register

In general, a register comprises two latches for each dual-rail signal, two latches for the input and output phase detector and one acknowledge latch [47]. In case of a single-bit register ($n = 1$), the input and output phase detector can be built using just an XOR gate, thus no latches are needed in this special case. The number of latches $|L(n)|$ versus the number of bits n can be calculated with

$$|L(n)| = 2n + 1 + 2(n > 1). \tag{4.39}$$

The number of 2-input gates in the register control block is 3 and independent of n. Thereby the inverter has been neglected. The number of 2-input gates for a phase detector is

$$|G_\varphi(n)| = n_{XOR} + (n-1)_{AND} + (n-1)_{NOR} = 3n - 2 \tag{4.40}$$

105

4. Fault Mitigation

as there are n XOR gates and two trees of 2-input AND/NOR gates that define the set and reset signals of the phase detector latch. The size of these trees is $n-1$, which can be checked by simple graph theory. Finally, the total number of 2-input gates $|G(n)|$ including two phase detectors and the latch control block is

$$|G(n)| = 2(3n-2) + 3 = 6n - 1. \tag{4.41}$$

The DRXS architecture requires two times the latches and gate resources plus additional hardware for synchronization. Regarding the implementation in Fig. 4.23(b) four AND-gates are needed to synchronize the set and reset signals of the two input phase detectors. To give a closed expression for the resource occupation, the latches are expressed in equivalent 2-input gates. Thereby each latch is counted as 5 gates, which will be discussed below. So the number of 2-input gates in DRXS is

$$\begin{aligned}|G(n)_{DRXS}| &= 2 \cdot (5 \cdot |L(n)| + |G(n)|) + 4 = \\ &= 2 \cdot (10n + 5 + 10(n > 1) + 6n - 1) + 4 = \\ &= 32n + 12 + 20(n > 1).\end{aligned} \tag{4.42}$$

Table 4.7 compares the hardware resources of a simple QDI register, with DRXS and calculates the overhead.

Table 4.7: Overhead of DRXS versus number of bits n by counting gates

	latches + 2-input gates		
n	simple	DRXS	overhead
1	20	44	120%
2	46	96	109%
4	78	160	105%
8	142	288	103%
16	270	544	101%
32	526	1056	101%

The previous assessment suffers from two uncertainties. First, the equivalent gate count of a latch is assumed to be 5 and second, each 2-input gate is counted equally. In reality, a NAND gate can be implemented quite efficiently using just 4 transistors, while e.g. an AND gate already requires 6 transistors. These numbers correspond to a simple CMOS implementation and may vary in other semiconductor processes. Thus the hardware overhead was investigated by implementing simple and DRXS registers using the LSI Logic 10K library. The gate level netlist was generated in Synopsys (Version C-2009.06-SP4) and the cell area was compared. The correspondence of 5 times the area of a simple 2-input NAND gate and a latch was actually derived from these experiments. Table 4.8 shows the results.

4.4. Duplication and Rail Cross-coupling

Table 4.8: Overhead of DRXS versus number of bits n by gate level synthesis

n	cell area in μm^2 simple	DRXS	overhead
1	37	94	154%
2	68	138	103%
4	120	228	90%
8	192	356	85%
16	354	654	85%
32	673	1252	86%

Surprisingly, the overhead of DRXS was less than 100% as it would have been expected merely due to the duplication. The reason lies in the physical implementation of the gates. A tree of 2-input gates can be implemented more efficiently in terms of transistor count by means of multiple input gates. That fact has not been taken into account by the gate counting method presented in Table 4.7. Further, the synthesis tool is not optimized for asynchronous designs and such results shall not be used to derive an absolute metric for the hardware overhead of QDI logic. To conclude, it was shown that the overhead of DRXS in addition to the duplication is negligible. Thus the DRXS method has a clear advantage compared to other duplex based systems that need dedicated comparators to detect a token error such as [93, 95] or [97].

4.4.4 Tolerance against multiple errors

The effects of multiple errors due to a single transient fault have been examined in 4.3.5. In this case, an n-bit sequential circuit will receive a trace with $k \leq n$ token errors. The fault trace is generated in combinational logic at locations (3) and (4) in Fig. 3.8. At the primary output of this circuitry, the trace will have a pre-defined order according to (4.22) While the trace propagates to the receiver that order may be (i) re-arranged arbitrarily according to (4.24) or (ii) it may be maintained.

Case (i) can be handled similar to single faults handled by (4.27) when n is substituted with $2n$ to consider the duplication:

$$FPP(T^f(+1)_{2n,k}) = \frac{\binom{2n}{k} \cdot (2k)! \cdot (2n)! \cdot \sum_{j=1}^{k} \binom{k}{j}}{\binom{2n}{k} \cdot \frac{(2n+2k)!}{2^k}}. \qquad (4.43)$$

For the two extremes $k = 1$ and $k = n$ that equation becomes:

$$FPP(T^f(+1)_{2n,1}) = \frac{2 \cdot (2n)!}{\frac{(2n+2)!}{2}} = \frac{2 \cdot (2n)!}{\frac{(2n+2)!}{2}} = \frac{4}{(2n+2)(2n+1)} \qquad (4.44)$$

4. Fault Mitigation

$$FPP(T^f(+1)_{2n,n}) = \frac{2^n \cdot (2n)! \cdot \sum_{j=1}^{n} \binom{n}{j}}{\prod_{i=1}^{2k}(2n+i)} \quad (4.45)$$

For an arbitrary order of the fault trace between the source of the error and the receiving circuitry, DRXS effectively reduces the fault propagation. As in a non-redundant QDI circuit, the higher the number of signals n, the smaller the fault propagation as shown in Table 4.9. For convenience, numbers smaller than 5E-06 are shown as zero.

Table 4.9: Fault propagation for multiple faults in DRXS with an arbitrary order

n	$k=1$	$k=2$	$k=4$	$k=8$
1	33.333%	-	-	-
2	13.333%	17.143%	-	-
4	4.444%	2.424%	1.865%	-
8	1.307%	0.248%	0.033%	0.011%
16	0.357%	0.020%	0.000%	0.000%
32	0.093%	0.001%	0.000%	0.000%

Example 4.4.4: Fig. 4.26 depicts the general case of multiple errors for the expected trace set $T_X^e = \{13\}!$ and $T_Y^e = \{57\}!$. A multiple fault described by t_{22} and t_{44} is imposed on $T_X^e \cup T_Y^e$ and the effect of this fault in a DRXS circuit is investigated. The example assumes that the prefix contains $k = n = 2$ faults. In Fig. 4.26(a) and (c) the fault is masked by DRXS, in Fig. 4.26(b) and (d) the fault propagates through the DRXS circuit.

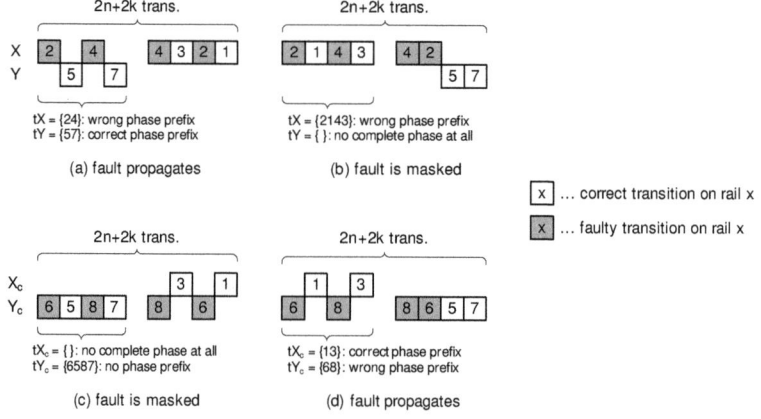

Figure 4.26: Definition of sensitive prefixes with multiple errors in a DRXS circuit

4.4. Duplication and Rail Cross-coupling

In case (ii), a receiver detects the same partial order $T^f(+0) \prec T^f(+1)$ as generated at the source of the error. A non-redundant QDI circuit is not be able to mask the preceding $T^f(+0)$ fault as it completes the code phase. A DRXS circuit will mask the premature $T^f(+0)$. To analyze the trace that is received by a DRXS register the main (X) and redundant (Y) trace are merged, with X having a fixed partial order as shown in Fig. 4.27.

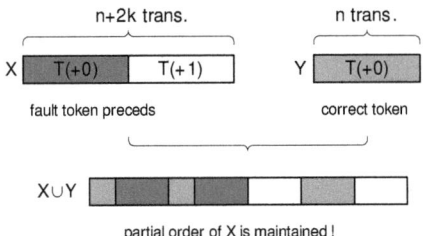

Figure 4.27: Merging of two traces, with a fixed partial order

A simple example illustrates that behavior and also points out the difference when the partial order is fixed on one path.

Example 4.4.5: Let's assume a 3-bit DRXS circuit with a faulty trace $t_f = \{1, 3, \overline{6}, 5, \overline{6}\}$ on X_c and the expected trace $t_e = \{7, 9, 11\}$ on Y_c. The number of faults is $k = 1$. If an arbitrary order is applied, the traces may be merged to e.g. $t_{xyc} = \{7, 1, 3, 5, \overline{6}, 9, \overline{6}, 11\} \in \{t_f \cup t_e\}$, which does not contain wrong phase prefixes. Applying (4.38), the circuit has an FPP of $4/(7 \cdot 8) = 7.14\%$.

If the partial order in t_f has to be maintained the previous scenario is illegal, since $\{1, 3, \overline{6}\} \prec \{5, \overline{6}\}$ does not hold in the merged trace t_{xyc}. One possible trace that maintains that partial order is e.g. $t_{xyc} = \{7, 1, 3, 9, \overline{6}, 11, 5, \overline{6}\}$. Here, the first $2n$ transitions contain a wrong phase prefix for X_c and a token error may be captured. The fault propagation probability for $n = 3$ and a fixed partial order is 1.79%. That result has been calculated with a Matlab script that counts all wrong phase prefixes within all legal traces due to a single fault and a fixed partial order.

The number of wrong phase prefixes for an arbitrary number of k faults in DRXS with a fixed partial order can be calculated analytically as shown in the following example. The criterion for a wrong phase prefix with k faults in a fixed partial order is that the last $2k$ transitions take place on exactly k signals.

Example 4.4.6: Fig. 4.28 derives the number of wrong prefixes for a fixed partial order assuming $n = 4$ and $k = 2$. Let's assume a faulty trace set $T_X^f = \{1, 3, \overline{4}, \overline{6}\}! \prec \{5, 7, \overline{4}, \overline{6}\}!$ on X and the expected trace set $T_Y^e = \{9, 11, 13, 15\}!$ on Y. The associated

4. Fault Mitigation

DRXS trace swaps all even indices as shown in the upper two rows of the figure. A wrong prefix completes the code phase of the DRXS circuit after $2n = 8$ transitions and has to be selected from the trace set $\{1, 3, \overline{12}, \overline{14}, 5, 7, 9, 11\}!$ where $\{1, 3, \overline{12}, \overline{14}\}! \prec \{5, 7\}! \equiv \{1, 3, \overline{4}, \overline{6}\}! \prec \{5, 7\}!$ must hold due to the fixed partial order. The fixed partial order applies to both the nominal and the cross-coupled traces.

The first n transitions of X are defined by the preceding $\{1, 3, \overline{12}, \overline{14}\} \in T(+0)$ token. The expected rail transitions $(5, 7)$ on the k faulty rails are successively moved from their most early position $n + 1$ to the end of the $2n$ long prefix trace. These transitions are highlighted for a better visualization. As the transitions on the two paths are not correlated, all transitions from Y may be merged with the preceding $T(+0)$ on X. So the number of wrong prefixes for that example are

$$|T^{44,66}(2n,k)| = (2k)! \cdot [n! \cdot \binom{n-k}{0} \cdot k \cdot (n-1)! + (n+1)! \cdot \binom{n-k}{1} \cdot k \cdot (n-2)! +$$
$$+ (n+2)! \cdot \binom{n-k}{2} \cdot k \cdot (n-3)!].$$

Plugging in the numbers for that example $n = 4$ and $k = 2$ gives

$$|T^{44,66}(8,2)| = 4! \cdot [4! \cdot \binom{2}{0} \cdot 2 \cdot 3! + 5! \cdot \binom{2}{1} \cdot 2 \cdot 2! + 6! \cdot \binom{2}{2} \cdot 2 \cdot 1!] =$$
$$= 24 \cdot [288 + 960 + 1440] = 64512.$$

The *FPP* for the general case can be derived from the previous example considering that there are $\binom{2n}{k}$ combinations to select k faulty rails within the total $2n$ unexpected rails of a DRXS circuit. The number of wrong prefixes becomes then

$$|T^{pf}(+1)^{fo}_{2n,k}| = \binom{2n}{k} \cdot (2k)! \cdot \sum_{j=0}^{n-k}(n+j)! \cdot k \cdot \binom{n-k}{j} \cdot (n-1-j)!. \qquad (4.46)$$

The size of the class fault set $T^f(+1)^{fo}_{2n,k}$ can be derived similarly to (4.46). First, the last $2k$ transitions are merged with the preceding $2n$ traces of the phase prefix. Second, it has to be ensured that the partial order on the faulty path is fulfilled in all permutations:

$$|T^f(+1)^{fo}_{2n,k}| = \binom{2n}{k} \cdot \sum_{j=0}^{n}(n+j)! \cdot 2k \cdot \binom{n}{j} \cdot (n-1+2k-j)!. \qquad (4.47)$$

Table 4.10 presents the fault propagation probability $|T^{pf}(+1)^{fo}_{2n,k}|/|T^f(+1)^{fo}_{2n,k}|$ for a fixed partial order using (4.46) and (4.47), respectively. The table shows all numbers smaller than 5E-06 as zero. Comparing with an arbitrary fault order shown in Table 4.9, the FPP with a fixed partial order is less for $n \leq 2$, while it becomes larger for $n > 2$.

4.4. Duplication and Rail Cross-coupling

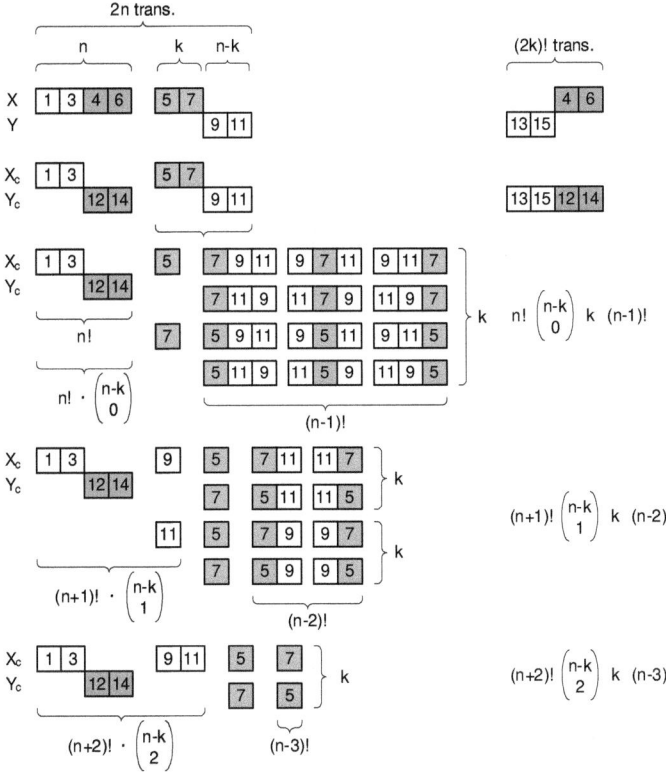

Figure 4.28: Wrong phase prefixes with k faults and a fixed partial order

Table 4.10: Fault propagation probability for multiple faults with a fixed partial order

n	$k=1$	$k=2$	$k=4$	$k=8$
1	25.000%	-	-	-
2	13.333%	3.571%	-	-
4	6.667%	0.943%	0.055%	-
8	3.268%	0.227%	0.004%	0.000%
16	1.604%	0.054%	0.000%	0.000%
32	0.793%	0.013%	0.000%	0.000%

The reason for that behavior is that the class fault set does not grow that fast compared to the wrong prefix set when a fixed partial order is maintained.

The fixed partial order constitutes the worst case for a QDI pipeline, as it assumes that a faulty $T^f(+1)$ trace always starts with a $T^f(+0)$ error. A simple QDI pipeline

4. Fault Mitigation

cannot prevent that error from being received, while the DRXS scheme reduces that probability significantly. As it is not possible to mitigate the class fault set $T^f(+1)$ on token / signal level, it will be investigated how such a fault will propagate once it has been received as error.

4.4.5 Fault propagation and storage in cross-coupled circuits

As subsections 4.4.3 and 4.4.4 have shown that DRXS cannot code mask all $T^f(+1)$ faults, the propagation and storage of wrong prefixes is investigated in more detail. Thereby it is assumed that the subsequent circuit stage also implements DRXS. After receiving a wrong prefix from a $T^f(+1)$ token, three possibilities emerge:

1. Although a wrong prefix triggers the storage process, the complete $T^f(+1)$ token is received before the storage can be completed. Eventually, the expected token is stored, while a $T^f(+1)$ trace propagates to the output.

2. Before the storage process is completed, additional transitions arrive. The register captures an inconsistent token as well as propagates a $T^f(+1)$ token.

3. The wrong phase prefix, described by $T^f(+0)$ is captured and propagated to the output. This scenario occurs when the receiving circuitry is very fast and immediately captures the detected prefix.

Case (1) simply shifts the fault to the next circuit stage without storing any wrong or inconsistent data. In fact, that scenario is like if the fault would have been generated in the subsequent circuit stage at all. The masking effects in that stage will determine whether the propagated $T^f(+1)$ will again lead to a wrong phase prefix or whether the fault is mitigated. The *FPP* in the subsequent stage can be calculated using (4.38). Thus the probability of a $T^f(+1)$ fault that passes the first stage and generates a wrong phase prefix in the subsequent stage is very unlikely, provided the trace distributions in the two stages are independent from each other. See Fig. 4.29(a) how a $T^f(+1)$ trace will propagate a multi-stage DRXS circuit.

Case (2) applies an inconsistent token to the subsequent circuit stage, which may lead to a deadlock if the propagated trace does not contain a phase prefix. Assuming a single fault, the inconsistent token is described by $2n+1$ transitions, where $\frac{1}{2n+1}$ traces contain a correct or wrong phase prefix, while $\frac{2n-1}{2n+1}$ traces lead to a deadlock. Thus the deadlock is the most probable result of this scenario.

Case (3) always leads to a deadlock since any $T^f(+0)$ fault will stop the circuit operation until the fault has been resolved – which will never happen. That scenario is depicted in Fig. 4.29(b).

Taking these scenarios into account, case (1) is the most preferable one as it prevents a deadlock of the circuit. If a wrong phase prefix is received, its storage should be

4.4. Duplication and Rail Cross-coupling

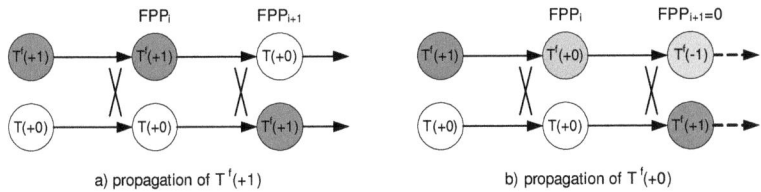

Figure 4.29: Propagation of faulty tokens in DRXS

prevented. Therefore, the rail cross-coupling principle is revised. As shown in Fig. 4.22, a received pair $T^f(+0)/T(+0)$ will be separated in the pair $T^f(+1)/T^f(-1)$, where the inhibited transition in $T^f(-1)$ will prevent the hazardous $T^f(+1)$ from being processed. The rail cross-coupling was applied to the input of a register to block any incoming wrong prefixes. Similarly, the same principle can be applied to the output detection of a register to prevent any wrong prefix from being captured. Such a modified DRXS register is depicted in Fig. 4.30. The *DRXS with cross-coupled completion detectors* is called *DRXX* to distinguish it from the ordinary DRXS scheme.

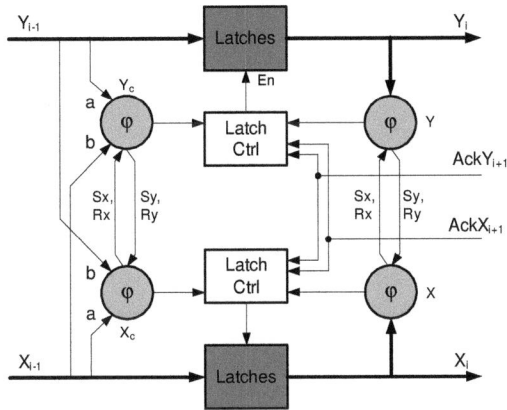

Figure 4.30: DRXS with synchronized completion detectors (DRXX)

The *FPP* of DRXX is identical to the ordinary DRXS, but the tolerance against deadlocks can be reduced. The upper part of Fig.4.31 shows the token sequence as it is received by the DRXX register. The transient fault generates the pair $T^f(+0)/T(+0)$ that triggers the storage process. Contrary to DRXS, the DRXX register passes the non cross-coupled data to the synchronized output phase or completion detectors as given in the lower part of Fig.4.31. Thus the output receives the pair $T^f(+1)/T^f(-1)$, which will delay the completion of the storage process until both paths get a phase prefix.

113

4. Fault Mitigation

In a fixed trace circuit, the order of the transitions as received at the input must not be changed, which applies to both the original non cross-coupled trace and the cross-coupled trace. Thus when the output has received the $T^f(+1)/T^f(-1)$ pair, the inhibited trace $T^f(-1)$ trace suppresses the completion of the storage process. The next transition either removes the fault (which is the preferred scenario) or generates a $T^f(+1)/T^f(+0)$ token pair at the output. Due to the synchronization of the completion detectors, the $T^f(+1)$ trace will now suppress the completion of the storage. That state is maintained until all transitions have taken place and the fault is removed.

Although a $T^f(+1)$ has been propagated, a fixed trace circuit prevents the capture of both $T^f(+0)$ and $T^f(+1)$ tokens and thereby prevents a deadlock in a DRXX pipeline due to transient faults. That principle is illustrated in a simple example.

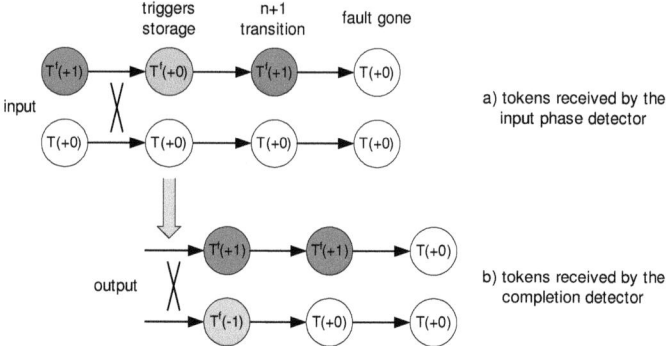

Figure 4.31: Fault propagation in a DRXX register

Example 4.4.7: The DRXX circuit according to Fig. 4.30 receives the expected trace $t_{xy} = \{1, 3, 5, 7, 9, 11\}$. A single fault applied on rail 6 leads to the trace $t_{xy}^f = \{1, 3, \overline{6}, 5, 7, 9, 11, \overline{6}\}$. The input phase detectors receive the cross-coupled trace $t_{xyc}^f = \{1, 3, \overline{12}, 5, 7, 9, 11, \overline{12}\}$, where the first $2n$ transitions complete the code phase on either path, as shown in Fig. 4.32(a). An ordinary DRXS circuit would receive the token error $t_y^f = \{\overline{12}, 7, 9\}$, which will lead to a deadlock if it is stored in the register.

In a DRXX register, the first $2n$ transitions of the original trace $t_{xy}^f = \{1, 3, \overline{6}, 5, 7, 9\}$ propagate through the latches as shown in Fig. 4.32(b). As the sub-trace $t_y = \{7, 9\}$ belongs to $T(-1)$ it will prevent the completion of the storage process. That completion is even prevented when the next transition 11 arrives, as the phase of X meanwhile holds an inconsistent token $t_x = \{1, 3, \overline{6}, 5\}$.

In a practical QDI register, the enable time of the register internal latches is typically longer than the input propagation delay, as described by Fig. 4.11 in 4.3.2. The partial

4.4. Duplication and Rail Cross-coupling

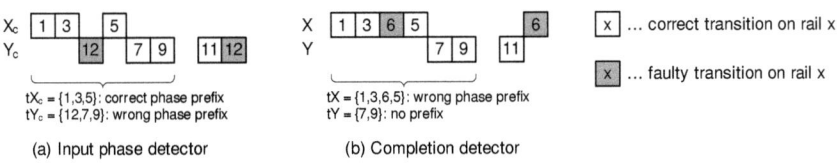

(a) Input phase detector (b) Completion detector

Figure 4.32: Different perception of traces in a DRXX register

order of a trace is likely to be destroyed as the transitions have already been applied to the register internal latch inputs when the latch is enabled. These timing constraints have no effect on the *FPP*, but they may lead to a re-ordering of the rail transitions when propagate through the latches to the output.

Applied to the previous example, the trace $t_{xy} = \{1, 3, \overline{6}, 5, 7, 9, 11, \overline{6}\}$ that is received at the latch inputs, may be perceived as $t_{xy} = \{1, 3, \overline{6}, 7, 9, 11, 5, \overline{6}\}$ at the synchronized completion detectors. That reordering would not be allowed in a fixed trace circuit but may be encountered if the asymmetric input delays are taken into account in a practical circuit realization.

The reduction of deadlocks only applies to faults that are introduced via the data path, see Fig. 3.8. Handshake faults or faults in the acknowledge section of a register may lead to a deadlock as they lead to a misalignment of the redundant pipelines. The treatment of deadlocks due to transient faults is not further investigated on theoretic level and will be handled by means of fault simulations in chapter 5.

Table 4.11 compares the overhead of a DRXX circuit with DRXS and a simple duplex architecture versus the number of bits n. The hardware resources have been evaluated by counting latches and 2-input gates. The synchronization of the output phase detectors requires 4 additional gates, thus the overhead is slightly more than for the original DRXS scheme given in Table 4.7. The table does not consider the additional interconnections that are needed to distribute the b-rails to both the main and redundant circuitry. If this rail distribution comes along without any buffers, there is no difference to the hardware need of ordinary DRXS. A performance impact is assumed as the splitting of the b-rails will increase the delay on this path as the load capacitance is increased. That impact is not further investigated as it is assumed to be minor.

So far, all token based methods have failed to mitigate a $T^f(+1)$ token when arbitrary delays have to be taken into account. It was not possible enforce the generation of a $T^f(-1)$ token in the presence of a $T^f(+1)$ fault that can be used to stop the processing of a wrong phase prefix. The solution is to place the comparison on rail level, as it allows to generate the essential $T^f(-1)$ token as shown in the next subsection.

4. Fault Mitigation

Table 4.11: Overhead of DRXX compared to a simple QDI register by counting gates

	latches + 2-input gates				
n	simple	DRXC	DRXS	DRXX	overhead
1	20	40	44	48	140%
2	46	92	96	100	117%
4	78	156	160	164	110%
8	142	284	288	292	106%
16	270	540	544	548	103%
32	526	1052	1056	1060	102%

4.4.6 Rail comparison

The comparison of rails has been introduced by Martin et al [18,93,94] as *duplication and double-checking*. This topic has been thoroughly investigated by the cited authors and has been summarized in 4.2.2. Now the function of this method is examined using the trace based model derived in this thesis. Fig. 4.33 shows the principle of operation. Each pair of redundant rails is synchronized via a dedicated Muller C-gate that acts as rail comparator. A transition is only passed if it occurs on both the main and redundant path.

The function of the double-checking can be described with the token class model from 3.4.3. Fig. 4.33 shows a $T^f(+1)$ fault that generates a rising edge on rail a_0. As long as the redundant rail a_1 is correct, the fault is ignored and the synchronized output $a_{0,syn}$ is not excited. The b-rails only carry expected transitions and $b_{0,syn}$ will be excited as expected.

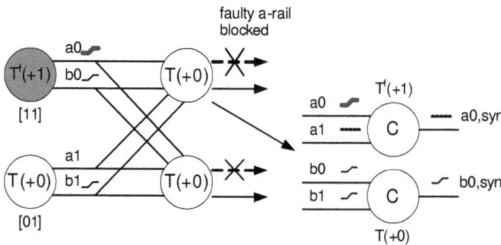

Figure 4.33: Principle of duplication and double-checking [93]

Fig. 4.34 illustrates the different possibilities of comparing rail transitions via a C-gate using token classes. Fig. 4.34(a) shows a nominal scenario. Both inputs receive an expected transition so the C-gate will also generate an output transition, which is described by $T(+0)$. In Fig. 4.34(b), one expected transition is inhibited, which corresponds to $T(-1)$. The C-gate will maintain its current output as it requires two transitions to change its output. Similarly, Fig. 4.34(c) shows the case where an unexpected rail is

4.4. Duplication and Rail Cross-coupling

excited, which forms a $T(+1)$ token. Since the second input has no transition, the C-gate will maintain its output. Finally, Fig. 4.34(d) depicts the only case where the rail comparison fails. Both inputs are subjected to a fault, which is illegal in a single-fault model. This scenario cannot be distinguished from a nominal case as the class $T(+0)$ is observed.

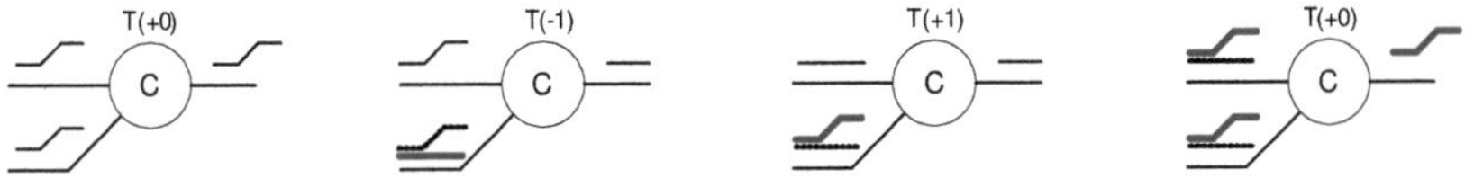

Figure 4.34: Different possibilities of comparing rail transitions

The benefit of comparing tokens on the rail level is that $T(+1)$ tokens are code masked. One additional, unexpected rail transition cannot trigger a code phase completion like in systems that compare at token level. A $T(+1)$ token does not comply to the specification of DI codes as it cannot be distinguished whether the first received rail transition is expected or unexpected. Only one transition is required to change the code phase. If the particular rails of a dual-rail signal are compared with a C-gate, two transitions are required to change the code phase. Thus a single rail fault cannot propagate.

In the original work by Martin, the duplication and double-checking method explicitly adds C-gates to the outputs of redundant gates, each checking the associated rails for equality. For sequential functions the method works similarly. Additionally, the acknowledge signals are also synchronized via C-gates. Fig. 4.35 shows the detailed designs of a simple and duplicated double-checking register implemented as so called pre-charge half buffer.

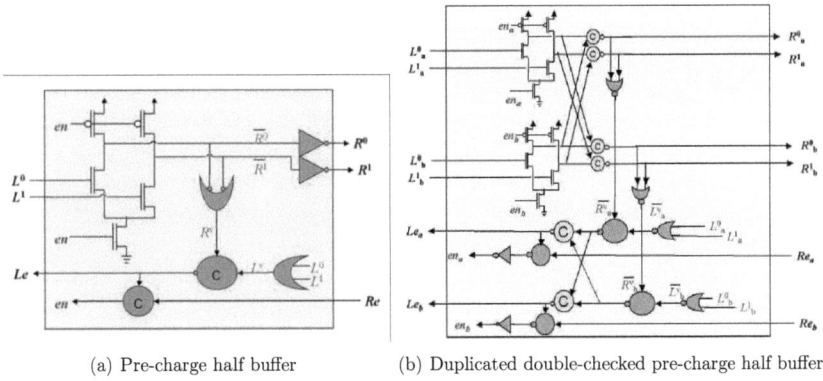

(a) Pre-charge half buffer   (b) Duplicated double-checked pre-charge half buffer

Figure 4.35: Simple and fault tolerance pre-charge half buffers [94]

4. Fault Mitigation

For this thesis, the adaptation of the duplication and double-checking method to FSL has been briefly investigated. Thereby the most common form of a QDI register implementation for a 4-phase protocol given by Fig. 3.21 is ported to FSL.

The duplicated version of a single-bit register is depicted in Fig. 4.36. Compared to the preferred implementation of an FSL register, the phase of each particular input signal is checked separately. The set and reset signals for each rail latch are synchronized via AND gates. That specific FSL implementation is referred to as *duplication and rail synchronization* (DRS). Contrary to the original duplication and double-checking scheme, the DRS method minimizes the hardware effort as it does not need to place explicit synchronizing C-gates at the output of a register, but already incorporates the rail synchronization within the register control signals. That approach also eliminates the dedicated C-gates to synchronize the acknowledge signals that are required in the duplication and double-checking circuits to prevent a synchronization error. A single fault on one acknowledge line will be ignored as the synchronized register control circuit prevents loading the next token as long as the redundant path does not receive an acknowledge as well.

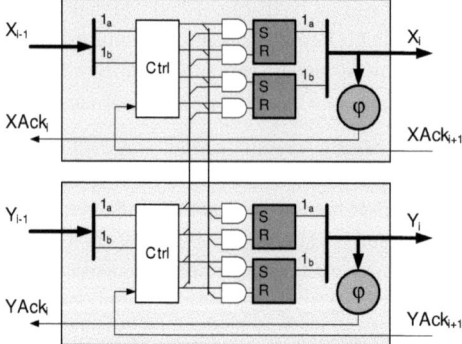

Figure 4.36: FSL register designed using DRS

Table 4.12 illustrates the *FPP* of an n-bit DRS register. All token classes that are produced by single faults that affect only one redundant rail at the same time are masked due to the comparison performed at rail level.

Table 4.13 compares the hardware overhead of DRS with DRXX versus the number of bits n by means of gate counting. A more efficient implementation at transistor level as in Fig. 4.35 is not considered in this work. Each redundant path has $2n$ latches for each signal and 1 latch for the completion detector. In case of a single bit register, the completion detectors do not require a latch:

$$|L(n)| = 2n + (n > 1)$$

The number of 2-input gates for the completion detector are calculated with (4.40). The combinational function to derive the distinct set/reset signals for the data latches

4.4. Duplication and Rail Cross-coupling

Table 4.12: Fault propagation probability of an n-bit DRS QDI function

n	$FPP(T^f(-1))$	$FPP(T^f(+0))$	$FPP(T^f(+1))$
1	0%	0%	0%
2	0%	0%	0%
4	0%	0%	0%
8	0%	0%	0%
16	0%	0%	0%
32	0%	0%	0%

requires $6n$ gates, the synchronization of the set/reset signals requires another $4n$ gates in either path. The total number of 2-inputs gates, where each latch is counted again as 5 gates like in 4.4.3, is

$$|G(n)_{DRS}| = 2 \cdot (5 \cdot |L(n)| + 6n + 4n + 3n - 2) =$$
$$= 2 \cdot (10n + 5(n > 1) + 13n - 2) = 46n - 4 + 10(n > 1). \quad (4.48)$$

Table 4.13: Overhead of DRS versus number of bits n by counting gates

	latches + 2-input gates				
n	simple	DRXX	DRS	overhead	
				vs simple	vs DRXX
1	20	48	42	110%	-13%
2	46	100	98	113%	-2%
4	78	164	190	144%	16%
8	142	292	374	163%	28%
16	270	548	742	175%	35%
32	526	1060	1478	181%	39%

For $n \leq 2$ bits, the DRS system is more area efficient than DRXX that is based on a register design according to Fig. 3.20. Although DRS comes along with fewer latches, the separate input phase detection for each bit begins to dominate the resources at higher number of bits. As for the resource estimate of DRXX, a latch was counted equivalent to 5 gates. That factor may depend on the physical implementation of the latch. A synthesis with Synopsys using the LSI Logic 10K library reported an even worse picture for DRS as given in Table 4.14. It has to be emphasized that the reported cell area shall not be used for a comparison with synchronous logic, as the device library is not well suited for asynchronous designs. The intention is to compare the relative overhead to a simple FSL design. Here DRS is only efficient for small numbers of n.

Table 4.14: Overhead of DRS versus number of bits n from gate level synthesis

n	cell area in μm^2			overhead	
	simple	DRXX	DRS	vs simple	vs DRXX
1	37	94	82	122%	-13%
2	68	138	152	112%	10%
4	120	228	308	150%	35%
8	192	356	560	183%	57%
16	354	654	1110	205%	70%
32	673	1252	2208	219%	76%

4.4.7 Summary

Several duplication based methods to mitigate single transient faults in QDI circuits were presented. Comparing the received data on the main and redundant path on the token level, no solution was found to mask a $T^f(+1)$ fault. Only the DRS method, which compares on rail level is able to reliably prevent this kind of fault class.

On token level, the DRXS scheme has evolved as promising candidate as it minimizes the hardware overhead in addition to the duplication and mitigates all $T^f(+0)$ faults. This kind of fault is expected to occur frequently if the receiver is connected to a combinational function, since a wrong intermediate result can be characterized by the sequence $T^f(+0) \prec T^f(+1)$. The DRXS scheme was improved with negligible overhead by synchronizing the completion detectors. The resulting DRXX method further stores the original non cross-coupled data and only cross-couples the rails that are evaluated by the input phase detectors, see 4.4.5. Both modifications do not have an impact on the *FPP* of $T^f(+1)$ faults but reduce the probability of storing a wrong or inconsistent token, which reduces the susceptibility of deadlocks.

An investigation of the hardware overhead has shown that DRS is efficient for small circuits, while DRXX becomes more efficient at larger circuits. Additionally, the *FPP* of a DRXX circuit is reduced the higher the number of input rails it receives. A strategic approach can be derived to adapt the fault mitigation technique depending on the number of input signals. For small circuits, such as glue logic, DRS is the optimum choice. The hardware overhead is kept small and the fault tolerance is optimized. For larger circuits, such as the data path or the arithmetic unit of a processor, DRXX is an alternative as it reduces the hardware overhead and still provides sufficient fault tolerance. The more signals a DRXX circuit receives, the higher is its code masking capability. So the implementation of a fault tolerance mechanism is getting application dependent as each method has its merits. Table 4.15 summarizes the *FPP* for all methods discussed in this chapter.

The fault propagation is zero for all $T^f(-1)$. Although this fact does not need to be illustrated, that token class is also depicted to highlight that fundamental property.

4.4. Duplication and Rail Cross-coupling

Table 4.15: Summary of fault propagation probability in an n-bit QDI register

	simple	DRXC	DRXS	DRXX	DRS
$FPP(T^f(-1))$	0	0	0	0	0
$FPP(T^f(+0))$	1	$\frac{1}{n+1}$	0	0	0
$FPP(T^f(+1))$	$\frac{4}{(n+1)(n+2)}$	$\frac{4}{(n+1)(n+2)}$	$\frac{4}{(2n+1)(2n+2)}$	$\frac{4}{(2n+1)(2n+2)}$	0

Nevertheless, an inhibited transition will lead to a deadlock as it does not complete the code phase. For this work, a deadlock is acceptable as long as the circuit does not stop its operation with a token error. The recovery from a deadlock is not scope of this thesis. The token class $T^f(+0)$ is dangerous, as it will always propagate a token error if no hardening methods are applied. The DRXS and DRXX method show the same properties, although DRXX is more robust against deadlocks – which is based on physical, reasonable timing constraints within a register design, but not included in the boundary conditions defined in 3.4.2. The DRS method does not propagate faults under these boundary conditions. However, even this type of QDI design requires gate and register internal timing constraints for a correct operation, while a network composed of DRS circuits is delay-insensitive.

A detailed assessment of the overhead in terms of power, speed, cost goes beyond the scope of this thesis. A general overview of the overhead of different asynchronous design styles is provided in [106]. So far, the hardware overhead for each particular hardening methods was only compared to an unhardened FSL circuit. As asynchronous logic is typically compared with synchronous logic, that overhead is briefly investigated on the example of unhardened as well as hardened register implementations. Fig. 4.37(a) shows a simple synchronous register with asynchronous clear and Fig. 4.37(b) depicts the TMR-hardened version, both circuits are extracted from [107]. Both synchronous and asynchronous FSL registers are synthesized in Synopsys (Version C-2009.06-SP4) using the LSI Logic 10K library, which has already been used in this chapter to estimate the circuit area.

The simple, unhardened FSL register design is based on Fig. 4.25. A dedicated clear input is added to make it functionally equivalent to its synchronous counterpart DFC1B. The fault tolerant FSL register is implemented using the DRXS method according to Fig. 4.23(b). That design is compared with the synchronous TMR cell DFC1B_TMR.

Table 4.16 compares the hardware resources and the overhead of simple FSL registers with synchronous DF1CB registers for different bit widths n. Both the overhead in terms of sequential elements (seq) and circuit area (μm^2) decreases at higher n. The FSL design is optimized for larger number of bits, since the overhead of the phase detector

4. Fault Mitigation

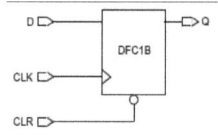

(a) Simple Sequential Cell (DFC1B)

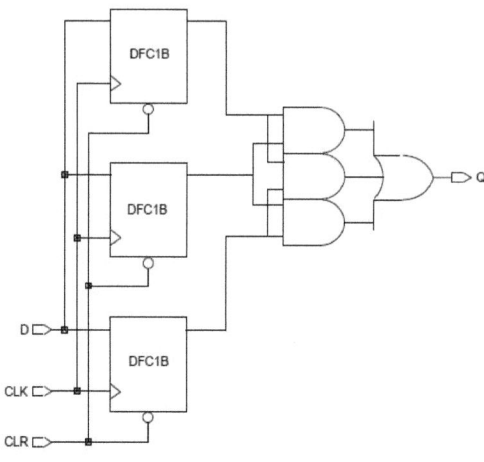

(b) TMR Sequential Cell (DFC1B_TMR)

Figure 4.37: Synchronous register implementations with asynchronous clear [107]

in Fig. 4.25 becomes less significant as the number of bits is increased. In general, the hardware overhead of FSL is significant. However, it should be mentioned that the used circuit library does not contain special asynchronous primitive blocks, such as Muller-C gates. Thus the hardware overhead cannot be assumed as being optimized.

Table 4.17 compares the overhead of the FSL-DRXS register with the synchronous DFC1B_TMR versus the number of bits n. Although the used circuit library is not dedicated to asynchronous designs, the duplication plus inherent comparison of DRXS instead of the triplication and the dedicated voter in TMR, significantly reduces the hardware overhead of the asynchronous solution. Especially at larger number of bits, the DRXS design nearly approaches the TMR register. Although, these results cannot be used as a general statement, they serve as an indication that it is indeed possible to build resource efficient fault-tolerant asynchronous circuits.

The comparison between asynchronous and synchronous logic was limited to register designs only. In combinational functions, the hardware overhead of asynchronous logic applies as well. That overhead highly depends on the type of the function and the

Table 4.16: Hardware overhead of FSL versus synchronous registers

	FSL register		Actel DFC1B		Overhead	
n	#seq	area (μm^2)	#seq	area (μm^2)	seq	μm^2
1	5	52	1	10	5.0	5.2
2	7	78	2	19	3.5	4.1
4	11	148	4	37	2.8	4.0
8	19	220	8	73	2.4	3.0
16	35	410	16	145	2.2	2.8
32	67	788	32	289	2.1	2.7

Table 4.17: Overhead of FSL-DRXS versus synchronous TMR

	FSL-DRXS		Actel DFC1B_TMR		Overhead	
n	#seq	area (μm^2)	#seq	area (μm^2)	seq	μm^2
1	10	112	3	43	3.3	2.6
2	14	160	6	83	2.3	1.9
4	22	266	12	163	1.8	1.6
8	38	418	24	323	1.6	1.3
16	70	764	48	643	1.5	1.2
32	134	1458	96	1283	1.4	1.1

asynchronous design style. Using *Null Convention Logic* (NCL) (see 3.5.2) it is possible to design more optimized combinational functions than using synchronous circuit libraries – as it was done in this thesis. An example of such an NCL gate is provided in Fig. 3.17, which shows an optimized full adder. With this technology, a hardware overhead in the range of 2–3 is achievable [108].

A detailed investigation requires to implement benchmarks or practical applications on different platforms, which is dedicated to future research. A brief examination is carried out in chapter 5 where circuits are simulated on gate level.

4.5 Fault Injection Overview

Fault injection is a common practice to evaluate a circuit's behavior under various types of faults as well as to assess hardening strategies. One common classification of fault injection methods distinguishes simulation based, hardware based and software based techniques as well as combinations of them called hybrid fault injection [109].

- Simulation based methods apply the faults in a simulation model of the system under test, which almost places no restriction on the type of fault to be injected, its duration, its location, etc. The system can be simulated on different abstraction levels depending what granularity shall be reached. That topic is investigated in chapter 5.

4. Fault Mitigation

- Hardware based methods, often referred to as *emulation* directly apply the fault in the target hardware. Thereby invasive elements such as *saboteurs* are added or *mutants* are used to replace nominal circuit components. That topic is investigated in chapter 6.

- Software based methods are targeting the application or operation software of a system. Faults are injected directly in the software that is executed. The system may be available as real hardware or as software model. The level of intrusiveness is not hat high as in hardware based methods. That topic is not examined in this thesis.

The following chapters 5 and 6 apply the trace based fault model and the DRXS/-DRXX/DRS methods to practical circuits. For the circuits under test both building blocks such as adders, comparators, ISCAS benchmark circuits as well as a real-life signal processing application are used. Rather simple circuits are selected to highlight the properties of the trace based fault assessment more clearly. These properties apply to complex, larger circuits and systems in the same way.

5
Simulation

The trace based model developed in chapters 3 and 4 is subjected to simulation based fault injection experiments. The simulation of faults provides a detailed insight compared to other methods. However, to simulate asynchronous QDI logic some adaptations to common fault simulation applied to synchronous circuits are needed.

5.1 Related Work

When dealing with synchronous integrated circuits, there exists a variety of fault injection tools covering simulation such as [64, 110, 111], etc. In the domain of asynchronous logic that list of tools becomes scarce. Especially due to the absence of a global clock, fault injection and simulation tools for synchronous circuits cannot directly be used in asynchronous circuits and vice versa [19].

A template based fault simulation that compares the sequence of signal transitions in a faulty circuit with the specified sequence in the correct circuit is presented in [19]. The idea of this simulator is to check whether the expected transition sequence of a QDI circuit occurs during a fault injection. If not, the specification of the circuit is violated and an error is reported. Fig. 5.1 shows a simple register and its corresponding signal sequence. The register is designed as pre-charged full buffer, which is one of the various QDI design styles. That style is similar to the design of an FSL register in Fig. 3.20. Both the input and output signals are connected to completion or validity detectors (LCD, RCD) that enable the calculation of the logic function F if the input is consistent and the buffer is ready for new data. In case of a simple register or buffer, F is just an identity function. The pre-charged style also allows any other logic function to be implemented. In this case, the circuit can be regarded as combinational circuit with a latched output. Fig. 5.1(b) shows the corresponding register timing.

5. Simulation

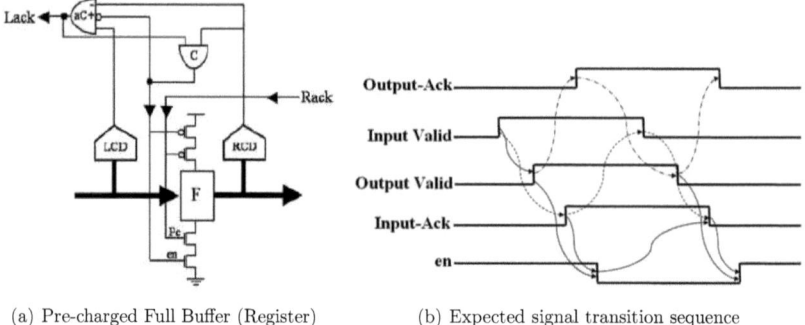

(a) Pre-charged Full Buffer (Register) (b) Expected signal transition sequence

Figure 5.1: Template Based Fault Simulator [19]

The template based method considers the simulation of random delays to modify the main signal sequence. Thereby the delays are extracted from the synthesized signal list. According to the actual fault location, the delays in the affected part of the circuit are randomly chosen, while the non-affected circuit parts are simulated with an average delay. Finally assertion statements are included in the synthesized code that check for the correct timing sequence as shown in Fig. 5.1(b) as well as monitor a deadlock by setting an upper boundary to the processing speed of these signals. The test patterns are calculated depending on the intended fault location to obtain an optimized test coverage.

Another method to simulate faults in QDI circuits is presented in [112]. The authors apply single stuck-at faults to QDI circuits and evaluate their effects by means of production rules [34]. The principle is depicted in Fig. 5.2.

The effects of single stuck-at faults are classified as token dropping and token generation, which are combined in the term token error in this thesis. Additionally, a single stuck-at fault may lead to a deadlock. It is concluded that the fault changes the number of tokens. This property is used to design a fault simulator on a high level of abstraction. The tool utilizes the token monitor in Fig. 5.2 to compare the number of input tokens to the number of output tokens to identify a faulty circuit. The expected token count is pre-evaluated for the circuit design before the synthesis takes place. The faults are then applied to the synthesized design. Similarly to the approach in [19], the delays for the selected fault location are adapted and the non-affected circuit parts are simulated with their inherent delays. Test vectors are selected carefully to obtain a high test coverage.

In [83] the sensitivity of an asynchronous circuit to transient faults is evaluated during simulation. The goal of this fault simulation method is to identify all valid sensitive states of a circuit. Thereby a gate is in a sensitive state when an input transition leads to an unexpected output transitions. Fig. 5.3(a) shows the expected behavior of a 1-bit QDI register designed in 4-phase dual-rail. In this example, only input I_0 is expected to

5.1. Related Work

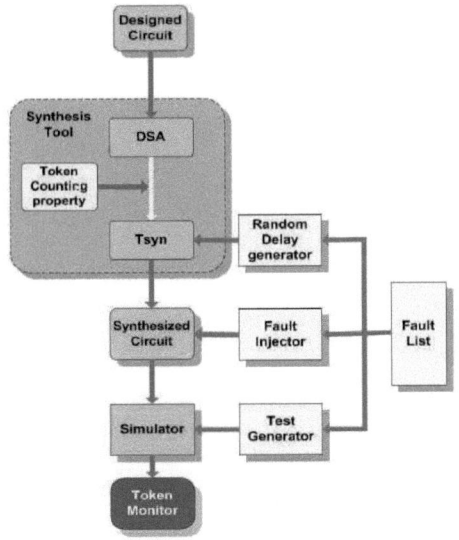

Figure 5.2: Token Counting Based Fault Simulator [112]

receive a transition, therefore the C-gate *M00* generates an output transition O_0. The register is sensitive to any input transition if $Ack = 1$ and $I_0 = I_1 = 0$. Fig. 5.3(b) shows an invalid sensitive state. The input I_0 receives a premature transition, which leads to the expected behavior. No error is memorized. Fig. 5.3(c) depicts a valid sensitive state where a transient on input I_1 leads to a wrong output transition on O_1.

A fault sensitivity tool analyzes each gate in the circuit for valid sensitive states. Thereby the natural timings from the gate level netlist after the place and route process are used. The tool computes a metric that corresponds to the total sensitive time of the circuit, which is used a measure for the circuit's robustness. The method can also be used to identify weak points that are in a sensitive state most of the time and apply local hardening strategies.

A comparison of transient fault effects in synchronous and asynchronous logic by simulation is presented in [65]. Faults are injected by means of simulator commands (*force*) into a gate-level netlist. The circuit timings are extracted from a Standard Delay Format (SDF) file that is obtained after the place and route process. Fig. 5.4 shows the flow and the methodology of the proposed fault simulation tool.

Faults are applied via the *pulse model* [64] that forces the signal to its inverse value for the time of transient fault width. The tool distinguishes two different simulation schemes for transient faults:

5. Simulation

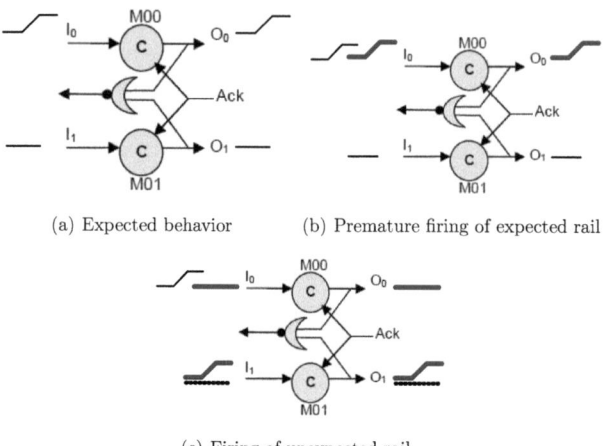

Figure 5.3: Example of sensitive states in a simple 1-bit QDI register

1. If the fault hits a combinational block or a C-element with equal input values, the output is simply forced to its faulty state for the transient fault duration. Fig. 5.5(a) shows a 2 ns long transient fault that is injected into a simple 2-input C-element. After the fault has vanished, the C-element will restore the initial output state logic 0, since both inputs are at logic 0.

2. If the fault directly hits a memory cell or a C-element with different input values, the faulty output is forced with the *deposit* option, which holds the subjected signal at the faulty state until it is updated by its driver. No fault width applies to this option. Fig. 5.5(b) shows how a transient fault in a C-element leads to a static soft error at the output. Due to the different inputs, the C-element will preserve the faulty output even after the fault has gone.

To apply the appropriate force method, the complete netlist of the circuit is processed. For each signal, the type of its associated drive circuitry (combinational or memory cell) and the actual input state at the moment of the fault injection are determined.

That overview focuses on fault simulation in QDI logic but is not exhaustive. Related work that mainly focuses on the testability of asynchronous circuits is found in [113, 114]. Others perform fault simulation in the analog domain using SPICE simulation [18]. A symbolic simulation that applies faults on token level depending on the state of the circuit is presented in [21]. The fault tolerance of a 2-phase 2-of-7 code used for the inter-chip connections in an asynchronous communication link is simulated in [115]. Random faults with different width and frequency are injected onto the post-synthesized circuit, although the simulation itself is not explained in detail.

5.1. Related Work

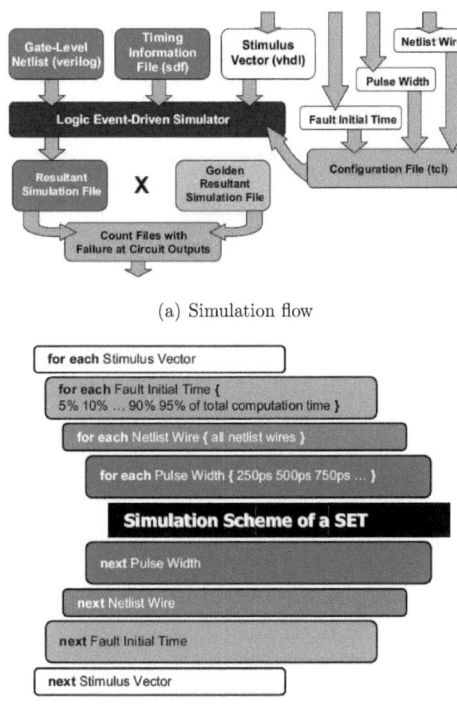

(a) Simulation flow

(b) Methodology

Figure 5.4: Simulation flow and methodology of [65]

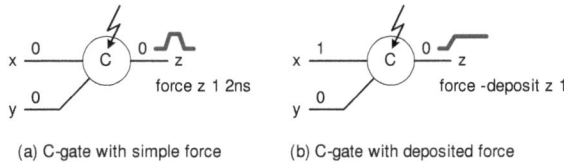

(a) C-gate with simple force   (b) C-gate with deposited force

Figure 5.5: Fault simulation of a C-element depending on its state

129

5.2 Fault Simulation in QDI Logic

A transient fault in a logic circuit has two principle effects. Fig. 5.6(a) shows a transient fault in a combinational function $z = f(x, y)$. The output z is only defined by the external inputs x, y. Provided the fault is not logically masked by the function itself, an SET will be observed at the output. In Fig. 5.6(b), a fault is injected in a sequential function $z = f(x, y, z)$, where the next output depends not only on the external inputs but also on the current output. A fault injected into a sequential circuit will be fed back. Depending on the external inputs x, y the faulty output state may be maintained even after the fault has vanished. The fault has become a soft error or an SEU.

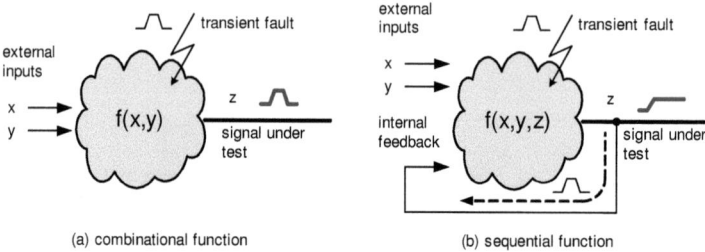

Figure 5.6: Fault injection in combinational and sequential circuits

In [65], this different behavior is taken into account by using the appropriate force command of the simulator. However, the subjected signal must be first identified to belong to a sequential gate. Second the external input state of that gate must be evaluated to determine whether the output state is defined by the feedback or not, which has been shown in Fig. 5.5. If the gate is in a sensitive state, the deposited force is used, otherwise the simple force is used.

Within this thesis, another method for the correct signal enforcement has been developed. Thereby no signal classification and state evaluation is necessary, which reduces the complexity of the simulation environment. The focus is placed on the fault injection method itself rather than on a comprehensive fault coverage. In general, the following approach would be desirable: First, the fault is applied to the signal under test. Then that faulty state is maintained for the complete fault duration. Finally, the fault is removed and the subjected signal is re-evaluated by the logic function it belongs to. The following examination is based on digital circuits designed and described in VHDL. All simulations are performed in ModelSim from Mentor Graphics.

To obtain the above behavior on register level a dummy signal *tForceEvent_S* was added to the sensitivity list of all processes in the VHDL design. This signal has no actual function and is solely used to interact with the simulator environment. A VHDL process will be only evaluated if any of the signals declared in its sensitivity list generates

5.2. Fault Simulation in QDI Logic

an event. Changing *tForceEvent_S* will re-evaluate each process of the design and if necessary, refresh any signal. That action has no impact on the function or performance of the circuit. The re-evaluation of the process simply acts as an additional calculation of the circuit state that is not necessary in the fault-free case. The fault injection will be performed as follows:

1. The logic state of the subjected signal for the fault injection is evaluated.

2. The signal is forced to the inverted logic state according to the pulse model [64] using the simple force command, which maintains the faulty state for the complete duration of the transient fault.

3. After the fault duration, the forced state is replaced by a deposited force command so the preservation of faults in sequential circuits is modeled correctly.

4. The *tForceEvent_S* signal is toggled and the circuit state is re-evaluated.

If the subjected signal is calculated by a combinational function, the re-evaluation of the signal's process will update the signal according to the current external input. If the signal's function is sequential and the external inputs are not taken into account, the faulty state will be preserved. The concept is illustrated using the behavioral VHDL model of a phase detector.

Example 5.2.1: A phase detector evaluates the code phase of the dual-rail word *rDataIn* and generates a logic 1/0 at its output *Phase_I* if all dual-rail signals of *rDataIn* are in the phase $\varphi 1/\varphi 0$. Otherwise the current phase is maintained. The corresponding VHDL design comprises two processes. The first one Set_P creates the set and reset signals for the RS-latch that is described in Latch_P. See also Fig. 4.25(b) for a schematic of the phase detector.

```
Set_P : process (rDataIn, tForceEvent_S)
  variable Set_V   : std_ulogic;
  variable Reset_V : std_ulogic;
begin
  Set_V   := '1';
  Reset_V := '0';
  for i in 0 to (rDataIn'length-1) loop
    Set_V   := Set_V and (rDataIn(i).a xor rDataIn(i).b);
    Reset_V := Reset_V or (rDataIn(i).a xor rDataIn(i).b);
  end loop;
  Set   <= Set_V;
  Reset <= not Reset_V;
end process Set_P;
```

5. Simulation

```
Latch_P : process (Set, Reset, tForceEvent_S)
begin
  if Reset = '1' then
    Phase_I <= '0';
  elsif Set = '1' then
    Phase_I <= '1';
  end if;
end process PD_P;
```

Next, a 10 ns long transient fault is injected onto *Phase_I* at $t = 38$ ns. We assume the RS-latch is opaque, i.e. $Set = Reset = 0$, $Phase\_I = 0$ and $tForceEvent\_S = 0$. First the simulation is run for $t = 38$ ns, then the current state of *Phase_I* is evaluated using the *examine* command in ModelSim. The force value is the opposite logic value. Next the fault is applied using the simple force method, which utilizes the *-freeze* option. The simulation is continued for the fault duration of 10 ns. A deposited force replaces the previous simple force via the *-deposit* option and *tForceEvent_S* is set to logic 1, which will re-evaluate **Set_P** and **Latch_P**. The deposited force maintains the forced *Phase_I* until it will be updated by an event on the *Set* or *Reset* signal of the latch.

```
run 38ns
if {[examine /uuti/Phase_I] == 1} {
  set fval 0
} else {
  set fval 1
}
force -freeze /uuti/Phase_I $fval
run 10ns
force -deposit /uuti/Phase_I $fval
force /uuti/tForceEvent_S 1 10ns
run 100ns
```

The presented approach can also be used on gate level. Since the synthesis process removes any unnecessary signals from the design, the *tForceEvent_S* signal was manually added to the gate level simulation models. It has to be emphasized again, that adding this signal does neither have an impact on the logic function nor, in case of the gate level, on the timings of the modified circuit.

Manipulating the *tForceEvent_S* signal in the process sensitivity list allows a realistic simulation of combinational and sequential circuits on register level. Especially in QDI logic, even combinational circuits contain latches that have to be simulated correctly. In the transparent phase, a latch behaves like a simple combinational function. In the opaque phase, it behaves like a sequential circuit that is solely defined by its internal feedback. The presented approach of adding a dummy signal to each process sensitivity list can also be applied to synchronous designs to perform a realistic simulation of both SET's and SEU's.

To simulate a circuit with representative timings there exist two choices depending on the level where the simulation takes place:

1. On register level, the timings have to be added explicitly e.g. by using the `after` statement in VHDL. Although this process generates considerable effort, it is a convenient way to model arbitrary delays.

2. On gate level, the synthesis tools provide a realistic simulation model using native components with their timings described in a *Standard Delay Format* (SDF) file. This file can be loaded in the simulator to run realistic timing simulations.

Both methods have their merits. On register level, the design and the impact of delays, faults, etc. are more easy to understand and to describe. In practical QDI circuits, the internal gate design anyhow depends on matched delays, while the connections between such atomic gates are delay-insensitive, as described in chapter 2. The timings of these connections define the circuit's trace and these few parameters can be modeled quite simple on register level. The transparent design allows to adjust these traces easily. This allows to easily study different scenarios and find clues for optimal routing.

On gate level, realistic timing figures are provided by the SDF file and the native components of the target platform. A fault injection simulation comes closer to reality than on register level. Since a circuit's robustness also depends on temporal masking, a realistic assessment of this figure requires a simulation with realistic parameters. To assess the fault tolerance of a particular design on a particular platform, a simulation of the gate level netlist is inevitable.

Within this thesis, the timings of the circuit are defined on register level for the testbench components only. These components are not related with the function of the design under test, such as testbench control functions or test vector memories. The design under test is simulated on gate level. Thereby all circuits are synthesized in a Xilinx Virtex-4 device using the Xilinx ISE 10.1 tool suite. The timings of the design under test are generated during the synthesis and implementation process and provided in an SDF file. A simulation of the design under test on register level is not performed.

5.3 The FOSTER Tool

To simulate the effects of transient faults in QDI logic, the **FO**ur **ST**ate **ER**ror (FOSTER) simulation tool was developed. The name originates from its original intended application, the examination of fault and errors in FSL circuits. However, it can be applied to other QDI implementations, such as 4-phase dual-rail or k-of-m codes as well. The

FOSTER tool allows to inject transient and permanent faults into the VHDL model of the design under test via the simulator environment. It has been fit to ModelSim from Mentor Graphics but can be adapted to other simulation tools as well. The functionality of the tool is similar to [116] developed for the European Space Agency (ESA). However, it is extended to simulate not only single event upsets, but in general all types of transient and permanent faults.

Since fault injection itself is not the main topic of this thesis, not too much effort has been spent on designing a sophisticated, highly customizable tool. The focus was set on the special needs for simulating faults in QDI logic.

5.3.1 Description of the Tool

The FOSTER tool was written in TCL/Tk, which is the scripting language not only for ModelSim but also for other digital design tools such as Xilinx ISE or Synopsys. It can be run either within ModelSim or from the command line. Fig. 5.7 shows a screen shot of the user interface. On top of the main window, a menu bar offers several options such as to define the simulation settings, to load new designs, to compare log files from different simulation runs, etc. In the center of the main window, the different signals of the design are listed. The user has the following options to perform fault injections:

- The disturbed signal can be selected manually, randomly or the tool may be setup to step through all signals of the circuit.

- The fault type can be either a stuck-at 0/1 or a pulse fault, see 2.2.3.

- The fault duration can be defined fixed or randomly.

- The moment of the fault injection can be selected manually, randomly or the tool may be setup to inject a fault every pre-defined time step.

- The primary input stimulus can be loaded from a file.

All these options can also be defined in a configuration file and the FOSTER tool can then be run from the command line using that configuration file.

The tool includes a parser that prepares the design for the fault injection. In the first step all internal signals of the circuit under test are extracted and compared with the file *ExcludeList.txt*. This file is used to manually exclude signals from the fault injection. In this thesis, all global *Reset* signals were excluded. Applying a fault on the reset will always produce an error, thus this net is a special case in any digital design and has been excluded.

Input and output ports are treated specifically. The *force* command in ModelSim does not allow to stimulate an input port that is connected to a higher level module.

5.3. The FOSTER Tool

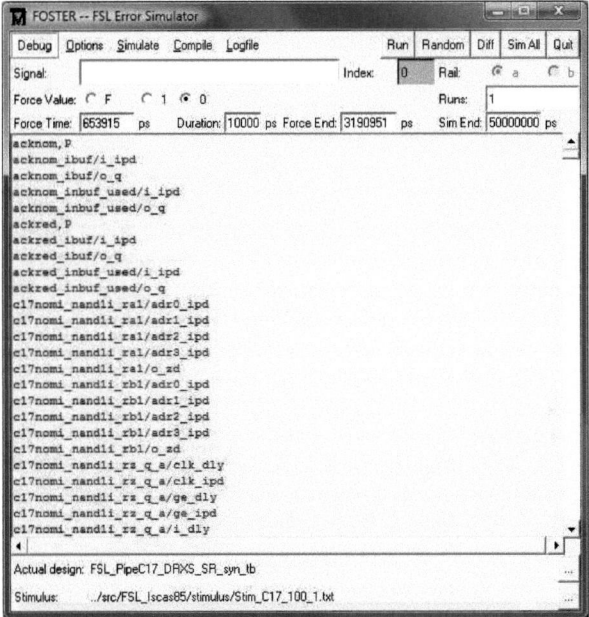

Figure 5.7: FOSTER - A simple fault injection tool for FSL circuits

Therefore only the input ports of the highest level – the primary inputs – are added to the list of fault injection signals. If the output port of a component is directly forced, all externally connected signals will follow the forced state but the internally connected signals of the component will be unaffected. That constitutes an undesirable and unrealistic behavior. Therefore, each output port will be connected to one dedicated internal signal. Instead of the port, only its internal signal will be subjected to fault injections. That approach leads to the desired effect, i.e. the fault will propagate externally via the port as well as internally.

```
entity FSL_NAND2 is
  port (
      rX       : in   fsl_ulogic;
      rY       : in   fsl_ulogic;
      rZ       : out  fsl_ulogic);
end FSL_NAND2;
```

5. Simulation

```
architecture rtl of FSL_NAND2 is
   signal rZ_Q : fsl_ulogic;
   ...
begin
   -- apply force to rZ_Q instead of port rZ
   rZ <= rZ_Q;
   ...
end rtl;
```

In a hierarchical design, the output port of a component is mapped to a higher level via an interconnection signal. This signal as well as the internal signal that has been introduced to stimulate the output port actually form a single physical net. For a correct fault evaluation a multiple stimulation of a net must be avoided. Therefore all signals that are connected to a port are labeled with the postfix _I to mark them as interconnections. These interconnection signals are removed from the fault signal list automatically.

Example 5.3.1: Fig. 5.8 shows a modular design that comprises three components $C1$, $C2$ and $C3$. The output ports of these components are $C1\_O$, $C2\_O$ and $C3\_O$. The logic state of these outputs is represented by the component internal signals $C1\_Q$, $C2\_Q$ and $C3\_Q$. The external connections of the output ports are formed by the signals $C1\_I$, $C2\_I$ and $C3\_I$. When generating the signal list for the fault simulation, the interconnection signals and component output ports are removed. Finally, the signal list comprises $\{PI1; C1\_Q; C2\_Q; C3\_Q\}$. Now each physical net of the shown design level is represented by one signal only.

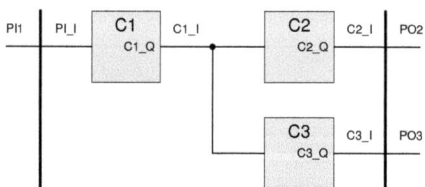

Figure 5.8: Signal connections in a hierarchical design

To interact with the simulator environment, the dummy signal *tForceEvent_S* was added to the sensitivity list of each process declaration. Thus, all signals ending with _S are also excluded from the fault signal list. After this selection process, each physical net of the design under test is described by one single signal no matter how many hierarchical levels the design has.

That process works for both register transfer level and gate level VHDL models. In gate level simulation models, the design is typically composed solely by interconnections of primitives such as buffers, latches, look-up tables, etc. These models are rather large VHDL files and it would be cumbersome to add the ending _I to the interconnection signals. Thus in gate level net lists, the top level signals are excluded from the fault injection in general. A flattened design is not used as it does not show the hierarchical levels, which eases the location of signals within the design. Additionally, gate level net lists contain global signals to define nets that are fixed strapped to logic 1 or 0 as well as unused signals for e.g. clock management units that are automatically synthesized in FPGAs. The FOSTER tool automatically excludes all fixed strapped and unused signals from the fault injection as they would falsify the result.

5.3.2 Error detection

The sensitivity of the circuit under test to the applied transient faults is evaluated by comparing the result at the primary output with a golden reference model that is obtained by simulating a fault-free circuit. All consistent, primary output data is written to a log file that is used for comparison. Thereby the logged time stamp is ignored as the timings may differ from run to run according to the simulation setup or to the fault impact. Only the data sequence is compared, since each consistent data must describe a valid token. If the fault has no impact, the token sequence of the faulty run must agree with the token sequence of the reference run.

That decoupling from time is only applicable up to a certain value. In the event of a deadlock, the circuit will have stopped and the number of logged tokens will be less than the number of expected tokens. The simulation time must be extended compared to the time needed for the reference run to take into account delay faults. However, it is quite easy to set the simulation time to a realistic upper boundary. If there are tokens missing after that time has expired, a deadlock will be indicated.

The FOSTER tool handles three different types of errors – deadlock, token error and synchronization error. Table 5.1 shows the log files of a 4-bit register output. The table only depicts the a-rail of the register output, which corresponds to the boolean value, see Table 2.1.

Table 5.1: Errors detected at a 4-bit QDI register output

Reference Data		Deadlock		Token Error		Synchronization Error	
49 ns	0100	49 ns	0100	49 ns	0100	49 ns	0100
68 ns	0011	68 ns	0011	68 ns	0011	68 ns	0011
98 ns	1110			98 ns	1110	98 ns	1110
122 ns	1001			120 ns	1101	124 ns	0101
143 ns	0000			141 ns	0000	145 ns	1100
171 ns	0101			169 ns	0101	173 ns	1010
189 ns	1100			187 ns	1100	191 ns	0001
219 ns	1010			217 ns	1010	221 ns	0110

A deadlock is detected by comparing the lengths of the recorded data and the reference data. In Table 5.1 only two tokens were recorded before the circuit deadlocked.

5. Simulation

Token and synchronization errors do not alter the length of the recorded data. The token error in column three solely corrupted the forth entry. The FOSTER tool indicates a token error if a single entry of the recorded data set differs from the reference data. A synchronization error will remove tokens from the recorded sequence. In Table 5.1 the token pair $\{1001; 0000\}$ is removed by a synchronization error, which is indicated by the horizontal line in the column. The FOSTER tool counts a synchronization error if one or two tokens are removed from the reference series but the content of the remaining tokens is not changed.

5.3.3 Random Tests

Chapter 3 has shown that the number of traces in a QDI circuit grows rapidly with the size of the circuit due to the usage of permutations. If faults are injected, the circuit trace set is extended to the fault trace set, which is even larger. An exhaustive fault injection requires an enormous effort even at moderate circuit complexity and becomes practically impossible for large and complex circuits. Therefore random fault injections in combination with probability theory are used in this thesis.

In general, a fault injection experiment can be regarded as Bernoulli experiment with the result being either a success (0) or a failure (1). A successful trial is defined when the injected fault did not lead to an error. The results of these experiments can be described by discrete random variables $X_k \in \{0; 1\}$, where k denotes the kth fault injection run. If N fault injection runs with randomly chosen parameters are performed, the *average soft error probability* $\hat{p}$ can be computed with

$$\hat{p} = 1/N \sum_{k=1}^{N} X_k = \frac{|T^f|}{N} \qquad (5.1)$$

which corresponds to the number of received errors $|T^f|$ divided by the total number of simulation runs N. If the number of runs is selected sufficiently high (ideally $N \to \infty$) the measured $\hat{p}$ will approximate the true mean value (typically denoted μ in statistics) of the discrete random variable X. Thereby the mean value describes the *true soft error probability* of a latch l that receives a specific trace set T: $\mu \equiv p \equiv P_f(l, T)$.

In case $N < \infty$, the average $\hat{p}$ will deviate from the real unknown mean p. A *confidence interval* $[p_u, p_o]$ can be given that encloses the real mean value $p_u < p < p_o$ with a certain probability. To determine that interval, the probability distribution of the random variables X_k must be known. In the case of a success/failure fault injection experiment, X_k follows a *binomial distribution*. Typically, that distribution is approximated by a normal distribution according to the central limit theorem as that distribution is more handy to work with. However, a normal distribution will not provide accurate results if the true soft error rate is anticipated low ($p < 0.1$) [117]. In this case, the binomial distribution is asymmetric and cannot be estimated very well by the Gaussian shape of the normal

5.3. The FOSTER Tool

distribution. Therefore, the confidence intervals in this thesis are determined by using the *Clopper-Pearson* method [118], which calculates $[p_u, p_o]$ using the binomial distribution itself and not any approximate distribution.

If not otherwise stated a confidence level of $\gamma = 1 - \alpha = 95\%$ is selected for p, i.e. the calculated confidence interval will contain the unknown mean p with a probability of 95%. The intervals are calculated using Matlab.

Example 5.3.2: A fault injection experiment with $N = 1000$ independent runs results in 38 errors in a latch l, i.e. $\hat{p} = 3.8\%$. The $100(1 - \alpha) = 95\%$ confidence interval is found using Matlab:

$$[phat, pci] = \text{binofit}(38, 1000, 0.05)$$
$$phat = 0.038$$
$$pci = [0.0270, 0.0518]$$

Thus the confidence interval is $[p_u, p_o] = [2.70\%, 5.18\%]$.

Table 5.2 shows the 95% confidence interval $[p_u, p_o]$ versus the average probability $\hat{p}$ and the number of runs N. For an accurate fault investigation based on random experiments a high number of runs has to be selected. Performing 1000 fault injections results in an acceptable simulation time, while it does not provide a satisfactory confidence interval especially for small $\hat{p}$. Making 10000 runs narrows the confidence interval but requires a high computation effort. As a compromise, the fault injection experiments in this thesis were generally performed with $N = 5000$ independent random runs if not otherwise stated.

Table 5.2: Confidence interval versus $\hat{p}$ and number of runs

$\hat{p}$	$N = 100$		$N = 1000$		$N = 5000$		$N = 10000$	
	p_u	p_o	p_u	p_o	p_u	p_o	p_u	p_o
0.1%	0.000%	3.823%	0.003%	0.556%	0.033%	0.233%	0.048%	0.184%
0.2%	0.000%	4.019%	0.024%	0.721%	0.096%	0.368%	0.122%	0.309%
1.0%	0.025%	5.446%	0.481%	1.831%	0.743%	1.316%	0.814%	1.215%
2.0%	0.243%	7.038%	1.226%	3.072%	1.630%	2.427%	1.735%	2.294%
5.0%	1.643%	11.284%	3.734%	6.539%	4.412%	5.641%	4.581%	5.446%
10.0%	4.901%	17.622%	8.211%	12.029%	9.182%	10.865%	9.419%	10.605%
20.0%	12.666%	29.184%	17.562%	22.616%	18.899%	21.136%	19.220%	20.798%
50.0%	39.832%	60.168%	46.855%	53.145%	48.604%	51.396%	49.015%	50.985%

Finally, a random fault injection experiment yields the soft error probability for the applied stimulus vector. For this thesis, the stimulus vectors were also selected randomly. The size of the code phase set for an n-bit wide test vector can be calculated according to (3.1). Thereby the factorial $n!$ considers the different possible arrangements of rail

5. Simulation

transitions in the trace, while the factor 2^n considers the number of distinct boolean values that can be described. For a process, which includes environmental impacts as well as the circuit layout, the observable sequences of rail transitions for a single boolean value is much smaller than $n!$ as there are only minor variations depending on which rail is excited, see 5.4.2. Therefore, the number of different code traces that is expected is in the range of 2^n. The length of the selected stimulus vectors in the fault injections has been selected $> 5 \cdot 2^n$ to ensure that each possible trace occurs several times in the test data. For example, the test vector for a 4-bit circuit has to contain at least 80 entries. The impact of the test vector length has been verified by means of experiments. Longer test vectors did not have any significant impact on the test results. A more detailed investigation of test vector length is left for future research.

5.3.4 Evaluation of Token Classes

The token classes were introduced in 3.4.3 as general property to describe the behavior of QDI signals with and without transient faults. The FOSTER tool allows to extract these token classes by using the *TraceLogger* component. Fig. 5.9(a) depicts the general logging circuitry. The data to be evaluated is *DataIn*, which is received by the register under test. That register is simulated as synthesized component with the timings defined in the SDF file. If the unit under test is placed within a pipeline, the successor stage(s) are also synthesized registers that belong to the circuit under test. The last stage of a pipeline is formed by a virtual testbench register. If it detects a new code phase, it will store the received token in the file *Result.log* and acknowledges its reception after a user-defined delay Δt. Thus in general, the testbench cannot be synthesized.

The *TraceLogger* records all transitions at the register input and stores them in *trace.log*. To convert the recorded transitions into code phase traces, a dedicated TCL script is used that stores them in *traceset.log*. Thereby each acknowledge event starts a new trace. The trace logger can be connected to an arbitrary net in the circuit to record the traces at that location. Thereby a fork is formed between the logged trace and the input trace of the monitored register under test. While that register receives the trace $t1$, the trace logger receives the trace $t2$. As the trace $t1$ shall be logged, all signals and buffers on the branch towards the trace logger are modeled with zero delay to ensure $t2 = t1$. That is accomplished by correcting the delays in the associated SDF file.

Additionally, no register duplication is allowed for the monitored signals. Register duplication is typically implemented by synthesis tools to reduce the loading of registers that drive multiple sinks. As the trace logger is a virtual testbench component, it has to be attached via primary output ports of the design under test. These ports constitute a high loading. So the driver that is connected to the root of the fork in Fig. 5.9(a), which is formed by a register in the preceding logic, will be typically replicated and each branch of the fork will be attached to a separate driver. Thus the trace logger may actually monitor a replicated signal with a different trace. The replication of registers is prevented in the configuration of the synthesis flow. It does not have any inadvertent effect on the simulation.

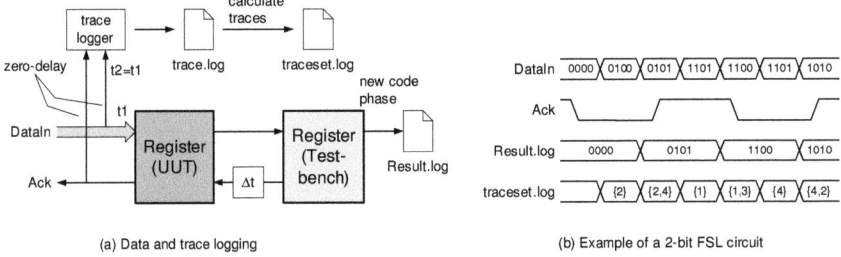

(a) Data and trace logging

(b) Example of a 2-bit FSL circuit

Figure 5.9: Logging the trace of a QDI circuit

Fig. 5.9(b) gives a simple example of a 2-bit FSL circuit. It shows the capture of the register output in the file *Result.log* and the evaluated code phase traces in *traceset.log*. The recorded trace set is used to determine the impact of the different types of error masking on the soft error rate.

5.3.5 Interpretation of Soft Error Probability

The soft error probability $P_f(T, l)$ of a register/latch that receives a specific trace set T is derived by counting the received errors $|T^f|$ within N independent fault simulations:

$$P_f(l, T) = \frac{|T^f|}{N}. \qquad (5.2)$$

The soft error probability can be expressed by code, logical and temporal masking as given in (4.4). Electrical masking is not considered as already described. Thereby the masking factors in (4.4) are now expressed as a function of the affected latch l and the received trace set T:

$$P_f(l, T) = \frac{|T^f|}{N} = P_{sens}(l, T) \cdot P_{latched}(l, T). \qquad (5.3)$$

So far, temporal masking has been excluded in this thesis. To examine its contribution, faults are injected directly at the primary inputs of a register. Thereby, temporal masking only applies if the register and the application is simulated with realistic timings. A register with zero delay would immediately capture a token error if the input receives a wrong phase prefix. That conservative assumption has been made in the assessment of the fault propagation in 4.3.1 but it will not hold in a real circuit. Similarly, in an infinite fast application a register will always be able to receive new data. In a real application, the register will not be sensitive to new data for a certain time due to the finite handshake period. To detect temporary masked traces, *traceset.log* is scanned for all traces t_i that may propagate an error, i.e. $FPP(t_i) = 1$, but that did not lead to a token error:

5. Simulation

1. The trace must be a member of the wrong prefix set T^{pf}, see 4.3.1

2. The simulation run must be successful, i.e. no error is reported

The FOSTER tool marks such simulation runs to indicate the suppression of wrong prefix traces by means of temporal masking.

Example 5.3.3: Transient faults were injected at the inputs of a 2-bit FSL register as shown in Fig. 5.9(a). Both the register internal timings and the timings of its environment are modeled by an SDF file. In the fault-free simulation the register receives the data sequence $rtOutP = \{1010; 0010; 0011\}$, which can be described by the trace $t_1 = \{14\}$. In a random simulation, a transient fault was injected on rail 3, which generated the trace $t_3^f = \{1\overline{3}4\overline{3}\}$ and the wrong phase prefix $t_3^{pf} = \{1\overline{3}\}$. A portion of the recorded data from the trace logger is given below. It shows that rail 3 is disturbed for a total time of 820354 - 818629 = 1725 ps, while the duration of t_3^{pf} is 819131 - 818629 = 502 ps. The simulator detected the transitions on rails 1 and 3 at the same time, although the trace based model does not consider concurrent events. This difference is not a limitation and has been discussed in 3.4.

Listing 5.1: Trace logger output with wrong prefix not captured

```
Time       : Data : Ack : Cons : Trace
...
803769 ps  : 1010 : 1   : 1    :
818629 ps  : 0000 : 1   : 0    : 1 3
819131 ps  : 0001 : 1   : –    : 1 3 4
820354 ps  : 0011 : 1   : 0    : 1 3 4 3
833200 ps  : 0011 : 0   : 0    :
851175 ps  : 0010 : 0   : –    : 4
...
```

Although the register received a wrong prefix, it did not capture a token error as illustrated in Fig. 5.10. The register input is described by the two top waveforms $rtOutP1/rtOutP0$. The register output is provided in $rOutP1/rOutP0$ below. The bottom waveforms show the acknowledge signal of the register (ack) and the boolean value of the register output ($dataout$). The duration of t_3^{pf} is not long enough to capture the wrong input $\langle \overline{0000} \rangle$. The fault even did not propagate to the register output as shown in waveform.

There exist two main reasons for the rejection of a wrong phase prefix:

1. In the definition of the *FPP* in 4.3, any $T(+1)$ token with a wrong phase prefix was counted as error, since it was assumed that the register is always ready for new data. In reality that is not always the case. If the register does not immediately

5.3. The FOSTER Tool

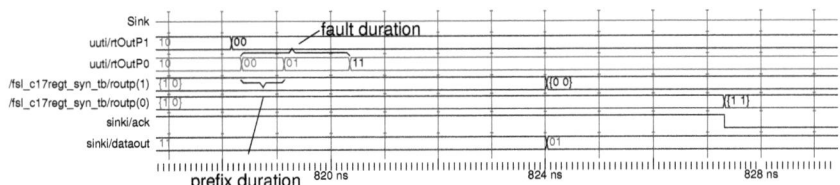

Figure 5.10: Temporal masking of a $T(+1)$ token error

process the wrong phase prefix, there exists a certain probability that the fault is removed before the register is able to receive it. Such a behavior is similar to the latching-window masking of synchronous circuits, if the fault is removed before the clock edge occurs.

2. Even if the register awaits the wrong prefix, the non-zero internal delays may prevent the capture of a token error. Either the fault duration is too short to be processed or several transitions are that close in time that a practical circuit cannot separate them. In this case an inconsistent token is sensed, which will be rejected. The previous example has shown such timing effects.

From the number of received token errors, the temporal masking effect can be calculated with

$$P_{latched}(l,T) = \frac{|T^f|}{|T^f| + |T_c^{pf}|} \tag{5.4}$$

where $|T_c^{pf}|$ denotes the number of wrong prefixes that lead to a correct result. The number of sensitive traces may be received as token error can be found by solving (5.3) for $P_{sens}(l,T)$:

$$P_{sens}(l,T) = \frac{P_f(l,T)}{P_{latched}(l,T)} = \frac{|T^f|}{N} \cdot \frac{|T^f| + |T_c^{pf}|}{|T^f|} = \frac{|T^f| + |T_c^{pf}|}{N}. \tag{5.5}$$

As $P_f(l,T)$ is a function of the actually received trace set T, different trace sets may lead to different results as well. For a generally valid soft error probability, the trace set must contain all possible code phase traces with a uniform distribution.

Example 5.3.4: A pipelined C17 benchmark circuit was simulated as shown in the setup of Fig. 5.16. Thereby a series of 1000 random 2 ns long transient faults was injected only at the inputs of the 2-bit receiving register. In total 23 token errors were recorded, while 29 traces had a wrong phase prefix, but did not trigger an error:

$$P_{latched}(l,T) = \frac{|T^f|}{|T^f| + |T_c^{pf}|} = \frac{23}{23 + 29} = 44.2\%$$

5. Simulation

$$P_{sens}(l,T) = \frac{|T^f| + |T_c^{pf}|}{N} = \frac{23+29}{1000} = 5.2\%.$$

The previous example showed 5.2% sensitive traces. This number deviates from the predicted *FPP* of a 2-bit FSL circuit, which is 33.33% as calculated in 4.3.1. The following reasons lead to this deviation:

1. The term $P_{sens}(l,T)$ includes logical masking, where a fault may hit a rail that is anyhow expected to be excited. A detailed investigation of the recorded trace set showed that 51.6% of all faults led to an expected rail transition. That comes close to the theoretic probability of 50% if all faults were injected uniformly across all dual-rail signals.

2. The *FPP* not only assumes that a fault solely generates unexpected rail transitions, it also assumes that all fault traces are uniformly distributed.

Both factors are eventually taken into account by the weights given in (4.8). Note that the *FPP* has been introduced to compare the robustness of a circuit independent of the actual trace set it receives. It will only become equal to $P_{sens}(l,T)$ if all fault traces are distributed uniformly and if all transient faults affect unexpected rails.

In the following, the fault trace distribution is examined more closely. Fig. 5.11(a) shows the inherent input trace distribution and Fig. 5.11(b) depicts the injected fault distribution from the previous example. The average is marked with a dotted line. While the fault distribution is rather uniform, the inherent trace distribution depends on the input data set as well as the circuit timings.

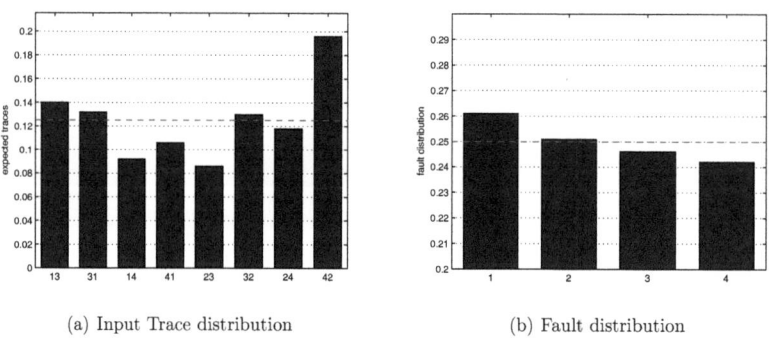

(a) Input Trace distribution   (b) Fault distribution

Figure 5.11: Simulated trace and fault distribution

Fig. 5.12 shows the distribution of all traces that led to an error. That figure is even more distorted as it would be expected from the input trace distribution in Fig. 5.11(a).

144

5.3. The FOSTER Tool

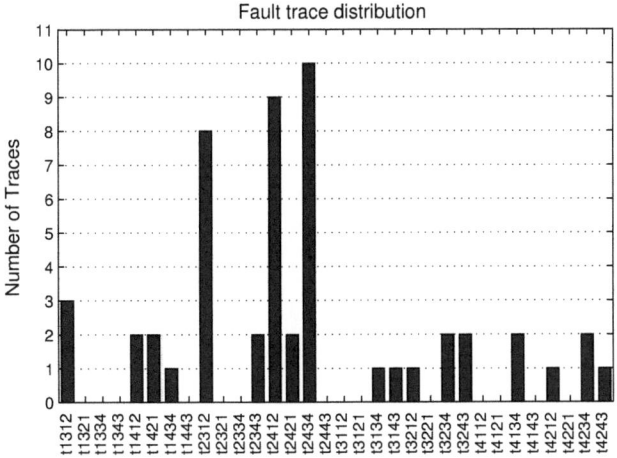

Figure 5.12: Actual fault trace distribution from Example 5.3.4

All traces where the faulty transitions are placed in between the nominal trace and not at the boundary, e.g. $\{3, \overline{1}, \overline{1}, 2\}$, did not occur. Looking at the signal waveform, it was found out that the skew on the signal under investigation (which is understood as the delay between the first and the last rail transition during the code phase change) was around 600 ps, which is much shorter than the fault duration of 2000 ps. Such a scenario is depicted by Fig. 5.13(a).

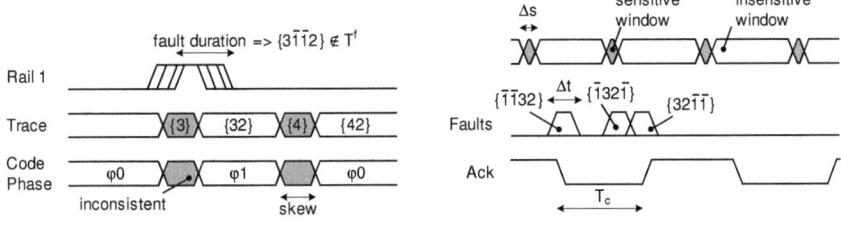

(a) Removal of fault traces depending on fault duration (b) Fault probability during a sensitive window

Figure 5.13: Impacts on fault trace distribution

Similarly, if the complete recorded trace set is examined, it was found out that 93.5% of all traces had both faulty transitions at their boundaries, e.g. $\{\overline{1}, \overline{1}, 3, 2\}$ or $\{3, 2, \overline{1}, \overline{1}\}$. These traces constitute the majority in the simulation and they do not lead to a token error as they do not comprise a wrong phase prefix. The reason for this non-

145

5. Simulation

uniform distribution is the rather long handshake cycle period T_c compared to the fault duration Δt. Fig. 5.13(b) illustrates that behavior. The handshake cycle can be divided in sensitive and insensitive windows. During the sensitive window, the register receives the n rail transitions that are needed to change the code phase. If the fault occurs during that window, it is able to generate a wrong prefix. The length of the sensitive window is defined by the skew on the data bus Δs. After a token has been captured and acknowledged, the register waits until the predecessor provides the next one. During that time, the register is not fault sensitive as a single fault alone cannot change the code phase (the only exception is a single-bit register, which is not regarded here). If the fault occurs in the insensitive window, it will generate a trace with all faulty transitions placed at the trace boundary. The combinational probability to get a faulty transition within the sensitive window is given by

$$p_w = \frac{\Delta t + \Delta s}{T_c}. \tag{5.6}$$

The average handshake period in Example 5.3.4 was $T_c = 31$ ns. That time was mainly determined by the input / output buffer delays that have been generated by the synthesis process and the artificial delays in the test bench. With the fault duration of $\Delta t = 2$ ns and the average skew of $\Delta s = 0.6$ ns, the probability to hit the sensitive window is only $p_w = 8.3\%$. That theoretic number almost correlates with the measured figure of $100\% - 93.5\% = 6.5\%$, which is obtained by excluding all traces with both faulty transitions at the trace boundaries. The difference mainly stems from the non-uniform distribution of the fault injection moments as well as from the variations of T_c and Δs between each particular handshake cycle.

The impact of the ratio of the handshake cycle to the fault duration was tested by reducing the average handshake period in Example 5.3.4 from 31 ns to 24 ns. That reduction was obtained by making the testbench circuits faster and by reducing the I/O delays of the circuit under test via its SDF file. As a result, the probability to hit the sensitive window p_w increases by $31/24 = 29.2\%$. A random fault injection scenario using this setup gave $P_{sens}(l,T) = 6.6\%$, i.e. the number of sensitive traces was increased by 26.3% compared to Example 5.3.4, which is almost the same factor as the increase in p_w.

To further examine the impact of the fault duration as well as the handshake cycle period, fault injections with different fault durations were performed. Thereby the fault duration was even extended beyond one handshake cycle.

Example 5.3.5: The fault injection experiments from Example 5.3.4 were repeated with fault durations $\Delta t = \{100 \text{ ps} \ldots 5 \text{ } \mu s\}$. The results are presented in Fig. 5.14. Both $P_f(l,T)$ and $P_{sens}(l,T)$ increase with a longer fault duration until they saturate at fault durations 50 ns and longer, when the fault duration exceeds the nominal handshake period.

5.3. The FOSTER Tool

Δt	$P_f(l,T)$	$P_{latched}(l,T)$	$P_{sens}(l,T)$
100 ps	0.4%	30.8%	1.3%
200 ps	0.6%	37.5%	1.6%
500 ps	3.2%	71.1%	4.5%
1 ns	3.5%	66.0%	5.3%
2 ns	3.8%	62.8%	7.8%
5 ns	4.8%	57.1%	8.4%
10 ns	5.7%	47.5%	12.0%
20 ns	7.9%	42.3%	18.7%
50 ns	9.1%	36.0%	25.3%
100 ns	9.1%	36.0%	25.3%
...	...	...	...
5 µs	9.1%	36.0%	25.3%

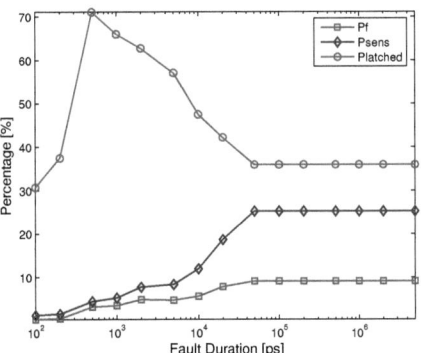

Figure 5.14: Fault sensitivity versus fault duration (Example 5.3.4)

At long fault durations with $\Delta t > T_c$, a faulty transition will always be present in the sensitive window and $p_w = 1$. The fault trace distribution will be even further distorted as the majority of all traces start and end with a faulty transition, e.g. $\{\overline{1}, 3, 2, \overline{1}\}$. Only faults that are applied during the sensitive window will not generate a trace that starts with a faulty transition, however, these traces are the minority as $\Delta t \ll T_c$. That can also be checked using Fig. 5.13.

The *FPP* of traces where a fault occupies the first and last transition of the trace can be calculated as follows. There are $n!$ total traces, where $(n-1)!$ have a wrong phase prefix as the last two transitions must take place on the same dual-rail signal, compare also with 4.3.1. So $FPP = 1/n$ or 50% for the 2-bit test circuit. Taking into account a uniform chance to hit an expected rail, reduces *FPP* by another 50%. Thus $P_{sens}(l,T) = 25\%$ in the theoretic case when all traces are uniformly distributed. Fig. 5.14 shows a high correlation to this theoretic boundary. However, as the trace distribution is not expected to be uniform (as shown in the previous investigations on this example) that correlation is rather coincidental. Repeating the experiment with different stimuli yielded to $P_{sens}(l,T) = 25\% \ldots 30\%$ and $P_f(l,T) = 5.9\% \ldots 9.1\%$.

Another property shown in Fig. 5.14 is the peaking of $P_{latched}(l,T)$. That peak could be reproduced also at other fault injections with different stimuli, although not that distinctive. A closer investigation has shown that the peak always occurred at $\Delta t \approx \Delta s$. At longer fault durations $\Delta t > \Delta s$, the number of wrong prefixes is getting larger as it is more likely to hit the sensitive window. Similarly, the number of wrong prefixes that do not lead to an error, $|T_c^{pf}|$, is also increasing. That number grows faster than the total number of received errors $|T^f|$, so (5.4) is decreasing. If the fault duration becomes $\Delta t < \Delta s$, both $|T_c^{pf}|$ and $|T^f|$ are decreasing, which eventually also reduces $P_{latched}(l,T)$. If the fault duration is in the range of the skew, the size of the fault trace set is a maximum, as the short fault duration permits all possible trace constellations,

5. Simulation

which leads to a maximum in $|T^f|$ compared to $|T_c^{pf}|$. A more detailed investigation of all the particular contributions to the soft error probability goes beyond the scope of this work, especially since nothing can be done against the fault duration on application level.

In Example 5.3.5 fault durations up to several microseconds were simulated. Such long fault durations are not realistic when speaking about transient faults. As already discussed in 2.2.2, transients fault durations range from 100 ps up to 1 ns, depending on the circuit environment and the manufacturing process.

A surprising result of the simulation was the occurrence of deadlocks, although these deadlocks should not occur when faults are injected at interconnections, as derived in 3.5.1. A closer examination of the simulations revealed that some faults violated timing constraints of the used circuit models, such as minimum set/reset pulse width, set/reset recovery time, etc. The simulation model reacts on these violations by setting the corresponding signal to an unknown state. An unknown boolean state eventually freezes the handshake as it cannot be interpreted as valid dual-rail code. A post-processing of the simulation results confirmed the theoretic assumptions, that no deadlocks are possible when faults are applied to pure interconnects. To solve this issue, the undefined state in the test result is detected and marked. Such a result is not counted as deadlock but highlighted to the user. A more detailed investigation of the drawbacks when simulating asynchronous logic is given in 5.4.

A real circuit should not be able to generate any undefined or unknown boolean states. The only exception is metastability when a logic signal is forced to the forbidden zone between logic 0 and logic 1. However, even those metastable states will resolve within some time and will not be permanent as in the simulation results. The generation of unknown states when simulating synthesized circuits has evolved as major drawback of fault simulation in general. A simulation is just as good and realistic as the model it uses. For the fault simulations in this thesis, only synthesized net lists after the place and route process were used. These are described by VITAL (VHDL Initiative Towards ASIC Libraries) compliant VHDL models that use platform dependent primitives. For this work the Xilinx Virtex-4 libraries were taken, since this FPGA will be used later for hardware implementations as well. The timings of the routed design are provided in an SDF file, which defines the parameters for the VITAL functions in the VHDL gate net list. In general this modeling approach generates a quite realistic behavior, although it cannot replace hardware based fault injections.

Nevertheless, simulation based fault injection provides a level of insight into a design that cannot be reached by hardware based fault injection. The effect of transient faults can be investigated down to the particular transistor that is actually affected by the transient fault incident. Further, the timings of the circuitry can be adjusted by e.g. placing dedicated statements in the code or by adapting the SDF file. Thereby, the fault tolerance to different trace settings can be evaluated easily. Chapter 6 will show a method how to modify the trace in hardware, however, the presented method limits the possible trace adjustments to a certain level of granularity that can be easily overcome in simulation. Thus both methods, simulation and hardware based fault injection have its merits. Finally, it depends on the scope of a fault injection program which methods is more suitable.

The previous examples have shown how to separate the particular masking effects that determine the soft error probability and its dependence on the distribution of the faults, traces and the fault duration. The next section presents fault injection experiments on different types of circuits using the rail cross-coupling methods that have been derived in chapter 4.

5.4 Simulation of DRXS Hardened Circuits

5.4.1 Test Setup

The test setup and method how QDI circuits are simulated using the FOSTER tool are demonstrated using the ISCAS-85 C17 benchmark circuit in Fig. 5.15(a). The circuit has five inputs, two outputs and comprises six NAND gates. The FSL design of such a 2-input NAND gate is depicted in Fig. 5.15(b). Each dual-rail output of the gate is generated from a RS-latch, whose set and reset inputs actually implement the logic NAND function. The fault injection setup of a typical pipeline stage is given in Fig. 5.16.

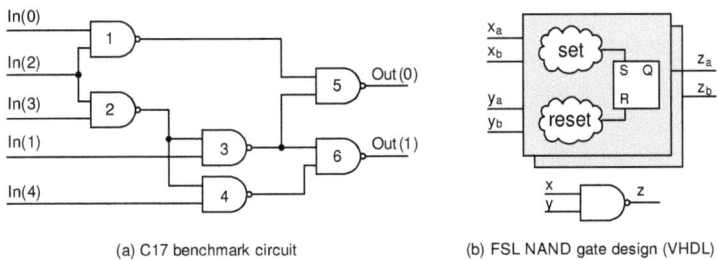

(a) C17 benchmark circuit   (b) FSL NAND gate design (VHDL)

Figure 5.15: FSL version of the ISCAS-85 C17 benchmark circuit

Only the shaded blocks are synthesized, with their timings provided by an SDF file after the place and route. All other functions are testbench models with user defined timings or ideal circuitries. The stimulus is a random 5-bit data word that is applied via a register model, whose timings are modeled using a timing package that can be generated manually or randomly. Faults are injected into the input register including the acknowledge signal and the C17 circuitry itself. All relevant signals that are subjected to faults are extracted from the cleaned-up signal list of the synthesized model. Thereby a dual-rail signal is replaced by two signals representing the two rails. The fault duration

5. Simulation

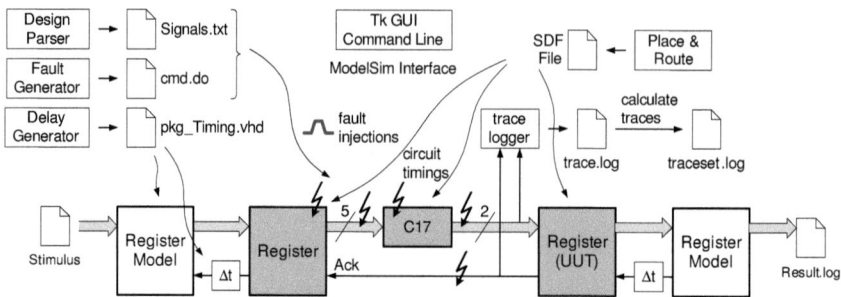

Figure 5.16: Typical fault injection setup

can be selected arbitrarily with the impacts as described in 5.3.5. No faults are injected in the receiving register (UUT), since $P_f(\text{UUT}, T)$ shall be investigated. The input trace of this register is recorded by a trace logger.

For each simulation run, the recorded data is compared with a fault-free reference run. In case of a difference, a token error, synchronization error or a deadlock is reported. Additionally, the trace logger detects all wrong prefix traces that do not lead to an error as described in 5.3.5.

Example 5.4.1: The setup according to Fig. 5.16 was simulated with 100 random input data. At simulation time 230 ns, a 2 ns long transient fault was injected in the output of the a-rail of NAND gate number 1 in Fig. 5.15. Fig. 5.17 shows the recorded output and its corresponding trace log.

Reference Data		Recorded Data	
145345 ps	11	134200 ps	11
173572 ps	11	150300 ps	11
199561 ps	11	167500 ps	11
228071 ps	11	183600 ps	11
253425 ps	11	200800 ps	11
281652 ps	11	216900 ps	11
306019 ps	01	230100 ps	**00**
334366 ps	01	246200 ps	01
362584 ps	00	263300 ps	00
389929 ps	00	279500 ps	00
418175 ps	11	296600 ps	11
446402 ps	11	312700 ps	11
471243 ps	01	327900 ps	01
500514 ps	01	343900 ps	01

Time	: Data	: Ack	: Cons	: Trace
...				
222900 ps	: 1111	: 0	: 0	:
229000 ps	: 0111	: 0	: –	: 1
230100 ps	: 0101	: 0	: 1	: 1 3
232000 ps	: 0111	: 0	: –	: 1 3 3
232100 ps	: 0110	: 0	: 1	: 1 3 3 4
236100 ps	: 0110	: 1	: 1	:
246200 ps	: 0111	: 1	: –	: 4
246200 ps	: 0011	: 1	: 0	: 4 2
...				

Figure 5.17: Token error due to a transient fault and corresponding trace log

Instead of the expected output $OutP = \langle 01 \rangle$ the erroneous result $OutP = \langle 0\overline{0} \rangle$ was received. The circuit expects the sequence $\{\langle 11 \rangle; \langle 01 \rangle\}$ or in dual-rail $\{\langle 1111 \rangle; \langle 0110 \rangle\}$.

5.4. Simulation of DRXS Hardened Circuits

Using the index notation, the expected trace set is $T^e = \{14; 41\}$. The trace logger shows the effect of the fault, which generates the faulty trace $t^f = \{1\overline{3}\overline{3}4\}$ and the wrong phase prefix $t^{pf} = \{1\overline{3}\}$. This time, no temporal masking prevented the capture of a token error and the receiver stored $OutP = \langle 01\overline{01}\rangle \mapsto \langle 0\overline{0}\rangle$.

5.4.2 Test Circuit Selection

The derived duplication and rail cross-coupling methods are applied to several test circuits, which have been selected according to their inherent trace distribution. In 5.3.5, it was shown that the fault trace distribution affects the amount of masking and eventually $P_f(l, T)$. The following circuits are selected:

- C17 benchmark (C17)
- 4-bit adder (Add4)
- 3-to-8 decoder (3to8)
- 4-bit greater or equal comparator (Geq4)
- 4-bit binary-to-gray decoder (B2G)

These circuits constitute typical building blocks of digital designs (the C17 benchmark is regarded as some kind of simple glue logic) and have different trace distributions. To better visualize the large number of different traces, the trace set of a fault-free reference run was parsed and each particular transition was assigned to its parent dual-rail signal. That process compresses the traces by a factor of two, which is a significant improvement regarding the factorial function that is used to calculate the permutations. Next, each particular transition is associated with an artificial, incremental time stamp that starts with 1 at the first transition and ends with n at the last transition.

Example 5.4.2: Let's assume a trace $t_1 = \{3, 8, 6, 1\}$. The sequence of rail transitions is converted to its equivalent signal trace $ts_1 = \{2, 4, 3, 1\}$ by evaluating the corresponding dual-rail signal of each rail transition. Thereby, the signals are labeled with the index i_s that can be calculated from the rail index i_r with $i_s = \text{floor}((i_r+1)/2)$. Finally, the artificial time stamp is associated to each signal, which yields the signal delay matrix $z_1 = \langle (1, 2); (2, 4); (3, 3); (4, 1)\rangle$.

With the above conversion, the signal delay matrices of the selected test circuits are plotted in Fig. 5.18 using the same random input patterns as in the following fault injection experiments. The Geq4 circuit provides a 2-bit output signal $\langle \text{greater,equal}\rangle = \langle 1, 2\rangle$. The equal output (signal 2) preceded the greater output (signal 1) in every code

5. Simulation

phase trace, which stems from the circuit architecture. In the C17 benchmark circuit, the most significant bit is faster than the least significant bit in the majority of the code phase traces. However, in some rare cases, the signal sequence is reversed, which is expressed by the slight deviation from the ideal 1:2 delay ratio. The B2G decoder also shows a clear order of precedence. The most significant bit is always the first one to be produced. Although the remaining bits follow in a sequence, some traces are re-arranged, which is indicated by the deviation from the ideal monotonic delays 2;3;4. The Add4 design has a monotonic signal delay matrix. All traces start with the least significant bit (signal 5) and end with the most significant bit (signal 1). That order comes from the ripple-carry structure of the adder. Finally, the 3to8 decoder shows a random signal delay distribution, which is based on the parallel processing of the input data.

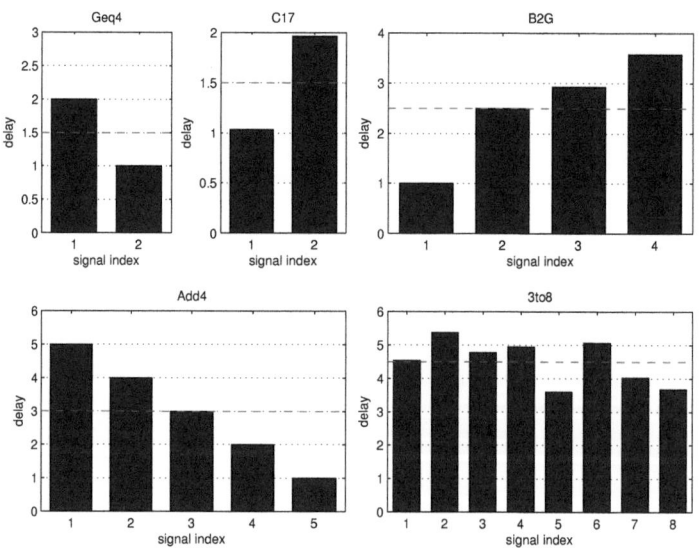

Figure 5.18: Trace distribution of test circuits expressed as signal delay

The test circuits were subjected to a random fault injection campaign using the setup described in Fig. 5.16. The circuit under test is composed of a pipeline with one input and one output register and the test circuit in between. The faults were injected on all circuit signals, except for the output register. For the experiments, the VHDL simulation model after the place and route process was taken. The timings were used from the associated SDF file, with the delays of path towards the trace logger set to zero as explained in 5.3.4. Additionally, all primary input and output delays were also reset

5.4. Simulation of DRXS Hardened Circuits

to zero delay to minimize the handshake cycle time T_c in the application and thereby to maximize the probability to hit the sensitive window p_w in (5.6).

For each test circuit, 5 random input stimulus vectors were generated. The length of the stimulus vector was set to 100 for the C17, 3to8 and B2G circuit and 1000 for the Add4 and Geq4 circuit. Each stimulus vector was subjected to 1000 random faults, so in total 5000 fault injection runs were performed. From the results of each stimulus the average was calculated. The fault injection runs were performed with a fault duration of {100 ps; 500 ps; 1000 ps}, which covers the typical variation of transient fault widths, see 2.2.2. Before a fault injection run is performed, a fault-free golden run is executed and the logged data is used for the comparison with the faulty runs. Further, the golden run determines the nominal execution time of the test vector $[t_{min}; t_{max}]$. The faults are injected within that time boundaries. The following pseudo-code illustrates the applied fault injection methodology.

```
for each Stimulus Vector {1 2 3 4 5}
  process Golden Run;
  get [t_min; t_max];
  for each Fault Duration {100ps 500ps 1000ps}
    i = 0;
    while i < 1000
      get random netlist signal;
      get random fault injection time (t_min ≤ t_f ≤ t_max);
      do fault injection;
      log results;
      compare with Golden Run;
      i = i + 1;
  next Fault Duration;
next Stimulus Vector;

process log files;
calculate average values for Deadlocks, P_f(l,T), P_latched(l,T), P_sens(l,T);
```

In addition, the fault tolerance was also examined in the test circuit according to Fig. 5.19. The test setup is identical to Fig. 5.16, but the output of the register under test is routed via an additional pipeline stage. That architecture has been selected to investigate the propagation of faulty traces. In the original test setup of Fig. 5.16, the register under test is directly evaluated by the testbench register model, which is not synthesized. Therefore, the additional pipeline stage was added to check the influence of the testbench model on the results of the fault injections. As a conclusion, no significant impact could be found. Therefore both setups, Fig. 5.16 and Fig. 5.19, could be applied. For simplicity and for higher simulation speed, the more simpler setup of Fig. 5.16 was chosen.

The next subsection presents the results of the fault injection simulation. First, the faults were applied to the unprotected test circuits, then the experiments were repeated with the DRXS, DRXX an DRS scheme applied.

5. Simulation

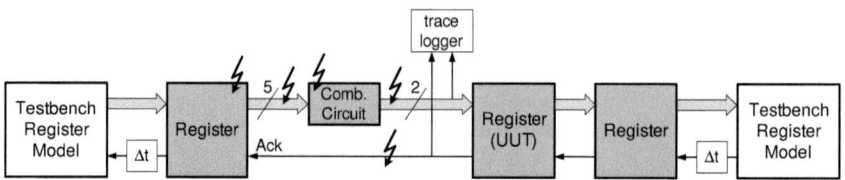

Figure 5.19: Typical fault injection setup using additional pipeline stage

5.4.3 Results

Table 5.3 shows the inherent fault tolerance of the selected test circuits. Most circuits showed roughly the same $P_f(l,T) = 2\%$ ... 3%. Only the B2G decoder had a higher $P_f(l,T) = 3\%$ ... 5%. That circuit is only composed of three XOR gates, so it does not provide a lot of logical masking capability.

Table 5.3: Inherent fault tolerance of test circuits

	Δt	Deadlocks	$P_f(l,T)$	$P_{latched}(l,T)$	$P_{sens}(l,T)$
C17	100 ps	0.00%	2.16%	86.40%	2.50%
	500 ps	0.00%	3.10%	94.51%	3.28%
	1 ns	0.00%	2.34%	86.67%	2.70%
Add4	100 ps	0.00%	2.54%	91.37%	2.78%
	500 ps	0.00%	2.76%	89.03%	3.10%
	1 ns	0.00%	1.94%	80.17%	2.42%
3to8	100 ps	0.00%	2.60%	97.35%	3.96%
	500 ps	0.00%	3.00%	86.71%	3.46%
	1 ns	0.00%	2.20%	97.35%	2.26%
Geq4	100 ps	0.06%	2.48%	99.20%	2.50%
	500 ps	0.10%	2.46%	97.62%	2.52%
	1 ns	0.08%	1.66%	92.22%	1.80%
B2G	100 ps	0.04%	4.82%	74.84%	6.44%
	500 ps	0.10%	5.42%	86.03%	6.30%
	1 ns	0.02%	3.04%	75.25%	4.04%

Checking the particular simulations, it was found out that two fault locations lead to the majority of the erroneous runs. First of all, the most failures were triggered by synchronization errors that emerged from transient faults in the handshake logic, such as the handshake lines themselves or the output phase detector. The second major group of failures were triggered by transient faults in the data path, which lead to both token and synchronization errors.

5.4. Simulation of DRXS Hardened Circuits

A small number of deadlocks was recorded in the Geq4 and B2G circuits. These deadlocks were checked, whether they result from model imperfections or whether they really stem from inconsistent data that stops the handshake process. It turned out that all deadlocks emerged from such inconsistent data that is stored in the input pipeline register. The probability to store a deadlock in a sequential circuit such as a register largely depends on the internal timings of that register. A detailed investigation of these timings as well as the impact of the internal register design on the capability to capture deadlocks is not investigated in this thesis. Nevertheless, the models that are used to simulate the QDI circuits in this work are investigated in more detail.

The results in Table 5.3 were obtained by using the default simulation settings of ModelSim. As already discussed in 5.3.5, the simulations were performed using VITAL compliant gate level models. These models do not only simulate the logic functions including the propagation delays, but also provide timing checks that imply whether a circuit will operate correctly or not. The VHDL code below shows an excerpt of the VITAL model of a simple latch.

```
architecture X_LATCHE_V of X_LATCHE is
  ...
  signal CLK_ipd   : std_ulogic := 'X';
  signal GE_ipd    : std_ulogic := 'X';
  ...
  -- FRI: tForceEvent_S added
  signal tForceEvent_S : std_ulogic := 'U';
  -- FRI: explicit output signal added
  signal O_Q            : std_ulogic := TO_X01(INIT);

begin
  ...
  VITALBehavior : process (CLK_dly, GE_dly, GSR_resolved, I_dly,
      PRLD_resolved, RST_dly, SET_dly, tForceEvent_S)
    ...
    variable PInfo_SET : VitalPeriodDataType := VitalPeriodDataInit;
    variable Pviol_CLK : std_ulogic          := '0';
    variable Violation : std_ulogic          := '0';
    ...

  begin
    if (TimingChecksOn) then
      VitalSetupHoldCheck (
        Violation       => Tviol_I_CLK_negedge,
        TimingData      => Tmkr_I_CLK_negedge,
        TestSignal      => I_dly,
        TestSignalName  => "I",
        TestDelay       => 0 ps,
        RefSignal       => CLK_dly,
        RefSignalName   => "CLK",
        RefDelay        => 0 ps,
        SetupHigh       => tsetup_I_CLK_posedge_negedge,
        SetupLow        => tsetup_I_CLK_negedge_negedge,
        HoldHigh        => thold_I_CLK_posedge_negedge,
        HoldLow         => thold_I_CLK_negedge_negedge,
        CheckEnabled    => TO_X01(((not RST_dly) and (GE_dly)
                                   and ((not SET_dly))) /= '0',
        RefTransition   => 'F',
        HeaderMsg       => "/X_LATCHE",
        Xon             => XON,
        MsgOn           => MSGON,
        MsgSeverity     => warning);
```

5. Simulation

```
        ...
    end if;
    Violation := Tviol_I_CLK_negedge or Tviol_GE_CLK_negedge or
                 Tviol_SET_CLK_negedge or Tviol_RST_CLK_negedge or
                 Pviol_RST or Pviol_SET or
                 Pviol_CLK;

    if((GSR_resolved = '1') or (PRLD_resolved = '1')) then
        O_zd := To_X01(INIT);
    elsif((GSR_resolved = '0') and (PRLD_resolved = '0')) then
        VitalStateTable(
            Result            => O_zd,
            PreviousDataIn    => PrevData_O,
            StateTable        => X_LATCHE_O_tab,
            DataIn            => (CLK_dly, I_dly, SET_dly, RST_dly, GE_dly));
        O_zd := Violation xor O_zd;
    end if;
  end process;
end X_LATCHE_V;
```

The VITAL model highlights the check for a proper setup and hold time. The applicable timing parameters are passed to the process *VitalSetupHoldCheck*, which sets the output variable `Tviol_I_Clk_negde` to 'X' if a timing violation is detected. Finally, all these violation variables are logically combined and eventually define the output of the latch, which is provided in `O_zd`. That timing check can be disabled by setting the variable `TimingChecksOn` to false. The effect of a timing violation is an undefined logic state 'X'. If that state applies for too long, the circuit may not be able to continue its operation and run into a deadlock.

Example 5.4.3: Fig. 5.20 depicts the timing simulation of a transient fault at the input of the final register in the pipelined C17 benchmark circuitry. The fault leads to the inconsistent register input $uuti/OutP = \langle 0\overline{0}, 01 \rangle$ and occurs during the storage process. The inconsistent token propagates to the register output */fsl_c17regt_syn_tb/ routp* and leads to a timing violation in the output phase detector *uuti/regouti_ phaseout_q_425* (1). The VITAL model responds with an undefined logic state that propagates via the acknowledge signal to the predecessor of the pipeline (2). That predecessor, which is the source testbench component, delivers the next token with undefined logic states (3). These undefined states propagate through the pipeline (4), as the VHDL models used in the simulation generate an undefined output if they receive an undefined input. Eventually, the sink testbench component receives an undefined logic state (5), which is never acknowledged and deadlocks the pipeline.

The previous example showed how a deadlock can be accidentally generated due to a timing violation of the used VITAL simulation model. These deadlocks due to undefined states are detected by the FOSTER tool. It is hard to predict how such an undefined state will resolve, whether it will really lead to a deadlock, whether it will generate wrong data or whether it will only delay the circuit execution. Due to this uncertainty, all simulation runs that lead to a deadlock due to undefined data were not considered at all, i.e. they

5.4. Simulation of DRXS Hardened Circuits

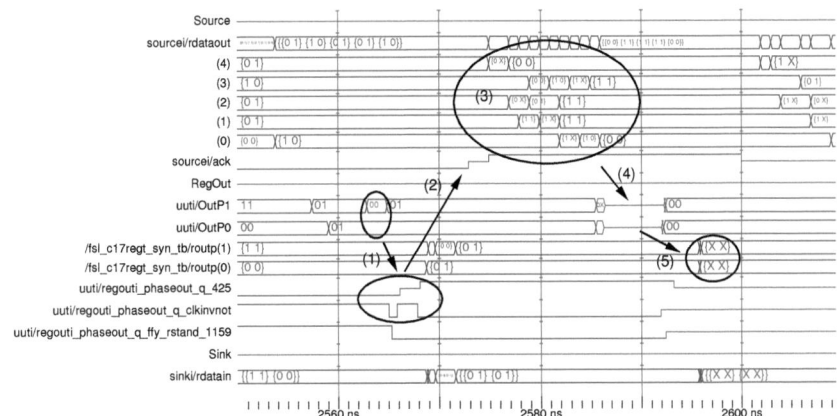

Figure 5.20: Undefined logic state due to timing violation leads to a deadlock

were neither counted as correct nor as wrong result. As the number of such runs was in the range of 2% that approach is acceptable.

In addition to the rather easy detectable deadlocks due to undefined states, the simulations presented in Table 5.3 contained many unexpected synchronization errors. Checking these faulty runs by inspection of the timing waveform in ModelSim revealed that they were also triggered by violations of the circuit timing models. These errors due to violations of the model's timing specification cannot be identified that easily as they are not distinguishable from real synchronization errors that emerge from handshake disturbances. It shall be further noted, that the VITAL models indeed notify the user of such timing violations. However, such notifications occurred rather often in the simulation as the injection of faults in an asynchronous circuit does not comply to the circuit timings at all.

Modelsim allows to disable the timing checks in the VITAL models using the command parameter +notimingchecks. The following example repeats the fault injection experiment from the previous one with disabled timing checks and shows the different behavior in the simulation of transient faults.

Example 5.4.4: Fig. 5.21 shows the same waveform as Fig. 5.20, with the timing checks of the VITAL models disabled. As depicted, the closely spaced input transitions of the output phase detector do not trigger an undefined state and consequently, no undefined state propagation occurs. The transient fault is masked and the circuit continues its nominal operation without reporting any errors.

To test the impact of the timing checks, all erroneous simulation runs from Table 5.3 were repeated with these timing checks disabled. The FOSTER tool allows to repeat a

5. Simulation

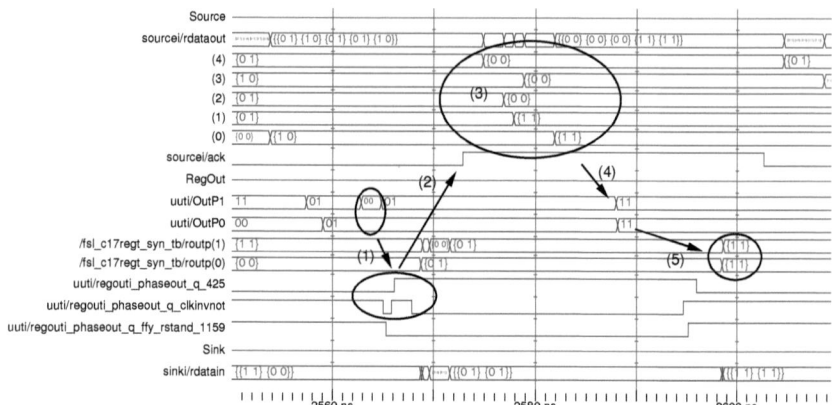

Figure 5.21: Suppression of undefined logic states by disabling the timing checks

simulation run with the same fault injection settings (signal under test, fault type, injection time, etc.) under different simulation parameters, such as different fault durations or different simulator settings. This procedure has the advantage that the result are not statistically distorted by running a new, independent random test. The summary of this second test run are presented in Table 5.4.

Table 5.4: Inherent fault tolerance of test circuits without timing checks

	Δt	Deadlocks	$P_f(l,T)$	$P_{latched}(l,T)$	$P_{sens}(l,T)$
C17	100 ps	0.00%	1.16%	96.67%	1.20%
	500 ps	0.00%	2.30%	96.64%	2.38%
	1 ns	0.02%	2.68%	100.00%	2.68%
Add4	100 ps	0.00%	0.64%	91.43%	0.70%
	500 ps	0.00%	1.50%	96.15%	1.56%
	1 ns	0.00%	1.48%	96.10%	1.54%
3to8	100 ps	0.00%	0.92%	97.87%	0.94%
	500 ps	0.02%	1.80%	95.74%	1.88%
	1 ns	0.04%	1.76%	94.62%	1.86%
Geq4	100 ps	0.12%	0.78%	90.70%	0.86%
	500 ps	0.22%	1.34%	95.71%	1.40%
	1 ns	0.14%	1.52%	97.44%	1.56%
B2G	100 ps	0.30%	1.14%	96.61%	1.18%
	500 ps	0.56%	2.60%	98.48%	2.64%
	1 ns	0.84%	2.38%	94.44%	2.52%

5.4. Simulation of DRXS Hardened Circuits

Without applying any timing checks the recorded $P_f(l,T)$ was generally reduced. An exception occurred in the simulation of the C17 benchmark, where the total number of errors with a fault duration of 1 ns was even larger without timing checks. An investigation of this unexpected results showed that some of the ignored runs with undefined results actually resulted in token errors. Thus a timing violation will not always resolve in a correct result. Deadlocks were even higher with timing checks disabled. The reason is that no undefined states are produced anymore. The FOSTER tool will disregard some undefined states, which would otherwise falsify the results. The disregarded undefined states are now inconsistent data that contribute to the number of deadlocks.

Taking into account timing checks allows to identify violations of the circuit's specification. These checks have their merits as a timing violation may lead to an undefined behavior such as metastability. As briefly noted above, it cannot be easily predicted how long such a metastable state persists and to what logic state it will resolve. Thus having timing checks enabled will lead to conservative results in terms of fault tolerance. On the other hand, omitting the timing checks will rather give best case results. Therefore, both methods provide a valuable output for the assessment of transient faults in QDI logic. For this work, the figures are regarded as lower and upper boundaries of the randomly evaluated fault tolerance. Of course, the confidence interval applies to both of them. This uncertainty in the simulation of QDI logic is another argument for performing hardware based fault injections in parallel to simulation based fault investigations. That topic will be tackled in chapter 6.

After performing fault injections with bare, unhardened QDI circuits, the selected test circuits are now implemented using the DRXS and DRXX methods, developed in 4.4. Thereby the same stimuli as for the inherent fault tolerance measurements were used. Due to the different circuit architecture, it is not possible to disturb the same nets as in the unhardened circuit and a random fault injection campaign was performed.

Table 5.5 shows the results of DRXS with the timing checks enabled. Table 5.6 depicts the results of DRXS with the timing checks disabled. Table 5.7 shows the results of DRXX with enabled timing checks. Table 5.8 shows the results of DRXX with the timing checks disabled. With the timing checks enabled, the fault tolerance of DRXS was generally better than DRXX, although both methods should behave identically in theory. The reason for this practical deviation was found in the tendency of DRXX to propagate token errors that are temporary mitigated in DRXS. The DRXX method performed better than DRXS when the timing checks were disabled, where the propagation of token errors generated by timing violations are reduced. Eventually, the DRXS/DRXX method significantly reduced $P_f(l,T)$ of all test circuits.

Table 5.5: Fault tolerance of test circuits using DRXS with timing checks

	Δt	Deadlocks	$P_f(l,T)$	$P_{latched}(l,T)$	$P_{sens}(l,T)$
C17	100 ps	0.08%	0.00%	0.00%	0.18%
	500 ps	0.10%	0.12%	42.86%	0.28%
	1 ns	0.00%	0.12%	54.55%	0.22%
Add4	100 ps	0.30%	0.44%	75.86%	0.58%
	500 ps	0.12%	0.42%	67.74%	0.62%
	1 ns	0.04%	0.26%	50.00%	0.52%
3to8	100 ps	0.46%	0.00%	0.00%	0.44%
	500 ps	0.62%	0.06%	23.08%	0.26%
	1 ns	0.02%	0.04%	50.00%	0.08%
Geq4	100 ps	0.16%	1.16%	93.55%	1.24%
	500 ps	0.14%	0.68%	87.18%	0.78%
	1 ns	0.00%	0.32%	66.67%	0.48%
B2G	100 ps	0.38%	0.00%	0.00%	0.56%
	500 ps	0.42%	0.10%	22.73%	0.44%
	1 ns	0.12%	0.22%	42.31%	0.52%

Table 5.6: Fault tolerance of test circuits using DRXS without timing checks

	Δt	Deadlocks	$P_f(l,T)$	$P_{latched}(l,T)$	$P_{sens}(l,T)$
C17	100 ps	0.00%	0.00%	-	0.00%
	500 ps	0.02%	0.20%	83.33%	0.24%
	1 ns	0.00%	0.16%	100.00%	0.16%
Add4	100 ps	0.00%	0.00%	-	0.00%
	500 ps	0.00%	0.10%	100.00%	0.10%
	1 ns	0.00%	0.14%	100.00%	0.14%
3to8	100 ps	0.00%	0.00%	-	0.00%
	500 ps	0.02%	0.02%	100.00%	0.02%
	1 ns	0.00%	0.04%	100.00%	0.04%
Geq4	100 ps	0.00%	0.02%	50.00%	0.04%
	500 ps	0.00%	0.04%	100.00%	0.04%
	1 ns	0.00%	0.02%	100.00%	0.02%
B2G	100 ps	0.00%	0.00%	0.00%	0.02%
	500 ps	0.02%	0.24%	92.31%	0.26%
	1 ns	0.06%	0.14%	100.00%	0.14%

Table 5.7: Fault tolerance of test circuits using DRXX with timing checks

	Δt	Deadlocks	$P_f(l,T)$	$P_{latched}(l,T)$	$P_{sens}(l,T)$
C17	100 ps	0.22%	0.40%	68.97%	0.58%
	500 ps	0.04%	0.60%	88.24%	0.68%
	1 ns	0.00%	0.42%	91.30%	0.46%
Add4	100 ps	0.10%	1.44%	90.00%	1.60%
	500 ps	0.10%	0.94%	79.66%	1.18%
	1 ns	0.02%	0.40%	57.14%	0.70%
3to8	100 ps	0.54%	0.10%	33.33%	0.30%
	500 ps	0.50%	0.50%	71.43%	0.70%
	1 ns	0.02%	0.22%	100.00%	0.22%
Geq4	100 ps	0.16%	0.86%	87.76%	0.98%
	500 ps	0.04%	0.48%	66.67%	0.72%
	1 ns	0.06%	0.20%	62.50%	0.32%
B2G	100 ps	0.32%	0.34%	42.50%	0.80%
	500 ps	0.34%	0.82%	80.39%	1.02%
	1 ns	0.14%	0.64%	86.49%	0.74%

Table 5.8: Fault tolerance of test circuits using DRXX without timing checks

	Δt	Deadlocks	$P_f(l,T)$	$P_{latched}(l,T)$	$P_{sens}(l,T)$
C17	100 ps	0.00%	0.00%	-	0.00%
	500 ps	0.00%	0.18%	100.00%	0.18%
	1 ns	0.04%	0.16%	100.00%	0.16%
Add4	100 ps	0.00%	0.00%	-	0.00%
	500 ps	0.00%	0.04%	66.67%	0.06%
	1 ns	0.00%	0.18%	100.00%	0.18%
3to8	100 ps	0.00%	0.00%	0.00%	0.02%
	500 ps	0.04%	0.30%	83.33%	0.36%
	1 ns	0.00%	0.16%	100.00%	0.16%
Geq4	100 ps	0.00%	0.00%	-	0.00%
	500 ps	0.00%	0.02%	100.00%	0.02%
	1 ns	0.00%	0.00%	-	0.00%
B2G	100 ps	0.00%	0.00%	0.00%	0.02%
	500 ps	0.04%	0.28%	82.35%	0.34%
	1 ns	0.06%	0.28%	100.00%	0.28%

5. Simulation

Table 5.9 and Table 5.10 show the results of DRS hardened circuits with and without timing checks enabled, respectively. The C17, 3to8 and B2G test circuit showed a better performance than DRXS/DRXX. That property was expected from the theoretical considerations. The soft error probability of the Add4 and Geq4 circuit, however, was in the same range as with DRXS/DRXX. These results were not expected, as the DRS should perform much better. A closer examination has shown that most of the recorded errors were accompanied with timing violation messages in the simulator. Comparing the results of DRS with the timing checks disabled, shows a general better performance than DRXS/DRXX. The unexpected high soft error probability of the DRS hardened circuits is another strong indication for the non-trivial simulation of faults in asynchronous circuits.

Table 5.9: Fault tolerance of test circuits using DRS with timing checks

	Δt	Deadlocks	$P_f(l,T)$	$P_{latched}(l,T)$	$P_{sens}(l,T)$
C17	100 ps	0.14%	0.00%	100.00%	0.00%
	500 ps	0.10%	0.00%		0.00%
	1 ns	0.00%	0.00%		0.00%
Add4	100 ps	0.12%	0.96%	100.00%	0.96%
	500 ps	0.14%	0.50%		0.50%
	1 ns	0.02%	0.14%		0.14%
3to8	100 ps	0.30%	0.02%	100.00%	0.02%
	500 ps	0.20%	0.00%		0.00%
	1 ns	0.00%	0.04%		0.04%
Geq4	100 ps	0.18%	1.00%	100.00%	1.00%
	500 ps	0.18%	0.42%		0.42%
	1 ns	0.00%	0.34%		0.34%
B2G	100 ps	0.34%	0.02%	100.00%	0.02%
	500 ps	0.26%	0.02%		0.02%
	1 ns	0.00%	0.00%		0.00%

Table 5.10: Fault tolerance of test circuits using DRS without timing checks

	Δt	Deadlocks	$P_f(l,T)$	$P_{latched}(l,T)$	$P_{sens}(l,T)$
C17	100 ps	0.00%	0.00%	100.00%	0.00%
	500 ps	0.00%	0.00%		0.00%
	1 ns	0.00%	0.00%		0.00%
Add4	100 ps	0.00%	0.00%	100.00%	0.00%
	500 ps	0.02%	0.00%		0.00%
	1 ns	0.04%	0.00%		0.00%
3to8	100 ps	0.00%	0.00%	100.00%	0.00%
	500 ps	0.00%	0.00%		0.00%
	1 ns	0.00%	0.04%		0.04%
Geq4	100 ps	0.00%	0.00%	100.00%	0.00%
	500 ps	0.00%	0.00%		0.00%
	1 ns	0.00%	0.04%		0.04%
B2G	100 ps	0.00%	0.00%	100.00%	0.00%
	500 ps	0.00%	0.02%		0.02%
	1 ns	0.00%	0.00%		0.00%

5.5 Summary

That chapter presents a method how to simulate transient faults in QDI logic. Thereby the FOSTER tool was introduced, which takes care of the peculiarities in QDI fault simulation and allows to separate the different masking effects during the fault evaluation process. A special test setup was created, which is capable of recording the different traces that are received by the circuit under test. Thereby different test circuits led to different trace distributions. Applying transient faults, generates a certain fault trace distribution, whose shape also highly depends on the fault duration and the handshake period. It was shown that a uniform trace distribution in practical circuits, especially when transient faults are applied, is rather a theoretic case.

During fault simulation experiments, different test circuits were subjected to transient faults of various durations. Thereby the circuits were simulated on gate level using VITAL models to obtain a realistic behavior. These models also check the timing specification of the particular components in the circuit. It was found out that transient faults may violate these timings, which may lead either to undefined circuit states but may also lead to errors without propagating undefined states. It is therefore difficult to assess, whether an error in a fault injection experiment stems from wrong data or from a violation of a component specification.

The DRXS/DRXX scheme influences $P_{sens}(l,T)$ as predicted in chapter 4. Comparing Table 5.3, Table 5.5 and Table 5.7 shows a reduced $P_f(l,T)$ when applying DRXS/-

5. Simulation

DRXX compared to the inherent fault tolerance of the unhardened test circuits. The DRS method even further improves that fault tolerance as shown by Table 5.9. However, in contradiction to Table 4.15, which predicts no fault propagation in a DRS hardened circuitry, a few token errors were observed in the fault simulations. That deviation came from the timing violations in the simulation models, which makes a correct evaluation of the fault injection results difficult.

Fig. 5.22 compares the average $P_f(l,T)$ of all test circuits versus the hardening strategy with and without applying timing checks. A quantitative comparison is difficult as all three architectures were subjected to independent, random fault injections. Nevertheless, the improved fault tolerance is evident. For instance, comparing $FPP(l,T)$ from a non-hardened circuitry with a DRXS/DRXX circuit gives a factor of 4, see Table 4.15. The same factor should be visible in $P_{sens}(l,T)$, provided the trace distribution between the non-hardened and the hardened circuit as well as the temporal masking expressed by $P_{latched}(l,T)$ are the same. That cannot be guaranteed, thus the improvement factor will deviate from that theoretic value. As expected, the DRS method shows the highest fault tolerance.

Table 5.11: Average $P_f(l,T)$ of DRXS, DRXX, DRS versus unhardened test circuits

	Timing checks	DRXS	DRXX	DRS
$\frac{P_f(l,T)_{unhardened}}{P_f(l,T)_{hardened}}$	enabled	3 ... 87	2 ... 10	4 ... 443
	disabled	15 ... 75	10 ... 121	121 ... ∞

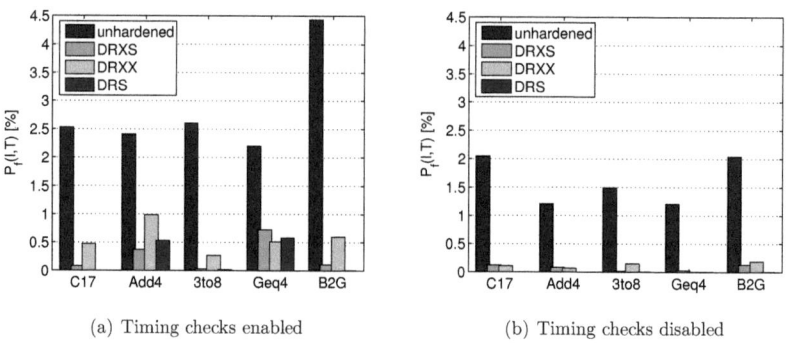

(a) Timing checks enabled (b) Timing checks disabled

Figure 5.22: Average $P_f(l,T)$ versus hardening strategy of test circuits

This chapter has shown that it is possible to improve the fault tolerance of a pipelined QDI circuit by means of DRXS/DRXX. The reduction in the error rate is significantly higher than the required additional hardware resources, which is only minimal larger than a factor of 2, see 4.4. The same applies for the DRS method.

No detailed investigation of the speed penalty due to the hardening methods was made. The average increase in the processing time was 15% compared to an unhardened test circuit. Thereby the smallest penalty was generated by the DRS method, followed by DRXS and DRXX, but the observed differences were rather small. The observed degradation in the processing of the hardening methods presented in this thesis is less than the 30 to 40% penalty that has been reported for the duplication and double-checking method, see 4.2.2. As the results are only based on a rather small number of tests, additional work is needed to draw a general conclusion.

The occurrence of timing violations had a significant impact on the simulation results and leaves many questions open that would go beyond the scope of this thesis and is reserved for future research. It has to be investigated whether these violations suppress any errors as well as whether they lead to wrong errors, which are actually only the result of an unexpected simulation behavior. The uncertainties in the fault simulation of QDI logic has also lead to hardware based fault injection experiments, which are discussed in chapter 6.

6
Emulation

Fault injection by means of simulation has shown some weak points. For instance, unexpected deadlocks have been generated by undefined logic states that did not resolve to a defined state within a finite time. Any simulation model will only be as good as its own specification within the model boundaries. Therefore fault investigations are extended by testing circuits directly in hardware using the trace based fault model developed in chapter 3.

6.1 Related Work

Similar to simulation based fault injection, there are several tools available although none of them has been developed for asynchronous logic. For instance, pin level fault injection is presented in [119]. In this method, stuck-at faults with various durations are applied to the I/O pins of the device under test by means of high-speed probes. Thereby the physical hardware of the tested design is not changed by the fault emulation environment. Injecting faults at the pin level imposes some limitations in terms of speed as well as restricts the locations of the fault origin to the device boundaries. FPGA-based fault emulation is provided in [120,121]. The circuit under test is implemented in an FPGA and special saboteur circuits are added to disturb the logic state of internal signals. These saboteurs influence the nominal circuit behavior. To minimize their impact, their number has to be limited. Thus for a high fault coverage, the FPGA has to be reprogrammed several times with saboteurs placed at different locations. A general overview of fault injection techniques including hardware based fault emulation is given in [109].

Physical fault injection in hardware by means of laser irradiation is presented in [122]. This approach allows to precisely inject faults into small circuit areas and at locations that cannot be reached by other means. This technique can be used to simulate the behavior of particle irradiation but cannot disturb a single net as the laser beam cannot

6. Emulation

be focused that high. The presented work uses a hardened Data Encryption Standard (DES) crypto-processor designed in 4-phase dual-rail. The laser beam was focused to a relative spot size of 1.9% of the circuit area, which definitely comprises several nets. Fig. 6.1 shows the principal test setup and the test sequence of the laser irradiation based fault injection. Drawbacks of this method are the necessity of a laser equipment and the associated costs. Further, the fault duration cannot be controlled directly, as it depends on the injected charge and the node capacitances.

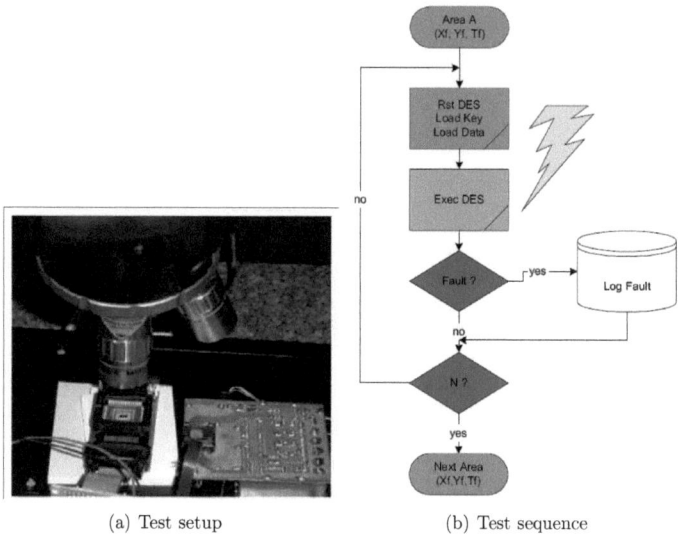

(a) Test setup (b) Test sequence

Figure 6.1: Laser irradiation based fault injection [122]

The inherent robustness of an asynchronous processor compared to its synchronous counterpart by means of hardware fault injection is investigated in [15, 63]. Fig. 6.2 shows the block diagram and the typical implementation of the saboteurs of the **F**lexible On-Chip Fault **I**njector for runtime **D**ependabilit**Y** Validation with target specific **CO**mmand language (FIDYCO). Saboteurs are placed at the desired locations of the circuit to generate faults at gate level. Both methodical and random faults are injected and their effects are evaluated. The tool compares the sequence of asynchronous events between a golden reference run and the faulty run, thereby the absolute time scale is not important. The experiments conducted in this work were limited to the data path of an asynchronous processor. Handshake faults were not generated, although the single-rail encoding of the handshake makes this path especially vulnerable to transient faults.

Hybrid solutions that combine the observability of a simulator with the performance of hardware based fault injection are presented in [123, 124]. The latter work introduces the

6.1. Related Work

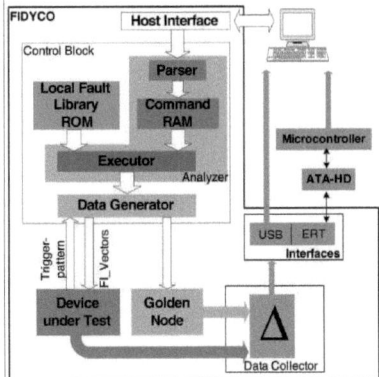

(a) Implementation of saboteurs

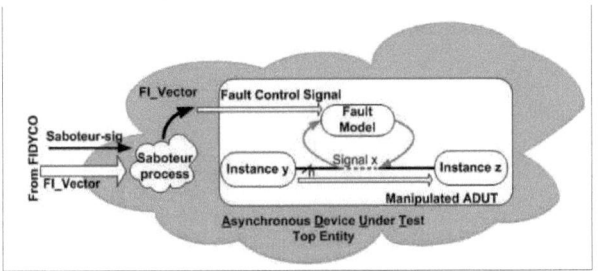

(b) Block diagram

Figure 6.2: Hardware based fault injection setup [63]

Fault injection **u**sing **SE**mulation (FuSE) tool. It allows to run certain parts of a design in an FPGA to speed up the simulation time. Although not dedicated for asynchronous circuits, it may be used to reduce the high simulation effort due to the larger circuit area. The tool is currently extended to asynchronous circuits.

Compared to simulation there are even less tools available to perform hardware based fault injection in QDI logic. Although it is assumed that such tools are used to overcome the bottleneck of simulation speeds, it seems that either not much effort is spent on the development of such a tool or it is assumed to be a straightforward task. This thesis also does not want to present a hardware based fault injection tool as main research topic alone, however, it wants to highlight some peculiarities that may be overlooked.

6. Emulation

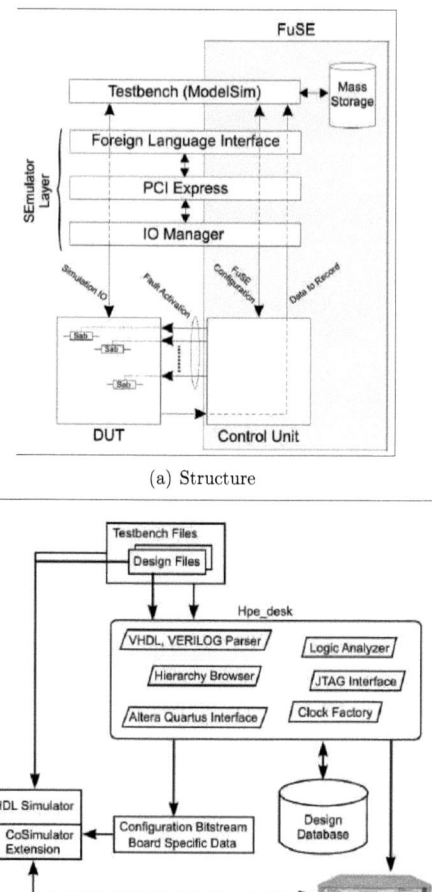

(a) Structure

(b) Overview

Figure 6.3: FUSE fault injection tool [124]

6.2 Fault Emulation in QDI Logic

This section briefly discusses the main requirements for a deterministic fault emulation in QDI logic. The key idea is to utilize the trace based model to ensure *full error coverage* and to obtain *reproducible results*.

6.2.1 Error Coverage

A fault injection tool shall be able to provoke all kind of errors in QDI logic, which are deadlock, synchronization error and token error, see 2.2.6. Deadlocks and token errors can be generated by solely corrupting the data path of a pipelined QDI circuit. To trigger a synchronization error the handshake has to be disturbed as well. Especially when faults are injected at register transfer level the acknowledge line(s) have to be included in the set of victim signals. Often these signals are omitted in fault injection tools.

Contrary to the fault simulation in chapter 5, the fault emulation method developed in this thesis, injects the faults solely at register transfer level, which comprises the data path as well as the handshake lines. Fig. 6.4(a) shows how simple single event transients are generated. The faulty state will be preserved only for the duration of the fault. A saboteur disturbs either the data rails or the handshake line for the desired fault duration. As discussed in 3.5, transient faults on the data path or the handshake will either generate token errors or synchronization errors. That statement holds as long as the circuit does not contain any redundant functions. If the circuit is hardened e.g. using DRXS, a synchronization error will turn into a deadlock if the two redundant tokens disagree. The same effect can be observed in any QDI circuitry that uses a synchronization between two redundant pipelines.

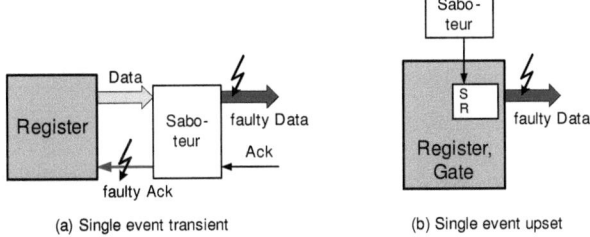

Figure 6.4: Different injection types in fault emulation

To produce a soft error or single event upset the principle in Fig. 6.4(b) is used. Here, the transient fault is directly applied to the set/reset inputs of a storage cell. Once the fault is removed, the erroneous state is maintained until the storage cell is refreshed. To ensure that soft errors can be provoked according to Fig. 6.4(b), each storage cell has to be designed using externally available set and reset inputs. As these ports are generally not needed, their implementation generates additional hardware overhead, which has to be considered when comparing the circuit occupation.

As described in chapters 3 and 4, the circuit trace determines the fault sensitivity of a circuit. The actual trace of a circuit depends on the inherent routing of the design, the data content, environmental conditions (temperature, supply voltage) and especially the process parameters, which suffer large variations [125]. A circuit that works correctly in one environment and with one set of process parameters might fail at different process parameters, which are additionally hard to predict. Thus if a comprehensive fault investigation in QDI logic shall be conducted, the circuit traces must be taken into account.

Reshuffling the rail transitions to modify the trace will help to detect all weaknesses. In simulation, that reshuffling can be accomplished by modifying the delay of the circuit. On gate level, the delays can be adapted by modifying the SDF file, on register level, the trace can be changed by using special delay statements in the source code, such as the **after** statement in VHDL. Such an artificial delay modification has already been performed in 5.3.4, where the propagation delays of the *TraceLogger* have been reset to zero in the SDF file to ensure the logged trace equals the monitored trace.

A modification of the circuit trace itself has not been performed in chapter 5. Although the particular components and gates can be identified in the SDF file, the synthesis software may obscure the physical assignment of the gates and signals by its optimization algorithms. Special statements allow to keep signal labels visible, however, a general processing of delay modifications in the SDF file has been analyzed being too complex, and would go beyond the scope of this thesis. A delay and trace modification on register level is not that complex, as the particular signals are kept visible to the user. However, a register level based simulation has been left out as that level does not include the timings of the target platform. The user would have to take care of all timings, which was regarded as leading to theoretical circuits without any connection to a physical device.

That situation is different for the fault emulation method applied in this thesis. To not disturb the internal timings of gates and registers (which require a certain matching to produce practical QDI circuits), saboteurs are only placed in the data and handshake path of the circuit as well as directly at the set / reset inputs of flip-flops and latches. Thus the fault emulation takes place on register level. As the emulated circuit already exhibits real timings, the user does not have to take care of the inherent delay settings – they are provided in a realistic manner. Thus a modification of the circuit trace is more easy to accomplish as it only requires to change the timings on the register level were the saboteurs have already been placed. However, to change the circuit trace in hardware, a special type of saboteur is needed, as presented in 6.3.2. Modifying the trace not only helps to check the robustness of a circuit in general but also supports a systematic verification as it allows to generate worst case scenarios more easily.

6.2.2 Reproducibility

The results of a fault injection shall be reproducible. Synchronous tools can always rely on consistent states to trigger an action. The clock edges are the only events that define the state of a circuit. In asynchronous circuits, each signal transition defines a new state as depicted by the state graphs in 3.3. The particular transitions may take place at any time and in theory even concurrently. In hardware experiments this trace is generally unknown, especially since the observability in hardware is much worse than in simulation where it is possible to monitor every signal, even internal ones. Hence for a reproducible fault injection in asynchronous circuits, it is vital to know the actual circuit trace. Otherwise, repetitive identical fault injections may lead to different results.

For a deterministic fault injection in asynchronous logic, the fault injection trigger has to be set on these signal events. Thereby the latency between the recognition of the trigger and the moment of the fault injection is critical. In synchronous logic, that latency must be smaller than a clock cycle so the fault will be present at the next clock edge – and thereby at the next state. In QDI logic, once a particular trace has been detected, it is generally arbitrary when the next signal transitions takes place. If a fault is injected in response to a trace or circuit state, it may happen that the next transition occurs before or just during the fault injection, which is not intended as it alters the current trace and thereby the behavior of the circuit. On the other hand, if the fault injector itself is a synchronous circuit it requires a synchronizer stage to process the asynchronous signal transition. The uncertainty of the synchronizer makes it nearly impossible to precisely control the moment of the fault injection as the recorded trace may differ from the real trace. Such effects have been identified in [63]. They add some unexpected noise to the fault injection scenario and require a more statistical fault evaluation.

Example 6.2.1: Fig. 6.5(a) shows a generic fault injection setup in a 2-bit QDI pipeline. Let's assume the circuit produces the expected trace $t_e = \{24\}$. A fault shall be injected on rail 3 after the first transition has been received and before the expected second transition on rail 4 arrives. That scenario is depicted in Fig. 6.5(b), with the intended faulty trace $t_f = \{2\overline{3}4\overline{3}\}$. That trace has a wrong phase prefix and may therefore lead to a token error in the receiver.

However, the fault injector will not be infinitely fast and propagation delays occur between the detection of a rail transition as well as the response of the fault injector, which has been highlighted by Δt identifiers. As long as these delays are smaller than the inherent skew Δs of the circuitry, the desired fault trace can be generated. However, if $\Delta t > \Delta s$ the fault injector will not be able to produce the desired fault trace as illustrated in Fig. 6.5(c). The delay until the fault is applied is too long and the expected transition occurs before the fault could be activated. The next stage receives the trace $t_3 = \{24\overline{33}\}$, which has the correct phase prefix. In this example, the fault has actually been transferred to the next handshake period. If it is short enough as shown in the waveform, it won't have any effect.

6. Emulation

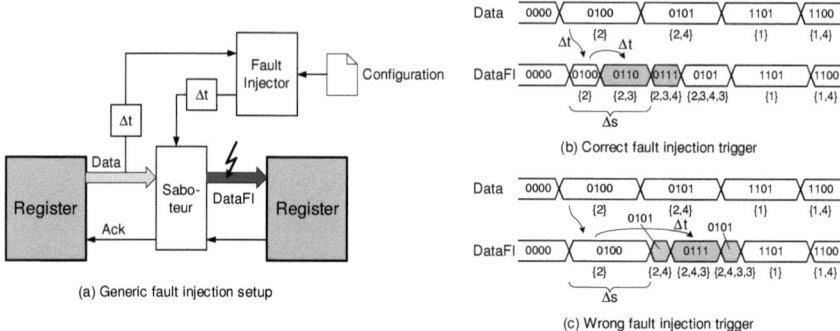

Figure 6.5: Trigger problem in QDI fault emulation

Although statistical investigations have their merits and shall exist in parallel, this work investigates how to obtain a reproducible environment, which has to take care of the trigger problem to aid a systematic validation of hardening strategies. One conclusion is that in QDI hardware fault injection, it is impossible to inject a fault in a specific state if the delay between the detection of the state (or more precisely the trace) and the time when the fault becomes active is longer than the minimum time between two arbitrary signal events on the subjected data path or signal. Since the delays are arbitrary in QDI logic and hence no lower bound on the distance between events can be given, such a fault injection method – detecting a trace and responding with a user-defined fault – will always fail.

6.3 The STEFAN Tool

To overcome the drawbacks presented in the previous subsection – consideration of error coverage and reproducibility – a novel tool for hardware based fault injection in QDI logic has been developed. The **S**ynthesizable **T**est **E**nvironment **F**or **A**synchronous **N**etworks (STEFAN) is not only able to control the logic value of a fault and the moment of its injection but also allows to control the circuit trace and thereby avoids the trigger problem in unbounded delay circuits.

6.3.1 Description of the Tool

Like the FOSTER tool presented in 5.3, the STEFAN tool was also written in TCL/Tk. That programming language was selected to ensure compatibility with the ModelSim simulator. That approach eases the debugging of the tool in the simulator

6.3. The STEFAN Tool

environment before the code is synthesized and programmed in the target hardware. As target, a Xilinx Virtex-4 FPGA (XC4VFX12-10FF668C) placed on an evaluation board from Memec was used. A functional block diagram of STEFAN is given by Fig. 6.6.

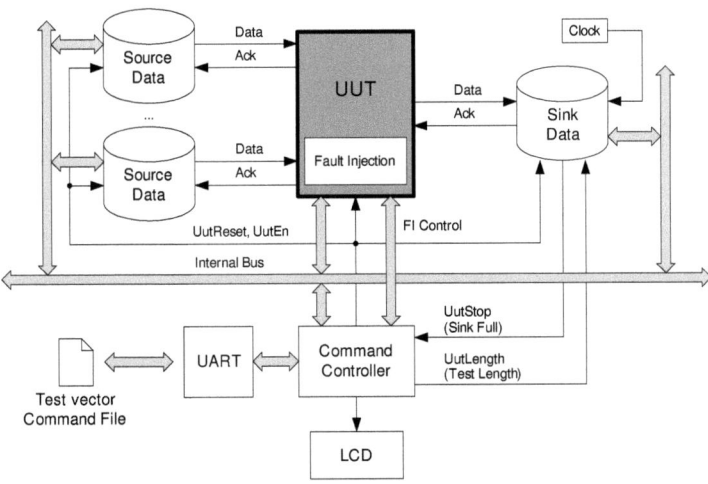

Figure 6.6: The STEFAN environment

The tool is operated via the USB from the PC. All components are attached to an internal bus that is handled by a command controller, which controls the complete application including the execution of test cases. Test data can be loaded into one or more source components. These sources are memories where test vectors can be written in single-rail logic. An integrated converter transforms that single-rail data into the appropriate dual-rail coded representation. The relevant output of the unit under test (UUT) is stored in one sink component. For this work only one common sink has been sufficient, however, the system can be easily extended due to the internal bus concept. The sink is designed as dual-rail memory and records the received data including code phase information and a time stamp in multiples of FPGA clock cycles. After all test vectors have been applied to the UUT, the sink is read out from the PC via an UART/USB bridge. That UART interface is the bottleneck in terms of speed, thus the concept does not allow arbitrary long test vectors to be processed in real-time. An interface with a higher throughput, e.g. PCI, would be needed to increase the performance of the emulation tool. Since the intention of STEFAN is only to proof the theory developed in this thesis rather than to be a competitive fault emulator, that drawback in throughput is accepted.

The architecture of STEFAN is generic and allows to operate common 4-phase dual-rail circuits as well as the FSL designs that are primarily investigated in this thesis. Other types of codes, such as generic 1-of-m codes or k-of-m codes are not supported. The

6. Emulation

architecture of STEFAN does not exclude these codes in principle, however, they require a modification of the source and sink memory structure.

To control STEFAN, a graphical user interface has been developed. Fig. 6.7(a) shows the main window of the application. Test vectors are defined in a command script. The fault injection setup can be defined via a command script as well or it can be entered manually. A list box displays any selected buffer memory of the tool such as source and sink data as depicted in Fig. 6.6. Two text boxes log the transmitted and received data from the target.

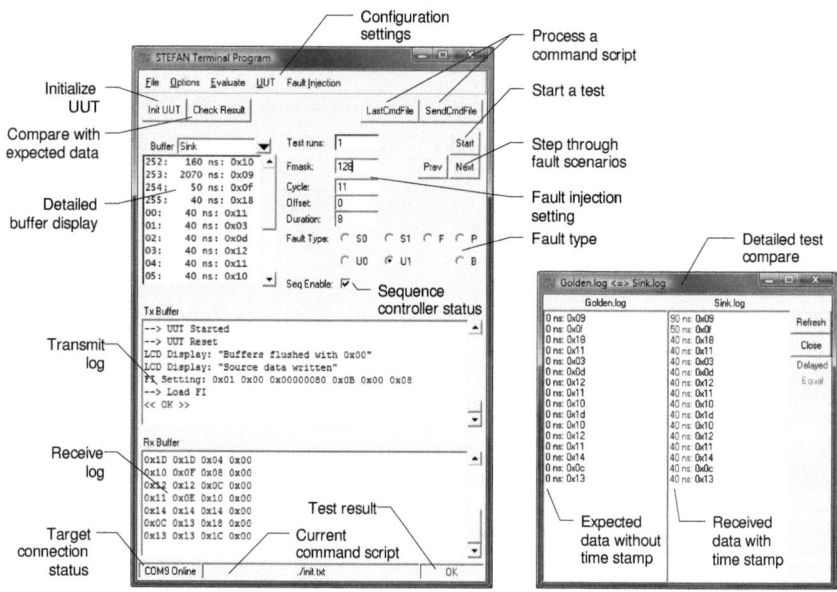

Figure 6.7: STEFAN graphical user interface

The tool supports user-defined as well as random fault injections. The command script also includes the expected results. After a test run, the received data is automatically compared with that expected data. Thereby the following results may occur:

- ERROR: At least one recorded token does not match the reference run.
- DEADLOCK: The number of recorded tokens does not match the expected length.
- DELAY: All tokens are equal to the reference run but at least one time stamp differs.
- OK: All tokens and all time stamps agree.

The result of a test run is immediately displayed on the main window. The user may also make a detailed comparison in the compare window as shown in Fig. 6.7(b), where the expected and received data are displayed side by side. The results of several test runs are logged in a separate log file. After a number of test runs, this log file is post processed to generate a failure statistics. Finally, the VHDL code of STEFAN can be loaded into a simulator, which accepts the same commanding syntax as the hardware. Thereby hardware tests can be compared with simulations.

6.3.2 A Versatile Saboteur

The key component of the STEFAN tool is the so called *versatile saboteur* (VS). A block diagram is shown in Fig. 6.8. The *VS* comprises three main elements:

- A *Sequence Controller* receives a token plus acknowledge and passes it to the output with a user-defined trace.

- The *Fault Injector* applies one or several faults into the reshuffled output of the sequence controller. The fault type, its duration and the moment of insertion are read from the internal bus of the STEFAN environment.

- The *Saboteur Process* eventually injects the fault and corrupts the selected rails.

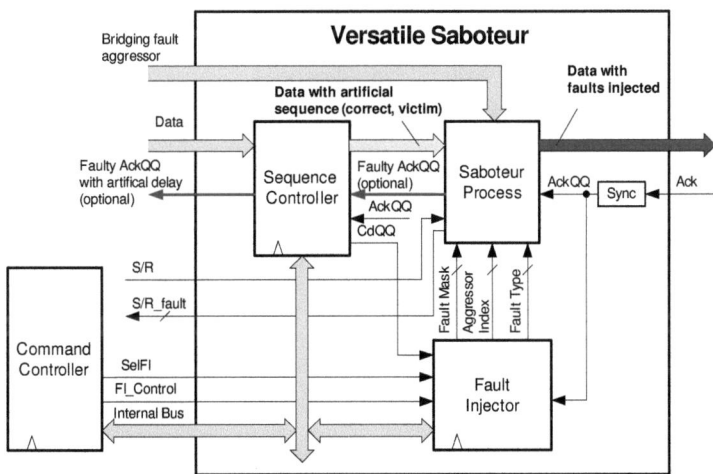

Figure 6.8: Block diagram of the versatile saboteur

The *VS* is configured by the STEFAN command controller via the internal bus of the test bench as depicted in Fig. 6.6. The *VS* can be placed at arbitrary positions of the

6. Emulation

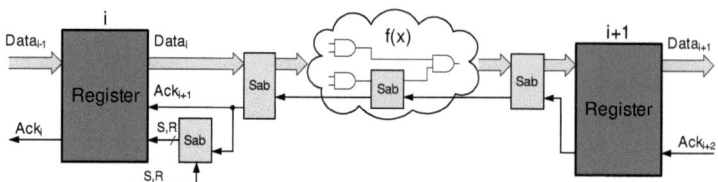

Figure 6.9: Placement of saboteurs

circuit. An example is shown in Fig. 6.9. These locations are the same as used for the description of the different fault effects in Fig. 3.8, see 3.4.2.

The sequence controller allows to reshuffle the transitions and thereby to define the circuit's trace. The block diagram and functional behavior in Fig. 6.10 illustrate the principle of operation. The sequence controller is based on a synchronous design. A state machine (FSM) checks whether a new token is received at the synchronized input $rDataIn$. In this case the first line of the configuration memory will be read. That memory is organized similar to the rail index notation that has been introduced in this thesis to describe a dual-rail code word. Each bit of that configuration is associated with one particular rail of the received token. The most significant bit of the configuration setting corresponds to rail index 1 and the least significant bit points to rail index N of an N-bit dual-rail signal. For example, a 4-bit dual rail sequence controller is organized as shown in Table 6.1.

Table 6.1: Sequence controller configuration

Config Bit	7	6	5	4	3	2	1	0
Rail Index	1	2	3	4	5	6	7	8
$rDataIn$	$(3)_a$	$(3)_b$	$(2)_a$	$(2)_b$	$(1)_a$	$(1)_b$	$(0)_a$	$(0)_b$

If a bit is set, the associated input rail will be passed to the output $rDataOut$, otherwise the old value of the rail is maintained. Listing 6.1 shows a snapshot of the VHDL code used in the sequence controller to illustrate that behavior.

Listing 6.1: VHDL design of the sequence controller configuration
```
for i in rDataOut'range loop
  if Config(i) = '1' then
    rDataOut(i) <= rDataIn(i);
  end if;
end loop;
```

To prevent deadlocking the circuitry, it has to be ensured that each expected rail transition is passed to the output. On the other hand, one can artificially delay a rail transition by setting the corresponding configuration bit to logic 0. The sequence controller in this thesis was designed 16-bit wide, i.e. a VS is capable to define the trace

6.3. The STEFAN Tool

of an 8-bit dual-rail signal. That size has been selected to limit the complexity of the implementation.

After reading a configuration line, the FSM waits for N clock cycles to check whether the actual output is acknowledged. Thereby the correspondence between the actual configuration and its impact is ensured. If no acknowledge is received, the next configuration is applied, otherwise the FSM waits for the next token. If all rails are enabled, the FSM returns to the initial state waiting for the next token. The N clock cycles are selected in such a way to ensure that each configuration is acknowledged before the next configuration is applied. The value of N depends on the worst case delay retrieved from the actual routing. The prototyping FPGA in this thesis runs with 100 MHz. Thereby one clock cycle delay has been analyzed as being sufficient to ensure the causality between a configuration setting and its associated acknowledge event.

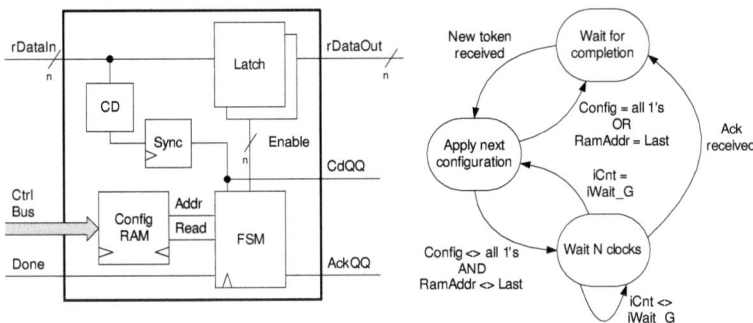

Figure 6.10: Sequence controller

No matter when the particular rail transitions are received at $rDataIn$, the output trace at $rDataOut$ will depend on the content of the configuration memory, which is user defined. One minor timing assumption remains: The theoretical unbounded delays between the output of the saboteur and the subsequent QDI circuit must not reorder the trace. This is prevented by the wait states between the configurations. As long as the practical delays are much shorter than these wait states no unintended reordering of the trace will take place.

Example 6.3.1: Fig. 6.11 shows how each rail of a 2-bit QDI signal $rDataIn$ is enabled by its associated bit in the configuration memory. The natural input trace is $t_{in} = \{14\}$, which corresponds to the sequence $rDataIn = \{0000; 1000; 1001\}$ as shown in the top waveform. In Fig. 6.11(a) a running 1 pattern enables each rail starting from rail index 4 down to 1. The first configuration '0000' disables all rails. The next setting '0001', enables rail 4 and generates the output $\langle 0001 \rangle$. The next three settings have no impact until the setting '1111' completes the output to $\langle 1001 \rangle$. The depicted configuration setting has modified the output trace to $t_{out} = \{41\}$ as

179

6. Emulation

shown in the bottom waveform. The end effect is not only a reversal of the trace but also an increase in the inconsistent time between the two code phases as $\Delta t_2 > \Delta t_1$. Fig. 6.11(b) shows a more arbitrary configuration pattern. In this example, $t_{out} \equiv t_{in}$. The only effect is a longer intermediate inconsistent phase due to the synchronized operation of the sequence controller, i.e. $\Delta t_2 > \Delta t_1$ still applies.

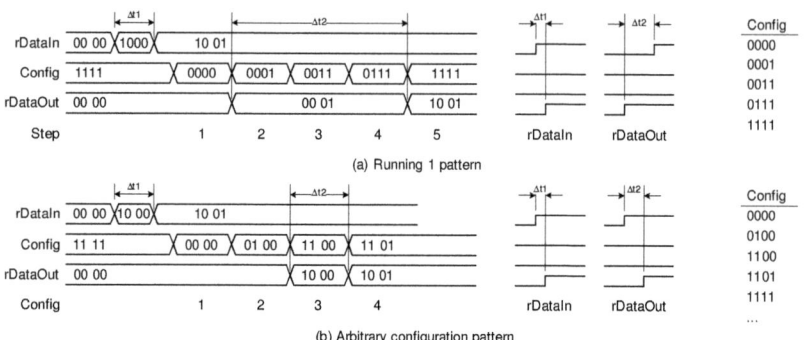

Figure 6.11: Example of trace modification by the sequence controller

In principle, the sequence controller converts the asynchronous QDI circuit trace in a synchronous state sequence. That conversion is valid, since synchronous circuits are covered by the unbounded delay model of QDI. That conversion also ensures the reproducibility, as the traces are now synchronized and the time of the next transition is not arbitrary anymore but well defined. Unfortunately, that approach reduces the performance of the circuitry as it prolongs the duration of the inconsistent state between the two code phases. Further, the maximum clock frequency of the sequence controller defines the minimum delay between two transitions. There is the possibility to excite several rails at once by setting more than one bit in the configuration line. Such a concurrent excitement will lead to an arbitrary trace, which should be avoided by the sequence controller. The FPGA used in this thesis runs at 100 MHz, i.e. the minimum amount of time between two transitions is 10 ns. It was tried to reduce the granularity by designing delay lines. Unfortunately, the used Virtex-4 FPGA only has dedicated tapped delay lines for its input ports. For internal delay lines, the timing reports have shown possible delays in the order of 5 ns, i.e. half a clock cycle. Since the reduction in granularity is not as much as expected, no further effort was spent on designing a fine grain delay line. The synchronized concept is sufficient to show the ideas of the versatile saboteur concept.

The fault injector receives a complete fault scenario including fault type, moment of injection and duration from the internal bus of the test bench. As QDI circuits are not bound to timing constraints, the moment of the fault injection is defined as a specific

6.3. The STEFAN Tool

number of handshake cycles after the start of the application. To allow a more detailed tuning, the fault injector allows to specify an offset in terms of application clock cycles within the injection handshake cycle. The fault duration is also specified in multiples of application clock cycles.

The fault injector is synchronized to the sequence controller, so the injection of a fault and the generation of a particular trace are well defined. Up to 32 victim rails can be subjected to the same type of fault. The fault injector allows to model stuck-at 0/1 faults, bit flip faults, pulse faults and bridging faults.

The saboteur process reads the output of the fault injector and eventually corrupts the selected rails according to the fault type. Stuck-at faults simply force the selected rail to the intended logic state. Bit flip faults invert the actual logic state. Like stuck-at faults, bit flip faults are generated by a simple combinational saboteur. Bit-flip faults are popular to model transient faults as they invert the logic value of the victim signal and avoid the masking effect of stuck-at faults. However, the simple inversion of the fault-free signal is not a good physical representation of a transient fault, since each transition of the fault-free signal within the fault duration is inverted as well. Therefore, the pulse model [64] is preferred as it maintains the faulty value for the complete fault duration and ignores any intermediate transitions of the victim. The pulse model is easy to simulate by using the `force` command in the simulator. In hardware, this fault model requires a more complex saboteur that includes a state holding element to preserve the inverted faulty state for the complete fault duration. Finally, to emulate bridging faults, the saboteur reads an aggressor index that replaces the selected victim signal by an aggressor signal.

Example 6.3.2: Let's assume a 2-bit FSL circuit with a fault-free data sequence as shown in the top signal D_{orig} of Fig. 6.12. The fault injector is set up to inject a stuck-at 1 fault on rail index 3 in handshake cycle number 2 with offset 1. The fault duration is 4 application clock cycles. The fault completes the code phase transition and leads to the wrong new token $D_{fault} = \langle 11\bar{1}1 \rangle$, which may be captured by the receiver provided it is ready for new data. In that example, it is assumed that the token error is blocked, thus after the fault has vanished the expected token $D_{fault} = \langle 1100 \rangle$ is applied to the receiver, which is captured and acknowledged.

Beside the constraint to adjust the sequence of the rail transitions only in multiples of application clock cycles, the fault duration is subjected to the same limitation as well, which forms another drawback of the emulation approach compared to fault simulations. In general, emulation does not provide that high level of insight as well as the adjustment capabilities that are offered by simulation. To reduce these disadvantages the approach to stick to a synchronized fault injection can be replaced by a pure asynchronous method where the fault duration is defined by e.g. delay lines to allow shorter transients.

Despite these drawbacks, the reproducible fault injection of the STEFAN tool by means of controlling the circuit trace is helpful in a systematic verification of hardening

6. Emulation

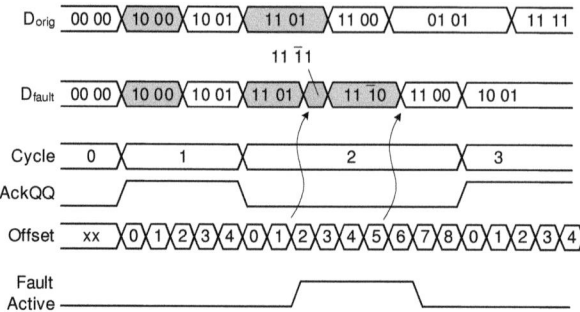

Figure 6.12: Example of the Fault Injector

methods. The higher speed of hardware based fault emulation allows to test a higher number of fault scenarios than a simulation based approach. Of course, a high-speed data interface is mandatory to take advantage of these benefits.

This work focuses on presenting a new hardware based fault injection method, which takes care on systematics and reproducibility. The application of the STEFAN tool is limited to the fault testing of a specific test circuit, which is presented in 6.4. A more detailed investigation as well as testing several circuit types and hardening methods would go beyond the scope of this thesis and is left for future research.

6.3.3 Usage

The STEFAN tool requires a synthesized design under test with versatile saboteurs placed at the desired locations. A unique address is assigned to each saboteur for commanding. The test vectors, the saboteur configuration and the expected result are provided in a command script. The syntax of such a command script is shown in Listing 6.2 and explained by comments. Especially the setup of the sequence controller shall be highlighted, which is defined as `WrBuf 6, 0xFC 0xFC 0xFC 0xFC 0xFF`. According to Table 6.1, that setting will delay the two least significant rails of the controlled data vector during the first four configurations (0xFC). Only in the fifth configuration (0xFF) all rails will be enabled to be passed to the output of the sequence controller.

6.3. The STEFAN Tool

Listing 6.2: Example of a STEFAN command script

```
—  Command file for STEFAN
—
—  WrBuf <Buffer>, <Data1> <Data2> ... <DataN> ... write buffer
—  RdBuf <Buffer>, <No of bytes to read> ... read buffer
—  SetLengh <Tokens> ... number of tokens to be processed in sink
—  Reset      ... reset UUT, after re-lease the UUT is stopped
—  Start      ... start a test
—  Exp <Length> <Byte0 Byte1 ... ByteN>
```

Reset
— *Fill the source buffer with test data, others use default setting*
WrBuf 0, 0x3 0x3 0xA 0xA 0x7 0x7 0xD 0xD 0xE 0xE 0xB 0xB 0x5 0x5
— *define the configuration setting for saboteur #6*
WrBuf 6, 0xFC 0xFC 0xFC 0xFF
— *define the length of the test and start it*
SetLength 14
Start
— *read the recorded data*
RdBuf 1, 64
— *define expected response for comparison*
—   *Length Bit0   1   2   3   4   5   6   7   8   9   10 11 12 13*
Exp: 0xE   0x0 0x0 0x7 0x8 0x7 0x7 0x7 0x9 0x9 0xC 0xC 0xC 0xF 0xF

The fault injection setup is input via the main window shown in Fig. 6.7 and internally defined as 72-bit structure. The particular fields of this structure are explained in Table 6.2. The injection setup defines fault type, duration and moment of occurrence as well as whether the fault shall be applied on the output of sequence controller or on the natural input data of the versatile saboteur. At the heart of that structure is a 32-bit fault mask that collects all data rails and acknowledge signals that eventually will be disturbed. The size of that structure has been selected for a moderately complex implementation. It can be resized according to the needs of the application.

To show the operation of the STEFAN tool and to test the efficiency of the different hardening methods from 4.4 in real hardware, a realistic application was used. For that purpose, a small portion of the video pre-processing algorithm of the GAIA space telescope has been implemented in FSL and subjected to transient fault injections.

6. Emulation

Table 6.2: Configuration of a fault injection scenario

Field	Reserved	SabEn	Reserved	SeqEn	Type	Reserved	Aindex	Fmask	Cycle	Offset	Duration
#Bit	1	1	1	1	4	3	5	32	8	8	8

Field	Function
Reserved	don't care
SabEn	0 ... Bypass the saboteur (general saboteur disable)
	1 ... Pass data via the saboteur
Reserved	don't care
SeqEn	0 ... Use the natural input data of the versatile saboteur
	1 ... Use the data after the sequence controller
Type	Fault type. Applied on all rails enabled in *Fmask*
	0000 ... no fault is injected (victim = expected data)
	0001 ... stuck-0 (victim forced to 0)
	0010 ... stuck-1 (victim forced to 1)
	0011 ... bit flip (invert victim rails)
	0100 ... pulse fault (victim forced to the inverted state at the injection moment)
	0101 ... bridging fault (victim forced to aggressor rail defined in *Aindex*)
	0110 to 1111 ... not used
Reserved	don't care
Aindex	Aggressor index. This setting only becomes effective if a bridging fault is applied (*Type* = 0101). It determines, which rail of the aggressor signal replaces the victim rails defined by *Fmask*.
Fmask	Fault mask. Determines the rail that is subjected to the fault injection. Each pair of 2 consecutive bits form a dual-rail signal in the form $D(n)_a, D(n)_b, ..., D(1)_a, D(1)_b$. For example 0x0010 will select $D(2)_b$.
Cycle	Determines the handshake cycle where the fault is applied, e.g. *Cycle* = 0x48 means the fault will be applied after 72 transitions of the synchronized acknowledge signals upon release of the reset.
Offset	Determines the exact time instant of the fault injection in terms of clock events after *Cycle* has been reached. In case *Offset*=0 the fault injection will take place immediately after the acknowledge event has been detected.
Duration	Defines the fault duration in multiples of clock cycles. If *Duration*=0 the fault will be applied permanently.

6.4 Application: The GAIA Video Pre-Processing Algorithm

6.4.1 The GAIA Mission

The *Global Astrometric Interferometer for Astrophysics* (GAIA) is a scientific mission of the *European Space Agency* (ESA) that is scheduled for launch in 2012 [126]. The mission places a large telescope at the Lissajous-type orbit around L2 to generate a precise three-dimensional map of our Galaxy. The *Video Processing Unit* (VPU) provides one of the central functions in GAIA. It pre-processes the digital data acquired by a large CCD array before it will be transmitted to Earth for the final analysis.

6.4.2 The GAIA Pre-Processing Algorithm

For performance reasons and due to the lack of an adequate, powerful space compatible processor, the various tasks in the GAIA VPU have been divided into hardware and software based algorithms. The following information is retrieved from the official invitation to tender for the VPU and is provided by courtesy of ESA and the prime contractor EADS Astrium [127]. A block diagram of the hardware algorithms in the GAIA VPU is shown in Fig. 6.13. For this thesis, a small portion of that algorithm, namely the preprocessing of the star mapper samples was selected, which is encircled in the figure.

The task of the star mapper preprocessing is to identify the particular stars within the huge amount of data provided by the CCD. A more detailed view of the algorithm is shown in Fig. 6.14. Although it only comprises a small portion of the complete VPU algorithms, the star mapper preprocessing already includes all typical functions used in signal processing applications, such as saturation checks, multiplication, addition, feedback filters, etc. Actually, it is composed of two main functions:

1. A linear correction checks for saturated values and applies column response and dark signal non-uniformity correction.

2. A dead column correction performs a simple neighbor interpolation for samples coming from pixels that are marked as dead.

The linear correction takes the raw samples *UNPREPRO_DATA[ac]* and compares them with a saturation level *SATURATION_LUT[ac]* for each CCD row *ac*. If the sample is saturated, it is replaced by the constant *SATURATED*. Otherwise a linear function correcting the *Dark Signal Non Uniformity* (DSNU) and the *CCD Column Response Non Uniformity* (CRNU) (both are parameters of the CCD) is applied:

6. Emulation

```
if UNPREPRO_DATA[ac] > SATURATION_LUT[ac]
    PREPRO_DATA[ac] = SATURATED
else
    crnu[ac] = trunc(UNPREPRO_DATA[ac] * CRNU_LUT[ac],15)
    dsnu[ac] = sat(crnu[ac],16) + DSNU_LUT[ac]
    PREPRO_DATA[ac] = sat(dsnu[ac],16)
end
```

The truncation operator $Y = \mathrm{trunc}(X, n)$ eliminates the n less significant bits of the input X and the saturation operator $Y = \mathrm{sat}(X, n)$ limits the input X to $2^n - 1$.

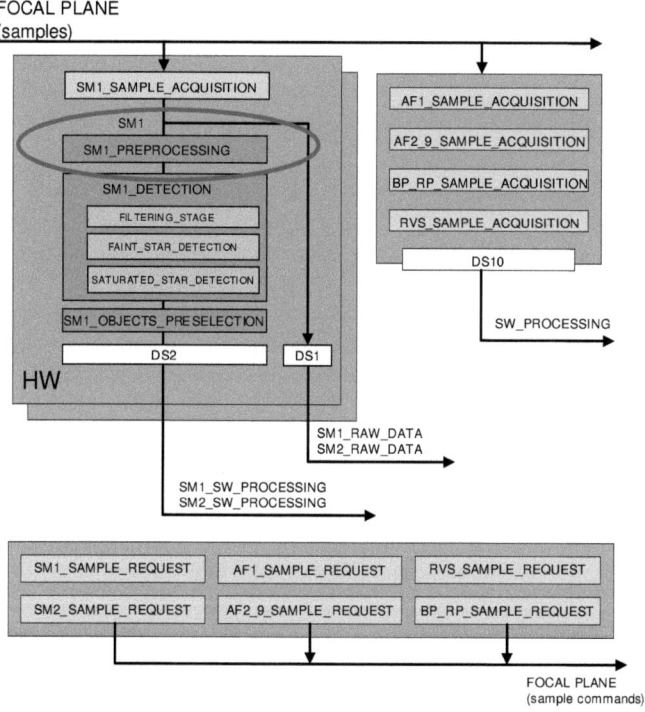

Figure 6.13: GAIA VPU hardware algorithms

The dead column correction performs a neighborhood interpolation as illustrated in Table 6.3. Dead columns are marked for each sample index ac in a separate buffer $DEAD\_LUT$. If an index is considered as unreliable, a '1' is written to the corresponding buffer location, while a '0' declares the index as correct. The algorithm takes the dead column marking of the current as well as the two previous samples $DEAD\_LUT[ac\text{-}2, ac\text{-}1, ac]$ and modifies the linear corrected samples $PREPRO\_DATA$ accordingly.

6.4. Application: The GAIA Video Pre-Processing Algorithm

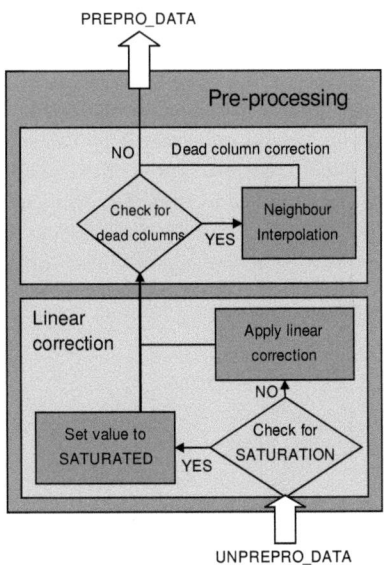

Figure 6.14: Principle of hardware pre-processing

Table 6.3: Principle of dead column correction

DEAD_LUT			PREPRO_DATA	
DL[ac-2]	DL[ac-1]	DL[ac]	PREPRO_DATA[ac-1]	PREPRO_DATA[ac]
0	0	0	Unchanged	Unchanged
0	0	1	Unchanged	PREPRO_DATA[ac-1]
0	1	0	(PREPRO_DATA[ac-2]+ PREPRO_DATA[ac])/2	Unchanged
0	1	1	PREPRO_DATA[ac-2]	Unchanged
1	0	0	Unchanged	Unchanged
1	0	1	Unchanged	PREPRO_DATA[ac-1]
1	1	0	PREPRO_DATA[ac]	Unchanged
1	1	1	Unchanged	Unchanged

6.4.3 FSL Implementation

The preprocessing is very well suited for a pipelined structure. According to [127], the un-preprocessed input data are 16-bit samples and the VPU has to process 983 rows within a period of 1 ms. To limit the complexity for the implementation in this thesis, the data width has been reduced to 4-bit and the memory size has been reduced to 64 rows. Both parameters are just a matter of scale.

6. Emulation

The linear correction in FSL is shown in Fig. 6.15. The circuit consists of a three stage pipeline. In the first stage $R1$, the saturation check is performed. Each raw sample $UNPREPRO[ac]$ is compared with the corresponding entry $SATURATION\_LUT[ac]$. The result of this check and the raw input data are stored in register $R1$. The second stage performs the column non-uniformity correction. The raw input $UNPREPRO[ac]$ is multiplied by $CRNU\_LUT[ac]$, truncated and limited to 4-bit. The result is stored in stage $R2$ together with the saturation information from the previous stage, which simply accompanies the data. The third stage adds the dark non-uniformity correction $DSNU\_LUT[ac]$ and limits the result to 4-bit. Depending on the saturation check performed in the first stage, either the result of the DSNU correction or the constant $SATURATE$ is stored in register $R3$.

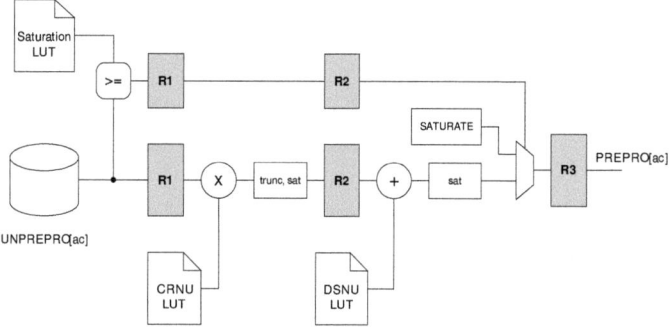

Figure 6.15: Implementation of the linear correction

The dead column correction is depicted in Fig. 6.16. This algorithm is more complex as the output depends on previous samples. Since the circuit uses feedback elements, phase inverters have to be deployed to ensure that all input data is applied in the correct code phase. See [46] for a detailed treatment of how to design non-linear FSL circuits. The dead column correction requires two pipeline stages $R4$ and $R5$, which hold $PREPRO[ac\text{-}1]$ and $PREPRO[ac\text{-}2]$, respectively. The input value to these registers depends on the content of the dead column look-up table, which is used to select the appropriate input via multiplexers.

6.4.4 Emulation of the GAIA Algorithm

The GAIA algorithm is emulated using the STEFAN tool. Thereby versatile saboteurs (*VS*) are placed at different locations of the circuit. The fault sensitivity is then tested for both a plain unhardened circuitry as well as for a DRXS hardened version.

Before the detailed test results are presented, the operation of the STEFAN tool and the *VS* is illustrated in more detail. Therefore, a *VS* has been placed at the output

6.4. Application: The GAIA Video Pre-Processing Algorithm

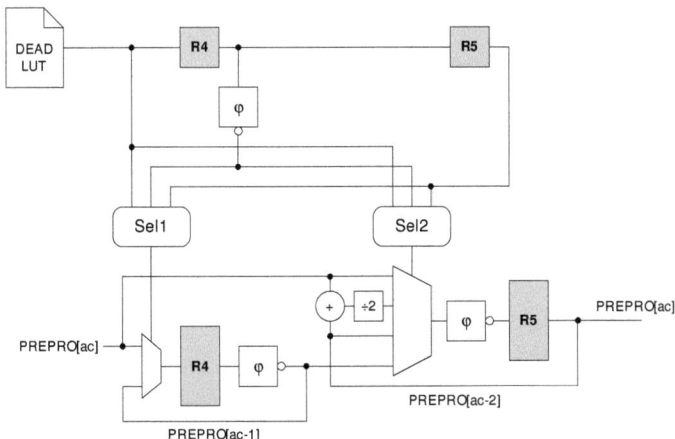

Figure 6.16: Implementation of the dead column correction

of the linear correction ($R3$), see Fig. 6.15. The command script used to test the circuit has already been presented in Listing 6.2. Fig. 6.17(a) shows the result with a stuck-at 0 fault applied to $PREPRO(1).b$. That fault accelerated the execution but it did not lead to a wrong result as the disturbed b-rail was anyhow expected to switch to logic 0. Fig. 6.17(b) shows the result with a bit flip fault applied to $PREPRO(0).b$. That fault did not lead to an expected transition and instead of the expected result sequence {0x0;0x0;0x7;0x8;0x7;...} the circuit captured {0x0;0x0;$\overline{0x6}$;0x8;0x7;...}, i.e. a token error did occur. The figure shows another user interface of the STEFAN tool, which provides two buffer listings on the main window instead of the fault injection controls. The readings of the sink buffer clearly show the expected result for the stuck-at-0 fault and the wrong result for the bit-flip fault.

To explain the operation of this hardware fault injection in more detail, the simulation interface of the STEFAN tool was used. Thereby, the GAIA circuitry was simulated with the same fault injection settings as depicted in Fig. 6.18. As described in Listing 6.2, the sequence controller delays the two least significant rails of $PREPRO$ by using the configuration FC. The next stage circuit $R4$ has to wait until all rails are enabled, which is signalled by the configuration FF, until the code phase can be completed. The operation of the sequence controller and the mapping of a particular rail index to a bit in the configuration is explained in Table 6.1 and Fig. 6.11. During the delayed state, the bit-flip fault was injected onto $PREPRO(0).b$. That fault completes the code phase and corrupts the output to $rDataOut=\langle 01, 10, 10, \overline{01}\rangle$=0x6 instead of the expected value $rDataOut=\langle 01, 10, 10, 10\rangle$=0x7. Without any fault applied, the artificial delay introduced by the sequence controller solely delays the execution of the circuit as shown at the right end of the waveform. If no fault is injected, the output data $rDataOut$ is delayed, but

6. Emulation

identical to the input data *rDataIn*.

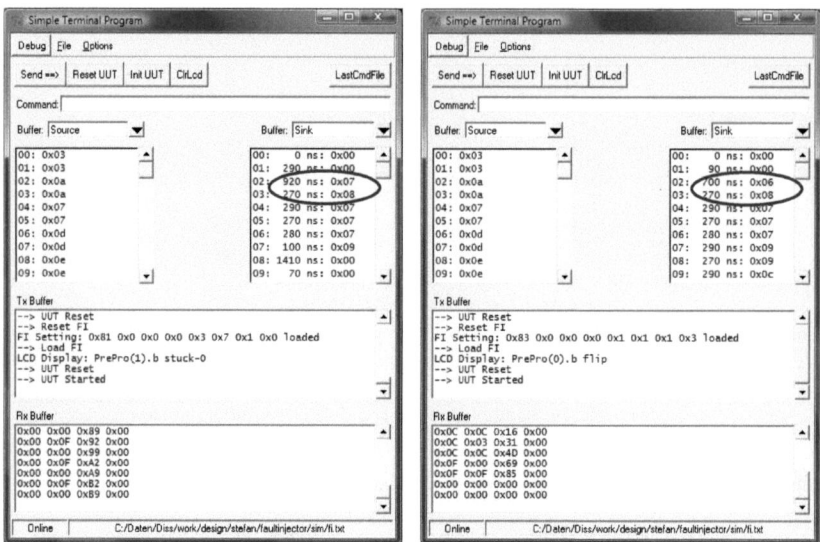

(a) Rejection of stuck-at 0 fault   (b) Error due to bit-flip 1 fault

Figure 6.17: Example of a token error emulation

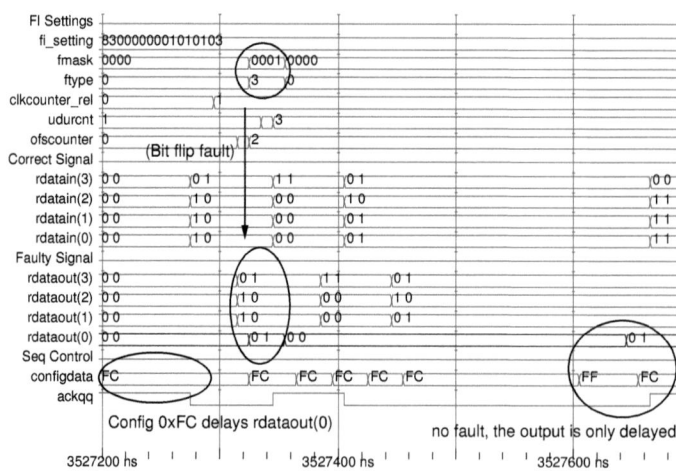

Figure 6.18: Generation of a token error by means of a transient fault

190

6.4. Application: The GAIA Video Pre-Processing Algorithm

Fig. 6.19 shows the fault emulation setup of the GAIA algorithm. The versatile saboteur $VS7$ was placed at the lower 4-bit output of $R1$ and the saboteur $VS13$ was placed at the lower 4-bit output of $R4$. The sequence controller in these saboteurs was setup using 4 different configurations: {FF00;FFFF}, {FFF0;FFFF}, {FFFC;FFFF} and {FFFF}. The objective of these configurations is to differently delay particular rail transitions and thereby to generate different traces and a different fault sensitivity. For each setting, 1000 random fault injection runs were performed using 5 different, randomly selected stimuli for all LUTs in the circuit. Each stimuli had a length of 16 entries. In total, 5000 fault injection runs were performed with $VS7$ and $VS13$, respectively. Thereby only one saboteur was activated.

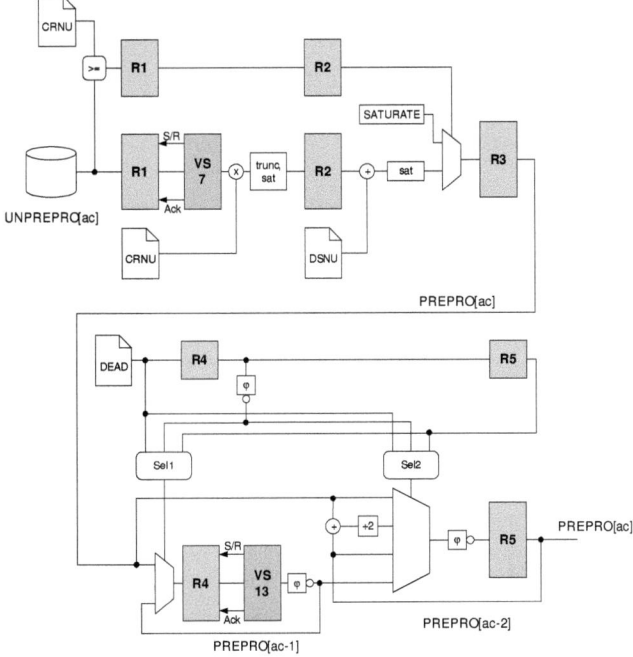

Figure 6.19: Fault emulation setup of the GAIA algorithm

Table 6.4 presents the first fault injection campaign using the unprotected GAIA test circuitry. The individual results of each saboteur and the average numbers are presented for each of the four sequence controller settings. The columns have to be interpreted as follows:

"VS" labels the saboteur (7, 13 or average of these two), "Seq" describes the sequence controller setting that has been used in that scenario. "OK" contains the per-

6. Emulation

centage of correct results. "Deadlock" collects all runs that have stopped the circuitry without producing erroneous data. "Errors" shows the relative number of emulation runs that produced wrong data at the GAIA output $PREPRO[ac]$, independent whether the expected number of data was recorded or whether the wrong data occurred together with a deadlock. "SEU" marks all runs that inject a stuck-at fault into the set/reset input of any rail latch of the associated register. "SEUD" and "SEUE" show the percentage of such fault injections that lead to a deadlock and wrong data, respectively. "SET" marks all runs that inject a stuck-at fault into the data path the saboteur is attached to. Thereby the acknowledge signal is also considered as victim signal. "SETD" and "SETE" show the percentage of such data path faults that lead to a deadlock and wrong data, respectively.

Table 6.4: Fault sensitivity of the GAIA test circuit

VS	Seq	OK	Deadlocks	Errors	SEU	SEUD	SEUE	SET	SETD	SETE
7	FF00	77.6%	17.2%	5.2%	49.0%	17.2%	2.4%	51.0%	0.0%	2.8%
	FFF0	85.4%	10.6%	4.1%	51.4%	10.6%	1.9%	48.6%	0.0%	2.2%
	FFFC	91.3%	4.7%	4.0%	50.5%	4.7%	1.8%	49.5%	0.0%	2.2%
	FFFF	97.7%	0.5%	1.8%	49.8%	0.2%	0.6%	50.2%	0.34%	1.1%
13	FF00	76.3%	18.0%	5.7%	50.2%	17.2%	2.5%	49.8%	0.88%	3.1%
	FFF0	87.0%	9.3%	3.6%	50.9%	8.6%	2.2%	49.1%	0.76%	1.5%
	FFFC	91.8%	4.0%	4.3%	49.7%	3.1%	2.5%	50.3%	0.82%	1.7%
	FFFF	97.3%	1.7%	1.0%	49.2%	1.2%	0.3%	50.8%	0.44%	0.7%
Average	FF00	76.9%	17.6%	5.4%	49.6%	17.2%	2.5%	50.4%	0.44%	3.0%
	FFF0	86.2%	9.9%	3.9%	51.2%	9.6%	2.0%	48.8%	0.38%	1.8%
	FFFC	91.5%	4.3%	4.1%	50.1%	3.9%	2.2%	49.9%	0.41%	2.0%
	FFFF	97.5%	1.1%	1.4%	49.5%	0.7%	0.5%	50.5%	0.39%	0.9%

The separate evaluation of faults that were injected into the set/reset input of the register latches and the data path stems from their different behavior with respect to deadlocks. In fact, transient faults on the set/reset input of the register latches did trigger the majority of deadlocks, while transient faults on the data path triggered much less deadlocks. The number of deadlocks is highly influenced by the setting of the sequence controller. A closer examination by means of simulating a fault injection scenario has shown that (i) the design of the sequence controller and (ii) the number of disabled rails determine the affinity to deadlocks.

It was shown that a transient fault in a register latch will upset the latch and generate a soft error. Using the definitions from 3.4.3, such an error may lead to a $T(-1)$ token if it affects a delayed rail and suppresses its transition, which is illustrated by an example.

Example 6.4.1: Fig. 6.20 shows a simulation that deadlocks due to a register upset. The register output of $R1$ is $rdataout = \langle 00, 00, 11, 00, 11, 00 \rangle$. The lower 4 dual-rail bits are passed to the sequence controller, which applies the configuration FFFC.

6.4. Application: The GAIA Video Pre-Processing Algorithm

First, it passes the inconsistent token $rfiout0 = \langle 11, 00, 11, 01 \rangle$ and delays the least significant bit 00. In this state a transient fault hits $set(0)$ and generates the inconsistent $R1$ output $rdataout = \langle 00, 00, 11, 00, 11, 0\overline{1} \rangle$. The next configuration of the sequence controller is FFFF, which will pass all $rdataout$ signals to the next stage, so $rfiout0 = \langle 11, 00, 11, 0\overline{1} \rangle$. The transition on the least significant bit is still missing, eventually generating a deadlock as it produces a $T(-1)$ token.

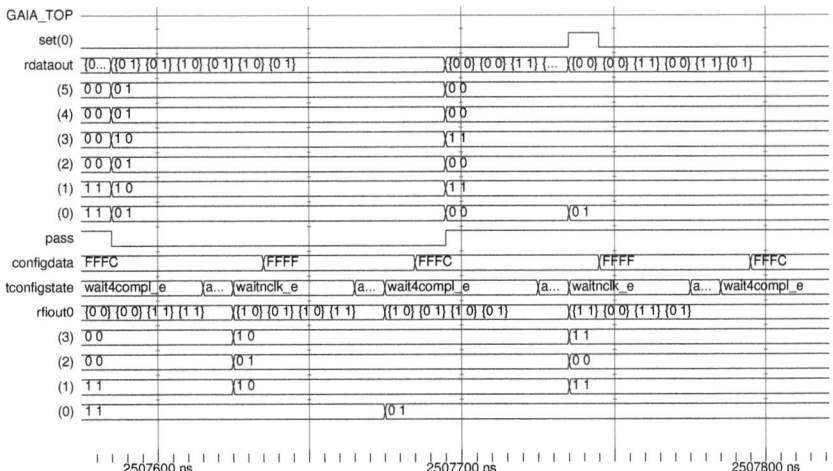

Figure 6.20: Deadlock due to hitting a delayed rail

The number of delayed bits is defined by the sequence controller configuration. For instance, {FFF0;FFFF} already delays the least 2 significant bits, i.e. the chance to hit one of this delayed rails in an error case is much higher than for {FFFE;FFFF}, which only delays the least significant rail. On the other hand, if the upset hits a rail that has already been enabled in the first iteration, the fault may generate a $T(+1)$ token if it hits a rail that is not expected to switch in the current code phase. Thereby, it depends on the local timings how such a token resolves.

Example 6.4.2: In Fig. 6.21, the simulation from Fig. 6.20 is repeated, but now a transient fault is injected on $clear(3)$. The output of $R1$ is modified to $rdataout = \langle 00, 00, 11, 00, 11, 00 \rangle \rightarrow \langle 00, 00, 11, 00, \overline{0}1, 00 \rangle$. That inconsistent token is stopped at the sequence controller until it applies the next configuration and generates the output transition $rfiout0 = \langle 10, 01, 10, 01 \rangle \rightarrow \langle 11, 00, 11, 01 \rangle \rightarrow \langle 11, 00, \overline{0}1, 00 \rangle$. The subsequent circuit stage sees two transitions on $rfiout0(1)$, which corresponds to a $T(+1)$ token. In the current simulation, the subsequent circuit stage resolves that hazard and processes the correct token $rfiout0 = \langle 11, 00, 11, 00 \rangle$. However, not all

193

6. Emulation

such $T(+1)$ tokens resolve to the correct data, some produce wrong data while others produce a deadlock.

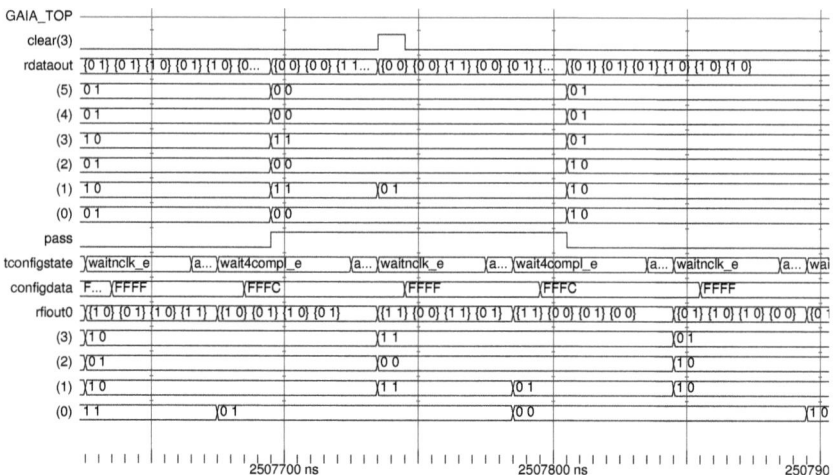

Figure 6.21: No deadlock due to sequence controller setting

Finally, the faults were randomly but uniformly applied at register level. Thus the number of faults that affect a register latch is approximately the same as the number of faults that are applied to the data path. In reality, the number of circuit nodes that contribute to the column "SEU" is less than the number of nodes that can be assigned to column "SET", since the register latches comprise only a few gates while the data path typically comprises complex combinational functions. Taking into account solely the faults on the data path provides a more realistic estimate of the overall fault tolerance. Regarding only the data path faults, the unhardened GAIA circuit showed an average fault tolerance between 0.9% and 3.0%. From all sequence controller configurations {FFFF} will be the most realistic one, i.e. the 0.39% deadlocks and 0.9% data errors are regarded as realistic property of the unhardened GAIA circuit within this fault emulation configuration.

Table 6.5 shows the results from fault injection campaign with a DRXS hardened GAIA circuitry. Thereby the same input stimulus and sequence controller settings as for the unhardened tests were used. The saboteurs $VS7$ and $VS13$ were placed at the same location as shown in Fig. 6.19. However, their scope was limited to the nominal path of the cross-coupled circuit and the faults were only injected into the nominal data path as well as into the nominal set/reset inputs of the register latches. That limitation has been performed for simplicity. Placing the saboteurs on the redundant path will lead to the same results.

6.4. Application: The GAIA Video Pre-Processing Algorithm

Regarding the number of deadlocks, no improvement with respect to the unhardened GAIA test circuit was observed. That is not unexpected, as nearly all deadlocks were triggered by upsets in the set/reset inputs of the subjected register latches (column "SEUD"). The DRXS cannot mitigate these deadlocks as the violate the fundamental handshake property of QDI circuits. However, no emulation run produced any wrong data, independent whether the fault was applied to the register latches or directly to the data path.

Looking at the most realistic sequence {FFFF}, the DRXS hardened GAIA circuit had only 0.01% deadlocks and 0.0% data errors for all data path faults. The improvement compared to the unhardened circuit is significant. The DRXS method is regarded as being fault tolerant with respect to the investigated implementation and the applied boundary conditions via the saboteurs, the circuit topology, the target platform, etc. A general fault tolerance cannot be assumed as the DRXS method has limitations with respect to $T(+1)$ as derived in chapter 4 and also confirmed by means of fault simulation in chapter 5.

Table 6.5: Fault sensitivity of the GAIA test circuit using DRXS

VS	Seq	OK	Deadlocks	Errors	SEU	SEUD	SEUE	SET	SETD	SETE
7	FF00	85.0%	15.0%	0.0%	51.4%	14.8%	0.0%	48.6%	0.22%	0.0%
	FFF0	91.5%	8.5%	0.0%	49.8%	8.3%	0.0%	50.2%	0.24%	0.0%
	FFFC	96.4%	3.6%	0.0%	49.7%	3.5%	0.0%	50.3%	0.06%	0.0%
	FFFF	100.0%	0.0%	0.0%	48.4%	0.0%	0.0%	51.6%	0.00%	0.0%
13	FF00	81.7%	18.3%	0.0%	50.0%	18.0%	0.0%	50.0%	0.30%	0.0%
	FFF0	90.3%	9.7%	0.0%	50.8%	9.4%	0.0%	49.2%	0.34%	0.0%
	FFFC	95.2%	4.8%	0.0%	49.8%	4.8%	0.0%	50.2%	0.00%	0.0%
	FFFF	99.4%	0.6%	0.0%	49.7%	0.6%	0.0%	50.3%	0.02%	0.0%
Average	FF00	83.3%	16.7%	0.0%	50.7%	16.4%	0.0%	49.3%	0.26%	0.0%
	FFF0	90.9%	9.1%	0.0%	50.3%	8.8%	0.0%	49.7%	0.29%	0.0%
	FFFC	95.8%	4.2%	0.0%	49.7%	4.2%	0.0%	50.3%	0.03%	0.0%
	FFFF	99.7%	0.3%	0.0%	49.0%	0.3%	0.0%	51.0%	0.01%	0.0%

Table 6.6 shows the results with a DRXX hardened GAIA test circuit. Looking at the total number of deadlocks shows a comparable performance as with the DRXS method. However, the deadlocks due to transient faults on the data path (column "SETD") are significantly reduced compared to DRXS. In principle, that is exactly the predicted difference between DRXS and DRXX, as described in 4.4.5 based on theoretic assumptions. The DRXX method is able to reduce the number of deadlocks due to data path faults, while it does not yield any improvement for deadlocks that are generated by register upsets due to direct hits. As for the DRXS runs, no wrong data was observed in any run.

Table 6.7 presents the results of a DRS hardened GAIA test circuit. Again, the number of deadlocks due to direct transient faults in the register latches remains approximately the same as for the DRXS and DRXX method. As predicted, the DRS method cannot reduce the sensitivity to deadlocks when the fault directly hits a register latch. However, contrary to the previous methods, none of the data path faults leads to

6. Emulation

Table 6.6: Fault sensitivity of the GAIA test circuit using DRXX

VS	Seq	OK	DEADLOCKS	Errors	SEU	SEUD	SEUE	SET	SETD	SETE
7	FF00	82.0%	18.0%	0.0%	49.9%	18.0%	0.0%	50.1%	0.02%	0.0%
	FFF0	91.8%	8.2%	0.0%	50.4%	8.2%	0.0%	49.6%	0.00%	0.0%
	FFFC	96.2%	3.8%	0.0%	50.2%	3.7%	0.0%	49.8%	0.06%	0.0%
	FFFF	100.0%	0.0%	0.0%	49.9%	0.0%	0.0%	50.1%	0.00%	0.0%
13	FF00	84.7%	15.3%	0.0%	49.6%	15.3%	0.0%	50.4%	0.00%	0.0%
	FFF0	91.4%	8.6%	0.0%	50.3%	8.6%	0.0%	49.7%	0.00%	0.0%
	FFFC	95.5%	4.5%	0.0%	50.2%	4.5%	0.0%	49.8%	0.00%	0.0%
	FFFF	99.1%	0.9%	0.0%	49.7%	0.9%	0.0%	50.3%	0.02%	0.0%
Average	FF00	83.4%	16.7%	0.0%	49.7%	16.6%	0.0%	50.3%	0.01%	0.0%
	FFF0	91.6%	8.4%	0.0%	50.4%	8.4%	0.0%	49.7%	0.00%	0.0%
	FFFC	95.9%	4.1%	0.0%	50.2%	4.1%	0.0%	49.8%	0.03%	0.0%
	FFFF	99.6%	0.4%	0.0%	49.8%	0.4%	0.0%	50.2%	0.01%	0.0%

a deadlock (column "SETD"). Thus the DRS method further improves the fault tolerance compared to the DRXX method, which also corresponds to the predicted behavior. Additionally, no transient fault in the DRS hardened GAIA test circuit produced wrong data, which already has been observed using the DRXS and DRXX method.

Table 6.7: Fault sensitivity of the GAIA test circuit using DRS

VS	Seq	OK	DEADLOCKS	Errors	SEU	SEUD	SEUE	SET	SETD	SETE
7	FF00	82.2%	17.8%	0.0%	49.6%	17.8%	0.0%	50.4%	0.0%	0.0%
	FFF0	91.3%	8.7%	0.0%	49.9%	8.7%	0.0%	50.1%	0.0%	0.0%
	FFFC	95.3%	4.7%	0.0%	49.9%	4.7%	0.0%	50.1%	0.0%	0.0%
	FFFF	100.0%	0.40%	0.0%	49.6%	0.0%	0.0%	50.4%	0.0%	0.0%
13	FF00	82.2%	17.8%	0.0%	49.6%	17.8%	0.0%	50.4%	0.0%	0.0%
	FFF0	91.3%	8.7%	0.0%	49.9%	8.7%	0.0%	50.1%	0.0%	0.0%
	FFFC	95.3%	4.7%	0.0%	49.9%	4.7%	0.0%	50.1%	0.0%	0.0%
	FFFF	100.0%	0.04%	0.0%	49.6%	0.0%	0.0%	50.4%	0.0%	0.0%
Average	FF00	82.2%	17.8%	0.0%	49.6%	17.8%	0.0%	50.4%	0.0%	0.0%
	FFF0	91.3%	8.7%	0.0%	49.9%	8.7%	0.0%	50.1%	0.0%	0.0%
	FFFC	95.3%	4.7%	0.0%	49.9%	4.7%	0.0%	50.1%	0.0%	0.0%
	FFFF	100.0%	0.04%	0.0%	49.6%	0.0%	0.0%	50.4%	0.0%	0.0%

Fig. 6.22(a) illustrates the number of deadlocks in the GAIA test circuit that have been observed in the particular test runs. Thereby the results of the different hardening methods are displayed for each sequence controller setting. The setting {FFFF} corresponds to the most realistic one taken into account the artificial synchronized design of the sequence controller. For this setting, (i) the number of deadlocks are minimized and (ii) the additional reduction in terms of deadlocks by applying a hardening method becomes evident.

In Fig. 6.22(b), the number of wrong data (consisting of token plus synchronization errors) is presented versus sequence controller setting and hardening method. The diagram

6.4. Application: The GAIA Video Pre-Processing Algorithm

is reduced solely to the display of wrong data in an unhardened circuitry, as all hardening methods (DRXS, DRXX, DRS) did not yield to any wrong data. The reduction of wrong data when applying a realistic sequence controller setting is also to be mentioned.

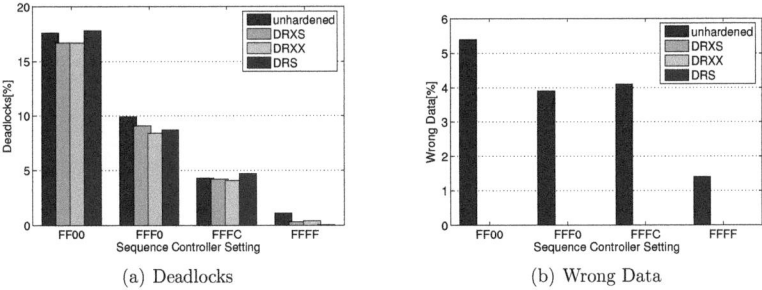

Figure 6.22: General fault sensitivity of the GAIA test circuit versus trace setting

Fig. 6.23 presents the same data as Fig. 6.22, however, it only considers the data path faults. Fig. 6.23(a) emphasizes the advantage of the DRXX method over the DRXS method in terms of less deadlocks. The DRS method provides the best performance regarding both register latch and data path fault injection. Fig. 6.23(b) shows the same shape as Fig. 6.22(b) when considering only data path faults. Contrary to the deadlocks, which are less than 0.5% when injecting the fault on the data path, the probability of getting a wrong data with such a fault injection is quite significant and can be compared as being equally probable as when the fault is injected directly into a register latch. Again, Fig. 6.23(b) only compares the sequence controller settings for the unhardened circuitry, since all hardening methods were immune to data path faults during the test campaign.

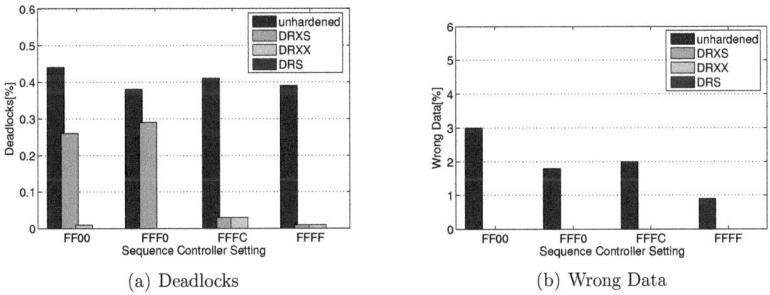

Figure 6.23: Data path fault sensitivity of the GAIA test circuit versus trace setting

6.5 Summary

That chapter presents a deterministic method to emulate transient faults in QDI logic using the STEFAN tool. Hardware fault injection has its merits due to the increased speed compared to simulation based methods. For instance, 1000 fault simulation runs of a simple 4-bit QDI adder using the synthesized netlist took approximately 1 hour on a commercial PC, using the simulation setup and the FOSTER tool as presented in chapter 5. A comparable scenario in the STEFAN tool was completed within 2 minutes. As example for the fault emulation, a portion of the GAIA video processing algorithm was chosen. Although that circuit only has a moderate complexity, it required several hours to simulate, while it the emulation only took a few minutes.

The STEFAN tool is able to place several versatile saboteurs within the circuit to be tested, which allow not only to inject different types of faults but also to reshuffle the particular rail transitions of the subjected signal. Thereby the circuit trace can be modified, which will give a different fault sensitivity and enables the investigation of different trace settings. The saboteurs have been implemented as synchronous circuitries, which complies to the unbounded delay requirement of QDI logic. The synchronization ensures that the fault injection will be reproducible and solves the trigger problem in QDI fault emulation. The STEFFAN tool also allows to reproduce a hardware fault injection by means of loading the same stimulus and fault injection setups to a simulator and investigate the fault behavior on a much finer granularity. This cross-checking allows to investigate the behavior of internal circuit nodes that are not visible in the hardware based emulation.

The drawback of this reproducibility is the limited separation of consecutive rail transition to multiples of the target platform clock period. Even if the clock runs at high speed, the minimum separation time between two rail transitions would be in the order of several nanoseconds. On the Virtex-4 platform that has been used for this thesis, that separation was bound to minimum 10 ns. In general, real-world circuits are able to cope with such timings quite easily. In a realistic QDI circuit, the separation of rail transitions is not bound and may range from a few picoseconds up to several nanoseconds, depending on a various number of parameters. The same restriction applies to the fault duration, i.e. the minimum fault duration in the STEFAN tool is one clock cycle, while in reality transient faults will be more than a order of magnitude shorter. Thus the STEFAN tool is not able to provoke all kind of fault behaviors due to these fundamental limitations.

A work around would be to modify the sequence controller by changing the trace via asynchronous delay lines, which will result in more fine grained traces. In addition, the fault injection itself could also be performed asynchronously. Both modification would result in a more realistic fault emulation, however, the reproducibility and the interchangeability with a simulator would be degraded. Such investigation goes beyond the scope of this thesis.

6.5. Summary

The results of the fault emulation by testing the GAIA test circuit have confirmed the theoretically derived properties of the different hardening methods postulated in 4.4. However, neither the DRXS nor the DRXX protected circuitry have shown any wrong data during the test campaign. That is in contradiction to the predicted behavior, as the DRXS and DRXX method should not be immune to $T(+1)$ tokens. The improved fault tolerance of DRXX versus DRXS in terms of deadlock reduction could be confirmed. As expected, the DRS method showed the best performance.

Table 6.8 shows the average relation in the number of deadlocks between the hardened GAIA circuit and the unhardened circuit. Considering all fault locations (columns "SEUD" + "SETD" in the tables of 6.4.4), the hardened GAIA circuit only shows a negligible improvement in the tolerance against deadlocks. However, when only data path faults are considered (columns "SETD" in the tables of 6.4.4) the significant improvement of the different hardening methods becomes evident. The DRXS method reduces the number of deadlocks due to data path faults by a factor of 2.75, DRXX already increases that factor to 32.4 while DRS lead to a deadlock immune circuitry, at least for that specific test campaign.

Table 6.8: Average improvement of deadlock reduction of versus hardening method

	fault location	DRXS	DRXX	DRS
$\frac{|DEADLOCKS_{unhardened}|}{|DEADLOCKS_{hardened}|}$	register latches + data path	1.09	1.12	1.06
	data path	2.75	32.40	∞

In contrast to the simulation based methods presented in chapter 5, the fault emulation in hardware by means of versatile saboteurs allowed quite easily to adapt the delays in a circuit and thereby to change the trace. It was shown by a number of random experiments that the trace setting has a significant impact on the fault sensitivity of QDI circuits, which confirms the theoretic expectations from chapter 3. Without modifying a circuit's trace, only a small portion of the possible delay scenarios a circuit will encounter in reality can be verified. Even if it is tested on the final hardware implementation, the unpredictable process and environmental impacts may lead to different delays and thus to a different fault sensitivity.

That thesis presented a first approach that supports the assessment of hardening strategies as well as serves helpful in the systematic verification of QDI circuits. The (reproducible) modification of a circuit's trace in hardware is a novel topic, which requires more research, especially to overcome the limitations due to the synchronized design of the STEFAN tool.

7

Conclusion

This chapter provides a brief summary of the work that is contained in this thesis. The key elements are summed up in the same logical order as they occur in the written text. Finally, an outlook to future research topics is given that could not be tackled in this thesis.

7.1 Summary

This work presents a novel treatment of transient faults in asynchronous QDI logic. Thereby *trace theory* has been selected as the main tool set for both description of transient fault effects and the assessment of hardening methods against such faults. Since traces are an established way to express the nominal operation of asynchronous circuits, it only seems to be natural to extend their usage to the characterization of faulty operations as well.

The operation of asynchronous QDI circuits is based on a local handshake between the sender and receiver of a piece of information. That handshake takes place in alternating code phases, each processing legal data also referred to as token. To model all kinds of fault effects on a token, three *token classes* $T(-1)$, $T(+0)$ and $T(+1)$ were introduced, which describe the number of additionally excited rails in a code phase compared to the nominal case. Each class has different fundamental properties and leads to different effects. It was investigated what kind of token classes are related to what kind of circuit topology and what fault effect may be provoked. Thereby the token class model has emerged as a general tool set that can be applied to unhardened and hardened QDI circuits as well as to different encoding schemes.

Within this thesis, the *duplication and rail cross-coupling* method was developed. The idea is to duplicate a QDI circuit and to swap one signal rail between the nominal

7. Conclusion

and redundant path. Thereby any mismatch between these two paths will stop the circuit. The advantage of this method is the minimum hardware overhead. No dedicated comparator is needed as the comparison is implicitly performed. Applying the token class model to that basic idea has shown some weaknesses and has led to the *synchronized duplicated and rail cross-coupled* (DRXS) method, which is able to mitigate most of the token classes. However, there exist some faulty traces of the $T(+1)$ class that remain undetected. Another improvement has been the *DRXS with cross-coupled completion detectors* (DRXX) method, which has the same fault detection properties as DRXS but additionally reduces the probability of deadlocks. Finally, it could be shown that the *duplication and rail synchronization* (DRS) method, which is one possible representation of Martin's duplication and double-checking method [93], is able to mitigate all token classes. However, the hardware overhead of DRS exceeds DRXS/DRXX at larger circuitries. Thus DRXS/DRXX is regarded as an alternative hardening method especially for complex architectures, which reduces the hardware overhead but still provides a high degree of fault tolerance.

The theoretic assumptions and hypotheses that have been derived in this thesis were confirmed by both simulation and hardware based fault injection experiments. The simulation of QDI circuits is not a trivial task as QDI logic has a fundamentally different behavior compared to synchronous circuits. To correctly simulate the effects of transient faults, the *FOSTER simulation tool* was developed. It is able to handle faults in both combinational and sequential circuits and correctly models their properties without making a time-consuming state evaluation, leading to a short simulation time while keeping the simulation model simple. The FOSTER tool is also able to record the different traces the circuit under test receives. Hence the connection to the token class model is established and the evaluation of the faults is done in a systematic way. Several test circuits have been subjected to transient fault injections and the different hardening methods have been evaluated. Both the DRXS and DRXX method significantly improved the fault tolerance. The DRS method showed the highest fault tolerance, although not as high as expected.

To be as realistic as possible, the fault injection was performed using VITAL compliant, synthesized netlists. Thereby a Virtex-4 FPGA has been selected as the target platform. Due to the asynchronous nature of both the QDI design itself and the fault injection, timing violations were reported frequently. Although most effects of these violations could be taken into account for the evaluation of the results, many effects remain questionable. So far no work is known that tackles that problem.

Since a simulation model is only as good as its specification, the transient fault behavior was also tested in hardware. For that reason, the *STEFAN emulation tool* was derived, which allows to test fault effects in QDI hardware in a reproducible manner. Thereby not only faults can be injected, but also the trace, which has a significant impact on the fault tolerance, can be modified. To keep the complexity of the STEFAN tool moderate, the fault injection and trace control mechanism was implemented by means of synchronous functions. That synchronicity does not impose a contradiction to the unbounded delay model, however, it limits the resolution of both the trace modification and the fault injection task. Thus the STEFAN tool also only draws a limited picture of the real world behavior of a QDI circuit and leaves improvements for future work. To test the properties of the hardening methods derived in this thesis, a real application was chosen: a small portion of the video processing algorithm of the European space mission GAIA. The hardening techniques performed even better than expected, no erroneous data was generated in a DRXS / DRXX / DRS protected system. Overall, the results of the emulation confirmed the theoretically derived expectations.

7.2 Outlook

Although this work tried to cover as much as possible in the field of transient faults in asynchronous QDI logic, a lot of topics could not be investigated within the scope of this thesis and are reserved for future research:

Metastability – It was shown that a fault of the class $T(+1)$ violates the delay-insensitive encoding of the data. That violation may result in a metastable behavior. It would be interesting whether hardening methods support the generation of such metastable states or whether they reduce their occurrence.

Analytical soft error calculation – There exists some work on the analytical calculation of soft error rates in conventional synchronous logic, while no research is known that tackles that topic in asynchronous logic. That thesis has shown the impact of the trace setting on the number of soft errors based on some selected test circuits. A more general approach that takes into account the actual trace distribution may lead to an estimate of fault tolerance of a circuit without needing time consuming simulations.

Encoding schemes – That thesis has only focused on dual-rail encoded QDI circuits. Especially networks-on-chip tend to use other, more efficient codes for data transmission channels. A different encoding scheme may have a direct influence on the fault tolerance and the selected hardening strategy.

Detailed assessment of overhead – That thesis has only investigated the hardware area overhead of different mitigation schemes. A more general assessment of the overhead a hardening method generates (in terms of power, speed, cost) will help to select the optimum method, depending on the main requirements of an application.

Recovery of deadlocks – It was shown that not only permanent but also transient faults may lead to a deadlock in QDI circuits. Although a deadlock does not explicitly produce wrong data and solely stops the circuit execution, such a behavior may be not acceptable from a system level perspective. For example, a safety system may cope with wrong data from one of its subsystems but it may not accept a subsystem that has stopped

7. Conclusion

working. The recovery of deadlocks is closely related to the treatment of permanent faults. For related work on this topic see [128].

Realistic simulation – The simulation of transient faults in QDI circuits has emerged as non-trivial, especially because of the occurrence of timing violations. The particular gates and sequential elements of a QDI circuit were modeled by means of conventional circuit libraries that are dedicated to synchronous designs. The usage of synchronous models goes along with the synchronous hardware platforms that are used as target for the circuit synthesis. The occurrence of timing violations within fault simulations makes the result of these simulations questionable. Thus a synthesis library that is based on an asynchronous target platform would improve the validity of QDI fault simulations. In addition, a modification of the circuit trace for the simulation would also be very helpful. A possible idea would be e.g. the automatic modification of the timings in the SDF file, so the circuit still complies with its specification, but faces a different trace setting that directly has an impact on its fault tolerance.

Realistic emulation – Testing the sensitivity of a circuit by means of hardware experiments yields to a high confidence on such results, provided the fault emulation does not have a significant impact on the behavior of the circuit. Although the presented fault emulator in this thesis leads to reproducible results, it is limited by its synchronous implementation. A pure asynchronous fault emulation will allow to modify the trace at a much finer level and to apply more realistic transient fault durations. It would be interesting how a more realistic fault emulator behaves. Additionally, random experiments should be performed as well to exclude systematic faults in the emulation setup. Thereby a trade-off with respect to reproducibility has to be made.

Bibliography

[1] Semiconductor Industry Association, "International technology roadmap for semiconductors (ITRS)," http://public.itrs.net, 2009.

[2] C. Constantinescu, "Trends and challenges in VLSI circuit reliability," *IEEE Micro*, vol. 23, no. 4, pp. 14–19, 2003.

[3] M. J. Gadlage, P. H. Eaton, J. M. Benedetto, M. Carts, V. Zhu, and T. L. Turflinger, "Digital device error rate trends in advanced CMOS technologies," *IEEE Transactions on Nuclear Science*, vol. 53, no. 6, pp. 3466–3471, 2006.

[4] R. Baumann, "The impact of technology scaling on soft error rate performance and limits to the efficacy of error correction," in *Proceedings of the IEEE International Electron Devices Meeting*, 2002, pp. 329–332.

[5] P. Shivakumar, M. Kistler, S. W. Keckler, D. Burger, and L. Alvisi, "Modeling the effect of technology trends on the soft error rate of combinational logic," in *Proceedings of the 2002 International Conference on Dependable Systems and Networks*, 2002, pp. 389–398.

[6] A. Dixit, R. Heald, and A. Wood, "Trends from ten years of soft error experimentation," in *Proceedings of IEEE Workshop on Silicon Errors in Logic - System Effects*, 2009.

[7] E. Normand, "Single event upset at ground level," *IEEE Transactions on Nuclear Science*, vol. 43, no. 6, pp. 2742–2750, 1996.

[8] P. Hazucha and C. Svensson, "Impact of CMOS technology scaling on the atmospheric neutron soft error rate," *IEEE Transactions on Nuclear Science*, vol. 47, no. 3, pp. 2586–2594, 2000.

[9] R. Baumann, "Radiation-induced soft errors in advanced semiconductor technologies," *IEEE Transactions on Device and Materials Reliability*, vol. 5, no. 3, pp. 305–316, 2005.

[10] G. Asadi and M. B. Tahoori, "Soft error rate estimation and mitigation for SRAM-based FPGAs," in *Proceedings of the 2005 ACM/SIGDA 13th international symposium on Field-programmable gate arrays*. New York, NY, USA: ACM, 2005, pp. 149–160.

Bibliography

[11] C. H. K. van Berkel, M. B. Josephs, and S. M. Nowick, "Scanning the technology: Applications of asynchronous circuits," in *Proceedings of the IEEE, 87(2), February 1999.*, 1999, pp. 223–233.

[12] J. Sparso and S. Furber, Eds., *Principles of Asynchronous Circuit Design - A Systems Perspective*. Kluwer Academic Publishers, 2001.

[13] A. J. McAuley, "Four state asynchronous architectures," *IEEE Transactions on Computers*, vol. 41, no. 2, pp. 129–142, Februray 1992.

[14] M. E. Dean, T. E. Williams, and D. L. Dill, "Efficient self-timing with level-encoded 2-phase dual-rail (LEDR)," in *Proceedings of the 1991 University of California/Santa Cruz conference on Advanced research in VLSI.* Cambridge, MA, USA: MIT Press, 1991, pp. 55–70.

[15] B. Rahbaran, "An experimental comparison of robustness between synchronous and asynchronous logic design," Ph.D. dissertation, Vienna University of Technology, 2005.

[16] N. Miskov-Zivanov and D. Marculescu, "Soft error rate analysis for sequential circuits," in *Proceedings of the conference on Design, automation and test in Europe.* San Jose, CA, USA: EDA Consortium, 2007, pp. 1436–1441.

[17] C. LaFrieda and R. Manohar, "Fault detection and isolation techniques for quasi delay-insensitive circuits," in *Proceedings of the 2004 International Conference on Dependable Systems and Networks (DSN'04).* Washington, DC, USA: IEEE Computer Society, 2004, pp. 41–50.

[18] W. Jang and A. J. Martin, "SEU-tolerant QDI circuits," in *Proceedings of the 11th IEEE International Symposium on Asynchronous Circuits and Systems*, 2005.

[19] A.-M. Rahmani, A.-A. Salehpour, M. Zamani, S. Mohammadi, and H. Pedram, "An efficient fault simulator for QDI asynchronous circuits," in *Proceedings of the 4th Southern Conference on Programmable Logic*, 2008, pp. 99–104.

[20] W. Bainbridge and S. Salisbury, "Glitch sensitivity and defense of quasi delay-insensitive network-on-chip links," in *Proceedings of the 15th IEEE Symposium on Asynchronous Circuits and Systems*, 2009, pp. 35–44.

[21] Y. Monnet, M. Renaudin, and R. Leveugle, "Formal analysis of quasi delay insensitive circuits behavior in the presence of SEUs," in *Proceedings of the 13th IEEE International On-Line Testing Symposium (IOLTS'07)*, 2007.

[22] V. Diekert, *The Book of Traces*, G. Rozenberg, Ed. River Edge, NJ, USA: World Scientific Publishing Co., Inc., 1995.

[23] S. Hauck, "Asynchronous design methodologies: An overview," *Proceedings of the IEEE*, vol. 83, no. 1, 1995.

[24] C. Myers, *Asynchronous Circuit Design*. JohnWiley & Sons, 2001.

[25] K. van Berkel, *Handshake circuits: An asynchronous architecture for VLSI programming*. Cambridge University Press, 1993.

[26] G. M. Birtwistle and A. L. Davis, *Asynchronous digital circuit design*. Springer, 1995.

[27] J. A. Brzozowski and C.-J. H. Seger, *Asynchronous Circuits*. Springer, 1995.

[28] M. M. Nystrom and A. Martin, *Asynchronous Pulse Logic*. Springer, 2002.

[29] K. Fant, *Logically Determined Design: Clockless System Design with NULL Convention Logic*. John Wiley and Sons, 2005.

[30] S. C. Smith, J. Di, and M. Thornton, *Designing Asynchronous Circuits Using Null Convention Logic (NCL)*. Morgan & Claypool, 2009.

[31] D. Huffman, "The synthesis of the sequential switching circuits," *Journal of the Franklin Institute*, vol. 257, no. 4, pp. 161–190, March 1954.

[32] D. Huffman, "The synthesis of the sequential switching circuits," *Journal of the Franklin Institute*, vol. 257, no. 3, pp. 275–303, April 1954.

[33] D. E. Muller and W. S. Bartky, "A theory of asynchronous circuits," in *Proceedings of the International Symposium on Theory of Switching*, 1959, pp. 204–243.

[34] A. J. Martin, "The limitations to delay-insensitivity in asynchronous circuits," in *Proceedings of the sixth MIT conference on Advanced research in VLSI*. Cambridge, MA, USA: MIT Press, 1990, pp. 263–278.

[35] S. M. Nowick and D. L. Dill, "Synthesis of asynchronous state machines using a local clock," in *Proceedings of the International Conference on Computer Design (ICCD)*. IEEE Computer Society Press, Oct. 1991, pp. 192–197.

[36] W. B. Toms, "Synthesis of quasi-delay-insensitive datapath circuits," Ph.D. dissertation, University of Manchester, 2006.

[37] A. Mitra, W. F. McLaughlin, and S. M. Nowick, "Efficient asynchronous protocol converters for two-phase delay-insensitive global communication," in *Proceedings of the 13th IEEE International Symposium on Asynchronous Circuits and Systems*. Washington, DC, USA: IEEE Computer Society, 2007, pp. 186–195.

Bibliography

[38] S. Ishihara, Y. Komatsu, M. Hariyama, and M. Kameyama, "An asynchronous FPGA using LEDR/4-phase-dual-rail protocol converters," in *International Conference on Reconfigurable Systems and Algorithms (ERSA)*, 2009, pp. 145–150.

[39] P. B. McGee, M. Y. Agyekum, M. A. Mohamed, and S. M. Nowick, "A level-encoded transition signaling protocol for high-throughput asynchronous global communication," in *Proceedings of the 14th IEEE International Symposium on Asynchronous Circuits and Systems.* Washington, DC, USA: IEEE Computer Society, 2008, pp. 116–127.

[40] K. Fant and S. Brandt, "NULL convention logic™: A complete and consistent logic for asynchronous digital circuit synthesis," in *Proceedings of the International Conference on Application Specific Systems, Architectures, and Processors (ASAP 96)*, 1996, pp. 261–273.

[41] I. E. Sutherland, "Micropipelines," *Communications of the ACM*, vol. 32, no. 6, pp. 720–738, 1989.

[42] T. Verhoeff, "Delay-insensitive codes – An overview," *Distributed Computing*, vol. 3, no. 1, pp. 1–8, 1988.

[43] S. Moore, R. Anderson, R. Mullins, G. Taylor, and J. J. A. Fournier, "Balanced self-checking asynchronous logic for smart card applications," *Microprocessors and Microsystems*, vol. 27, no. 9, pp. 421–430, 2003.

[44] C. LaFrieda, B. Hill, and R. Manohar, "An asynchronous FPGA with two-phase enable-scaled routing of delay-insensitive modules," in *Proceedings of the 16th IEEE International Symposium on Asynchronous Circuits and Systems*, H. Fuchs, Ed., 2010, pp. 141–150.

[45] R. R. Dobkin, R. Ginosar, and A. Kolodny, "Fast asynchronous shift register for bit-serial communication," in *Proceedings of the 12th IEEE International Symposium on Asynchronous Circuits and Systems.* Washington, DC, USA: IEEE Computer Society, 2006, pp. 117–126.

[46] M. Delvai, "Design of an asynchronous processor based on code alternation logic - treatment of non-linear data paths," Ph.D. dissertation, Vienna University of Technology, 2004.

[47] W. Huber, "Design of an asynchronous processor based on code alternation logic - exploration of delay insensitivity," Ph.D. dissertation, Vienna University of Technology, 2005.

[48] J. Laprie, Ed., *Dependability: Basic Concepts and Terminology.* Springer-Verlag, 1992.

[49] A. Avizienis, J.-C. Laprie, and B. Randell, "Fundamental concepts of dependability," in *Proceedings of the 3rd IEEE Information Survivability Workshop (ISW-2000)*, 2000, pp. 7–12.

[50] D. J. Sorin, *Fault Tolerant Computer Architecture*, ser. Synthesis Lectures on Computer Architecture. Morgan & Claypool Publishers, 2009.

[51] J. F. Ziegler, "Terrestrial cosmic rays," *IBM J. Res. Dev.*, vol. 40, no. 1, pp. 19–39, 1996.

[52] R. Baumann, T. Hossain, S. Murata, and H. Kitagawa, "Boron compounds as a dominant source of alpha particles in semiconductor devices," in *Proceedings of the International Reliability Physics Symposium*, 1995, pp. 297–302.

[53] T. May and M. Woods, "Alpha-particle-induced soft errors in dynamic memories," *IEEE Transaction on Electron Devices*, vol. 26, 1979.

[54] G. C. Messenger, "Collection of charge on junction nodes from ion tracks," *IEEE Transactions on Nuclear Science*, vol. 29, pp. 2024–2031, 1982.

[55] D. G. Mavis and P. H. Eaton, "Soft error rate mitigation techniques for modern microcircuits," in *Proceedings of the 40th Annual Reliability Physics Symposium*, ser. 216–225, 2002.

[56] P. E. Dodd, M. R. Shaneyfelt, J. A. Felix, and J. R. Schwank, "Production and propagation of single-event transients in high-speed digital logic ICs," *IEEE Transactions on Nuclear Science*, vol. 51, no. 6, pp. 3278–3284, 2004.

[57] R. Naseer, J. Draper, Y. Boulghassoul, E. Dasgupta, and A. Witulski, "Critical charge and set pulse widths for combinational logic in commercial 90nm CMOS technology," in *Proceedings of the 17th great lakes symposium on Great lakes symposium on VLSI*. ACM Press, 2007, pp. 227–230.

[58] European Cooperation for Space Standardization (ECCS), "Methods for the calculation of radiation received and its effects, and a policy for design margins (E-ST-10-12C)," http://www.ecss.nl/, 2008.

[59] A. Holmes-Siedle and L. Adams., *Handbook of Radiation Effects*. Oxford University Press, 2002.

[60] A. H. Fischer, A. von Glasow, S. Penka, and F. Ungar, "Electromigration failure mechanism studies on copper interconnects," in *Proceedings of the 2002 IEEE Interconnect Technology Conference*, 2002, pp. 139–141.

[61] J. R. Carter, S. Ozev, and D. J. Sorin, "Circuit-level modeling for concurrent testing of operational defects due to gate oxide breakdown," in *Proceedings of Design, Automation and Test in Europe (DATE)*, 2005, pp. 300–305.

Bibliography

[62] B. Johnson, *Design and Analysis of Fault Tolerant Digital Systems*. Addision Wesley, 1989.

[63] B. Rahbaran and A. Steininger, "Is asynchronous logic more robust than synchronous logic?" *IEEE Transactions on Dependable and Secure Computing*, vol. 6, no. 4, pp. 282–294, 2009.

[64] D. Alexandrescu, L. Anghel, and M. Nicolaidis, "Simulating single event transients in VDSM ICs for ground level radiation," *Journal of Electronic Testing-Theory and Applications*, vol. 20, pp. 413–421, 2004.

[65] R. P. Bastos, Y. Monnet, G. Sicard, F. Kastensmidt, M. Renaudin, and R. Reis, "Comparing transient-fault effects on synchronous and on asynchronous circuits," *IEEE International On-Line Testing Symposium*, vol. 0, pp. 29–34, 2009.

[66] S. Peng and R. Manohar, "Self-healing asynchronous arrays," in *Proceedings of the International Symposium on Asynchronous Circuits and Systems (ASYNC)*, 2006, pp. 34–45.

[67] G. Rui, C. Wei, L. Fang, D. Kui, and W. Zhiying, "Modified triple modular redundancy structure based on asynchronous circuit technique," in *Proceedings of the 21st IEEE International Symposium on on Defect and Fault-Tolerance in VLSI Systems*. Washington, DC, USA: IEEE Computer Society, 2006, pp. 184–196.

[68] T. Chu, "Synthesis of self-timed VLSI circuits from graph-theoretic specifications," Ph.D. dissertation, MIT, 1987.

[69] H. Saito, A. Kondratyev, J. Cortadella, L. Lavagno, and A. Yakovlev, "What is the cost of delay insensitivity?" in *Proceedings of the 1999 IEEE/ACM international conference on Computer-aided design*. Piscataway, NJ, USA: IEEE Press, 1999, pp. 316–323.

[70] J. Cortadella, M. Kishinevsky, A. Kondratyev, L. Lavagno, A. Yakovlev, and N. R. England, "Petrify: A tool for manipulating concurrent specifications and synthesis of asynchronous controllers," *IEICE Transactions on Information and Systems*, vol. 80, pp. 315–325, 1997.

[71] J. C. Ebergen, "A formal approach to designing delay-insensitive circuits," *Distributed Computing*, vol. 5, no. 3, pp. 107–119, 1991.

[72] J. L. A. van de Snepscheut, "Trace theory and VLSI design," Ph.D. dissertation, Eindhoven University of Technology, 1983.

[73] M. Rem, "The nature of delay insensitive computing," Eindhoven University of Technology, Tech. Rep., 1990.

Bibliography

[74] C. E. Molnar, T.-P. Fang, and F. U. Rosenberger, "Synthesis of delay-insensitive modules," in *1985 Chapel Hill Conference on Very Large Scale Integration*, H. Fuchs, Ed. IEEE Computer Society Press, 1985, pp. 67–86.

[75] J. A. Brzozowski and J. C. Ebergen, "On the delay-sensitivity of gate networks," *IEEE Transactions on Computers*, vol. 41, no. 11, pp. 1349–1360, Nov. 1992.

[76] A. Lines, "Asynchronous interconnect for synchronous soc design," *IEEE Micro*, vol. 24, pp. 32–41, 2004.

[77] A. J. Martin and M. Nyström, "Asynchronous techniques for system-on-chip design," in *Proceedings of IEEE*, vol. 94, no. 6, 2006, pp. 1089–1120.

[78] G. Fuchs, M. Fuegger, and A. Steininger, "On the threat of metastability in an asynchronous fault-tolerant clock generation scheme," in *Proceedings of the 15th IEEE Symposium on Asynchronous Circuits and Systems*, 2009, pp. 127–136.

[79] W. Kuang, P. Zhao, J. Yuan, and R. F. DeMara, "Design of asynchronous circuits for high soft error tolerance in deep submicron CMOS circuits," *IEEE Transactions on Very Large Scale Integration (VLSI) Systems*, vol. 18, no. 3, pp. 410–422, 2010.

[80] Y. Monnet, M. Renaudin, and R. Leveugle, "Asynchronous circuits sensitivity to fault injection," in *Proceedings of the 10th IEEE International On-Line Testing Symposium (IOLTS'04)*. Washington, DC, USA: IEEE Computer Society, 2004, pp. 121–126.

[81] A. J. Martin and P. J. Hazewindus, "Testing delay-insensitive circuits," in *Proceedings of the 1991 University of California/Santa Cruz conference on Advanced research in VLSI*. Cambridge, MA, USA: MIT Press, 1991, pp. 118–132.

[82] T. A. Henzinger, "Two challenges in embedded systems design: Predictability and robustness," *Philosophical Transactions Of The Royal Society*, vol. 366, pp. 3727–3736, 2008.

[83] Y. Monnet, M. Renaudin, and R. Leveugle, "Asynchronous circuits transient faults sensitivity valuation," in *Proceedings of the 42nd Design Automation Conference (DAC'05)*, 2005.

[84] G. Asadi and M. B. Tahoori, "An analytical approach for soft error rate estimation in digital circuits," in *Proceedings of the IEEE International Symposium on Circuits and Systems (ISCAS)*, 2005, pp. 2991–2994.

[85] F. Wang, Y. Xie, R. Rajaraman, and B. Vaidyanathan, "Soft error rate analysis for combinational logic using an accurate electrical masking model," in *Proceedings of the 20th International Conference on VLSI Design*, 2007, pp. 165–170.

Bibliography

[86] K. Mohanram and N. A. Touba, "Cost-effective approach for reducing soft error failure rate in logic circuits," in *Proceedings of the International Test Conference*, 2003, pp. 893–901.

[87] V. F. Bashkirov, N. V. Kuznetsov, and R. A. Nymmik, "An analysis of the SEU rate of microcircuits exposed by the various components of space radiation," *Radiation Measurements*, vol. 30, no. 3, pp. 427–433, 1999.

[88] C. Inguimbert and S. Duzellier, "SEU rate calculation with GEANT4 (comparison with CREME 86)," *IEEE Transactions on Nuclear Science*, vol. 51, no. 5, pp. 2805–2810, 2004.

[89] "The cosmic ray effects on micro-electronics (CREME)," https://creme-mc.isde.vanderbilt.edu/.

[90] T. Panhofer, W. Friesenbichler, and M. Delvai, "Fault tolerant four-state logic by using self-healing cells," in *Proceedings of the 2008 International Conference on Computer Design (ICCD'08)*, October 2008, pp. 1–6.

[91] P. D. Hyde and G. Russell, "ASSEC: An asynchronous self-checking RISC-based processor," in *Proceedings of the Digital System Design*, ser. DSD'04, 2004, pp. 104–111.

[92] S. Peng and R. Manohar, "Fault tolerant asynchronous adder through dynamic self-reconfiguration," in *Proceedings of the 2005 International Conference on Computer Design*. Washington, DC, USA: IEEE Computer Society, 2005, pp. 171–179.

[93] W. Jang and A. J. Martin, "Soft-error robustness in QDI circuits," in *Workshop on System Effects of Logical Soft Errors - SELSE1*, 2005.

[94] W. Jang and A. J. Martin, "A soft-error-tolerant asynchronous microcontroller," in *13th NASA Symposium on VLSI Design*, 2007.

[95] Y. Monnet, M. Renaudin, and R. Leveugle, "Hardening techniques against transient faults for asynchronous circuits," in *Proceedings of the 11th IEEE International On-Line Testing Symposium (IOLTS'05)*, 2005, pp. 129–134.

[96] Y. Monnet, M. Renaudin, and R. Leveugle, "Designing resistant circuits against malicious faults injection using asynchronous logic," *IEEE Transactions on Computers*, vol. 55, no. 9, pp. 1104–1115, September 2006.

[97] J. Di, "A framework on mitigating single event upset using delay-insensitive asynchronous circuits," in *Proceedings of the 2007 IEEE Region 5 Technical Conference*, 2007, pp. 354–357.

Bibliography

[98] S. Peng and R. Manohar, "Efficient failure detection in pipelined asynchronous circuits," in *Proceedings of the 2005 20th IEEE International Symposium on Defect and Fault Tolerance in VLSI Systems (DFT'05)*, 2005.

[99] D. A. Rennels and H. Kim, "Concurrent error detection in self-timed VLSI," in *FTCS-24. Digest of Papers, Twenty-Fourth International Symposium on Fault-Tolerant Computing*, 1994, pp. 96–105.

[100] K. J. Kulikowski, M. G. Karpovsky, E. Taubin, Z. Wang, and A. Kulikowski, "Concurrent fault detection for secure QDI asynchronous circuits," in *Proceedings of the 17th Workshop on Dependable and Secure Nanocomputing (WDSN)*, 2008.

[101] N. Minas, M. Marshall, G. Russell, and A. Yakovlev, "FPGA implementation of an asynchronous processor with both online and offline testing capabilities," in *Proceedings of the 2008 14th IEEE International Symposium on Asynchronous Circuits and Systems*, 2008, pp. 128–137.

[102] S. Almukhaizim and Y. Makris, "Concurrent error detection methods for asynchronous burst-mode machines," *IEEE Transactions on Computers*, vol. 56, no. 6, 2007.

[103] M. Goessel, V. Ocheretny, E. Sogomonyan, and D. Marienfeld, *New Methods of Concurrent Checking*, ser. Frontiers in Electronic Testing. Springer, 2008.

[104] J. Waddle and D. Wagner, "Fault attacks on dual-rail encoded systems," in *Proceedings of the 21st Annual Computer Security Applications Conference*. Washington, DC, USA: IEEE Computer Society, 2005, pp. 483–494.

[105] S. Moore, R. Anderson, P. Cunningham, R. Mullins, and G. Taylor, "Improving smart card security using self-timed circuits," in *Proceedings of the Eighth International Symposium on Asynchronous Circuits and Systems (ASYNC.02)*, 2002.

[106] M. Delvai and A. Steininger, "A practical comparison of logic design styles," *The 3rd International Conference on Cybernetics and Information Technologies, Systems and Applications - Volume 3*, Jul. 2006.

[107] Actel Application Note, "Using synopsys to design actel's radiation-hardened FPGAs," http://klabs.org/richcontent/fpga_content/synopsis_actel.pdf (17.12.2010), 1997.

[108] R. Smith and M. Ligthart, "High-level design for asynchronous logic," in *Proceedings of the 2001 conference on Asia South Pacific design automation*, 2001, pp. 431–436.

[109] A. Benso and P. Prinetto, *Fault Injection Techniques and Tools for Embedded Systems Reliability Evaluation*. Norwell, MA, USA: Kluwer Academic Publishers, 2003.

Bibliography

[110] R. Leveugle and K. Hadjiat, "Multi-level fault injections in VHDL descriptions: Alternative approaches and experiments," *Journal of Electronic Testing*, vol. 19, no. 5, pp. 559–575, 2003.

[111] J.-C. Baraza, J. Gracia, S. Blanc, D. Gil, and P.-J. Gil, "Enhancement of fault injection techniques based on the modification of VHDL code," *IEEE Transactions on VLSI Systems*, vol. 16, no. 6, pp. 693–706, 2008.

[112] B. Ghavami, A. Tajary, and H.-R. Z. H. Pedram, "High-level fault simulation methodology for QDI template-based asynchronous circuits," in *Proceedings of the 2009 IEEE Region 10 Conference (TENCON 2009)*, 2009, pp. 1–6.

[113] S. Sur-Kolay, M. Roncken, K. Stevens, P. P. Chaudhuri, and R. Roy, "Fsimac: A fault simulator for asynchronous sequential circuits," in *Proceedings of the 9th Asian Test Symposium*. Washington, DC, USA: IEEE Computer Society, 2000, pp. 114–119.

[114] F. Shi and Y. Makris, "Fault simulation and random test generation for speed-independent circuits," in *Proceedings of the 14th ACM Great Lakes symposium on VLSI*. New York, NY, USA: ACM, 2004, pp. 127–130.

[115] Y. Shi, S. B. Furber, J. Garside, and L. A. Plana, "Fault tolerant delay insensitive inter-chip communication," in *Proceedings of the 2009 15th IEEE Symposium on Asynchronous Circuits and Systems*. Washington, DC, USA: IEEE Computer Society, 2009, pp. 77–84.

[116] D. G. Gutierrez, "Single event upsets simulation tool," http://www.esa.int/TEC/Microelectronics (06.05.2008).

[117] K. S. Trivedi, *Probability and statistics with reliability, queuing and computer science applications*, 2nd ed. Chichester, UK: John Wiley and Sons Ltd., 2002.

[118] C. J. Clopper and E. S. Pearson, "The use of confidence or fiducial limits illustrated in the case of the binomial," *Biometrika*, vol. 26, no. 4, pp. 404–413, 1934.

[119] R. J. Martínez, P. J. Gil, G. Martín, C. Pérez, and J. J. Serrano, "Experimental validation of high-speed fault-tolerant systems using physical fault injection," in *Proceedings of the conference on Dependable Computing for Critical Applications*. Washington, DC, USA: IEEE Computer Society, 1999, pp. 249–265.

[120] K. Cheng, S. Huang, and W. Dai, "Fault emulation: A new methodology for fault grading," *IEEE Transactionson Computer-Aided Design of Integrated Circuits and Systems*, vol. 18, no. 10, pp. 1487–1495, 1999.

[121] P. Ellervee, J. Raik, K. Tammemae, and R.-J. Ubar, "FPGA-based fault emulation of synchronous sequential circuits," *Computers and Digital Techniques*, vol. 1, no. 2, pp. 70–76, 2007.

[122] Y. Monnet, M. Renaudin, R. Leveugle, N. Feyt, P. Moitrel, and F. M. Nzenguet, "Practical evaluation of fault countermeasures on an asynchronous DES crypto processor," in *Proceedings of the 12th IEEE International Symposium on On-Line Testing*. Washington, DC, USA: IEEE Computer Society, 2006, pp. 125–130.

[123] A. Ejlali and S. G. Miremadi, "Error propagation analysis using FPGA-based SEU-fault injection," *Microelectronics Reliability*, vol. 48, no. 2, pp. 319–328, 2008.

[124] M. Jeitler, M. Delvai, and S. Reichoer, "FUSE - A hardware accelerated HDL fault injection tool," in *Proceedings of the 5th Southern Conference on Programmable Logic*, 2009, pp. 89–94.

[125] S. Bhunia, S. Mukhopadhyay, and K. Roy, "Process variations and process-tolerant design," *International Conference on VLSI Design*, vol. 0, pp. 699–704, 2007.

[126] European Space Agency, "The GAIA Mission," http://sci.esa.int/gaia/ (16 Nov 2009).

[127] EADS Astrium, "VPU Algorithms Requirements Specifications," Invititation to Tender for GAIA VPU, 2006.

[128] T. Panhofer, "Self-healing asynchronous circuits for high-reliability applications," Ph.D. dissertation, Vienna University of Technology, 2012.

i want morebooks!

Buy your books fast and straightforward online - at one of world's fastest growing online book stores! Environmentally sound due to Print-on-Demand technologies.

Buy your books online at
www.get-morebooks.com

Kaufen Sie Ihre Bücher schnell und unkompliziert online – auf einer der am schnellsten wachsenden Buchhandelsplattformen weltweit! Dank Print-On-Demand umwelt- und ressourcenschonend produziert.

Bücher schneller online kaufen
www.morebooks.de

VDM Verlagsservicegesellschaft mbH
Heinrich-Böcking-Str. 6-8   Telefon: +49 681 3720 174   info@vdm-vsg.de
D - 66121 Saarbrücken   Telefax: +49 681 3720 1749 www.vdm-vsg.de

Printed by Books on Demand GmbH, Norderstedt / Germany